International Anti-trust Law

International Anti-trust Law

Volume I

A Review of National Laws

Edited by

Julian Maitland-Walker
Solicitor

ESC Publishing Limited
Oxford 1984

Published by ESC Publishing Limited
              25 Beaumont Street
              Oxford OX1 2NP

ISBN 0 906214 19 X

Phototypeset by Getset (BTS) Ltd, Eynsham, Oxford
Printed and bound in Great Britain by Billings & Sons Limited, Worcester

Contents

Introduction

The rapid expansion in world trade in the decades following World War II, the increasing level of concentration in many sectors of industry and the development and expansion of that much maligned creature, the multinational, has resulted in the mushrooming growth of anti-trust regulations throughout the world.

But businessmen and lawyers are confronted by an increasing need to consider a multiplicity of national and sometimes *supra*-national anti-trust rules in planning cross-frontier transactions, and often find themselves trying to reconcile the irreconcilable.

Despite efforts by UNCTAD and others to establish guidelines for the international regulation of anti-trust, nation states inevitably structure their laws to meet the needs of their own country, for the protection of their own industry; the world recession has simply compounded this trend, as witness the spate of national legislation to frustrate the enforcement of foreign anti-trust laws.

The object of the first International Anti-trust Law Conference held under the auspices of the *European Competition Law Review* was to provide a forum for discussion among anti-trust lawyers throughout the world, representing both administration on the one hand and trade and commerce on the other.

As the contributions which appear in this book reveal, the Conference provided fascinating insights into national anti-trust laws and their interface with anti-trust legislation in other jurisdictions.

The decision was taken to publish the contributions in book form in order to benefit a wider audience, and the summary of national laws of each Member State provided will, it is hoped, comprise an invaluable handbook for those industrialists and lawyers involved in international business.

I should like to express my personal thanks to all those who participated in the Conference, in addition to those contributors to this book. The success of the First International Anti-trust Law Conference has laid the foundations for an annual Conference on the topic, and it is hoped that further contributions will be published from time to time.

Julian Maitland-Walker
August 1983

AUSTRALIA

The Licensing of Intellectual Property Rights in Australia

LINDSAY R. NAYLER

While for many purposes it may be convenient to consider Australia as a single country, for the purposes of the law it is a federation in which the legislative power is divided between the Government of the Commonwealth, which has limited powers under the Australian constitution and the various States of the Commonwealth, which have the residual powers.

All intellectual property rights relating to patents, trade marks and copyrights are created under statutes of the Commonwealth Parliament and are interpreted by Commonwealth as distinct from State law. Intellectual property licences, however, are contracts and contracts are governed by the laws of the State or Territory concerned, whether as a matter of express choice of law or in accordance with the private international law rules.

To add to this confusion, while in recent years a system of federal courts has been created, original jurisdiction in matters which concern intellectual property rights, which was formerly reserved to the Australian High Court, has now been given to the State courts, with the exception that if such matters are associated with a matter which falls within the original jurisdiction of the Federal Court (for example proceedings under the Australian Trade Practices Act), jurisdiction of the Federal Court is then extended to enable it to hear and determine all the matters in dispute.

Thus, in order to minimise the confusion which can arise from the different jurisdictions which may be involved in any licensing arrangement, it is always necessary, as a matter of course, to specify the governing law as either that of the Australian State or Territory in which the party concerned has its principal place of business, or that of the overseas country, as a first point of reference. In this respect, it should also be noted that the legal profession in Australia is organised on a State by State basis, so that it would not be reasonable to expect to find a lawyer in, say, Victoria with any detailed knowledge of the laws of New South Wales or, indeed, of any other Australian State.

The basis of all Australian law which is likely to be relevant to intellectual property rights and intellectual property licensing is English law, in that the Australian statutes are closely related to the corresponding English statutes, although to assert Australian independence and to increase the cost to litigants and the corresponding prosperity of the legal profession within Australia a number of amendments (most of which are inconsequential) have been introduced. There are also some amendments of substance, which will be referred to later.

So far as restrictive trade practices are concerned, the relevant legislation is contained in the Trade Practices Act 1974 of the Commonwealth and Part IV of this Act imposes onerous restrictions on commercial dealings which are thought to inhibit competition, in a general sense. However, section 51(3) contains a series of exemptions which relate to statutory intellectual property rights.

So far as rights which arise under patents are concerned, section 51(3) of the Act provides that:

> A contravention of a provision of this Part other than Section 46 or 48 shall not be taken to have been committed by reason of -
> (a) the imposing, or giving effect to, a condition of -
> (i) a licence granted by the proprietor, licensee or owner of a patent . . . or by a person who has applied for a patent
> to the extent that the condition relates to -
> (iii) the invention to which the patent or application for a patent relates or articles made by the use of that invention . . .

Section 46, to which the exemptions do not apply deals with monopolisation which is defined in terms of a corporation, which is in a position substantially to control a market for goods, using its market power to eliminate or inhibit a competitor or potential competitor; section 48 deals with retail price maintenance.

The application of the relevant provision of the Trade Practices Act to rights under patents was considered by the Australian High Court in *Transfield Pty Ltd v Arlo International Ltd* (1980) 30 ALR 201 in which the High Court gave a wide meaning to the exemptions.

The granting of exclusive licences is contemplated by the Patents Act 1952 of the Commonwealth and, accordingly, despite the apparently clear language of section 46 of the Trade Practices Act, which prohibits 'monopolisation', there does not seem to be any impediment to the granting of exclusive licences in Australia, or indeed licences which are limited to particular States or Territories or which are limited geographically in some other way - at least as far as Australian law is concerned. Further, there does not seem to be any impediment to the imposition upon an Australian licensee of a prohibition against exports although, as a matter of prudence and common sense, if any such limitation is included in a licensing agreement, notification ought to be given to the Trade Practices Commission under section 51(1)(g) of the Trade Practices Act. This confers a blanket exemption on a provision in 'any contract, arrangement or understanding being a provision that relates exclusively to the export of goods from Australia . . .' provided that the particulars of the provisions are notified to the Commission within fourteen days of the relevant agreement.

So far as provisions which require a licensee to obtain articles or a class of articles not protected by the patent from specified sources are concerned, the situation is much the same as in the United Kingdom in that there are corresponding prohibitions in the Patent Acts of both countries with the practical consequence that if any such restriction is contemplated, then the situation under both the Patents Act and the Trade Practices Act would need to be considered carefully, taking the particular restriction into account.

At present there is no problem with the payment of royalties, save of course that the licensing agreement, as indeed all agreements between an Australian resident and any overseas entity, will need to be approved by the Australian Reserve Bank, under the Banking (Foreign Exchange) Regulations. In most cases this is a formality, but it is a formality which must be observed and it is usual to seek approval to enter into an agreement either by submitting the agreement in draft form or by expressly including a provision in the agreement to the effect that it will not become effective until approval has been obtained. The standard form of approval does not carry any commitment by the Australian Government to approve the payment of royalties. This approval must be sought as and when royalties become payable but it will contain 'words of comfort' indicating that such approval is likely to be given while present policies continue.

Any attempt to impose a restriction as to price on the licensee could lead to great difficulty. Very often draft licences originating from overseas attempt to impose such an obligation. In such a case, the exemption from the provisions of the Trade Practices Act would not apply and the Act prohibits any form of retail price maintenance in very positive terms. However it seems that it would be possible for the licensee specifically to exercise some control over such matters as packaging and get-up of the patented article.

One of the provisions in the Australian Patents Act which may assume some importance is set out in section 112(4) to the effect that a patent licence can be determined by either party on three months' notice after the expiration of the last of the relevant patents which was in force at the date the licence was entered into. This corresponds with section 58(1) of the 1949 UK Act which now appears at greater length as section 45 of the 1977 Act.

The position as to trade marks in Australia is governed by the Trade Marks Act 1955 of the Commonwealth, which again has a number of features in common with the Trade Marks Act 1938 of the United Kingdom, but there are some important differences so far as competition law is concerned.

In *Pioneer Electronic Corporation v Registrar of Trade Marks* 17 ALR 43 the Australian High Court held that an importer of goods who merely sells the goods in the Australian market 'uses' the trade mark which has been applied to the goods by the overseas registered proprietor and is entitled to become a registered user of this mark. Then, in 1981, in *Atari v Dick Smith* (1980/1981) 33 ALR 20 the Victorian Supreme Court granted an interlocutory injunction to restrain Dick Smith from importing and selling Atari video tape recorders in Australia, on the basis that to sell these tape recorders in Australia would be to infringe the rights of Atari as the registered proprietor of the Australian trade mark. There was no question but that the tape recorders with which Dick Smith was concerned were quite genuine Atari tape recorders, but nevertheless the injunction was granted. Although an appeal was lodged against the decision, it is understood that this appeal was not proceeded with. It follows that if a licence is granted to use a trade mark in Australia by the registered proprietor of the mark, then goods originating from the registered proprietor can be kept off the Australian market, to the advantage of an importer who may or may not be a registered user of the mark in Australia.

The Trade Practices Act exempts agreements and arrangements concerning trade marks from the provisions of that Act which apply to restrictive trade practices (except for the monopolisation and resale price maintenance provisions to which reference was made earlier) if the provisions relate to the 'kinds, qualities or standards of goods bearing that mark that may be produced or supplied . . .' However, the appointing of a single registered user would not be a contravention of section 46 of the Act.

While the exemption is perhaps in narrower terms than in the case of patents, nevertheless it seems that all the normal provisions which appear in a Registered User Agreement may be included in such an agreement which relates to the use of a trade mark in Australia. In this respect, it should be noted that the Trade Marks Act 1955 provides for the removal of a mark if, up to one month before the date of application, a period of three years has elapsed during which the mark was not used.[1] It may be recalled that under section 26(1)(b) of the UK Act (which is the corresponding provision) the period is five years, not three years.

There have been a number of cases in which trade marks have been registered as a protective measure by overseas proprietors and later removed for non-use under this provision and if any licence concerning trade marks is granted, then any such licence should provide strictly for such minimum use as will preserve the mark, if for any reason there is some prospect of delay in the continuing commercial use of the mark.

The next type of tangible industrial property to be mentioned is registered designs. Again, the thought behind the registered designs legislation is the same as in the United Kingdom. The controversy as to the scope of protection to be given to designs, the shapes of which are dictated by function, is presumably common general knowledge. If it is proposed to license the manufacture in Australia of any article which is of an original design, or which has an original design applied to it, then it is suggested that before commercial production begins an application should be made for registration of the design, notwithstanding that the shape may be dictated by the function. The Australian Act has recently been amended specifically to permit the registration of designs which include features which are dictated by function and in addition, there is a substantial body of opinion to the effect that if a design which is registrable

---

1   Section 23(1)(b).

under the Act is not registered, then it loses all protection. Thus, the position may possibly be different from the position in the United Kingdom and, although there may be some residual protection by way of proceedings for passing off in a limited number of cases, there are also a number of cases in which copies of various designs have been produced in the far east for sale on the Australian market to the detriment of an importer or an Australian licensee, who does not have the intellectual property rights implied (but not promised) by the licence.

So far as registered designs are concerned, there is an exemption in the Trade Practices Act from those provisions which apply to restrictive trade practices (again, except for monopolisation and retail price maintenance) provided that the restriction in question relates to '. . . goods in respect of which the design is, or is proposed to be, registered and to which it is applied'. It follows that there is unlikely to be any impediment to the usual type of licence which applies to registered designs.

Turning to artistic and literary copyright, the position is much the same as in the United Kingdom. Australia is a party to the Berne Convention and also to the Universal Copyright Convention as well as a number of subsidiary conventions, and there is a similar exemption under the Trade Practices Act in relation to copyright words as exists in relation to the other tangible intellectual property rights.

However, Australia has taken a parallel position in copyright matters to that in relation to trade marks. In *Interstate Parcel Express Co. Pty Ltd v Time Life International* (1977) 15 ALR 353 the Australian High Court considered a factual situation in which the owner of the copyright in certain books had granted an exclusive licence to sell the works in Australia to the Interstate Parcel Express Co. Pty Ltd which carried on business in Australia under the name of Angus & Robertson. A chain of retail booksellers purchased copies of the books in question from a source in the United States of America, which was also licensed under the copyright and was not restricted under this licence in the manner in which it sold the books produced under the licence. However, the High Court held that the importation of the books into Australia and the sale of the books in Australia was an infringement of the copyright and upheld a decision of the Supreme Court of New South Wales granting an injunction against the sale of the books in Australia.

Accordingly, it would seem possible to grant an exclusive copyright licence in Australia and to prevent the importation of works which are subject to the copyright which originate either from the licensor or from some other licensee. Again, the exemption in the Act applies to the work or subject matter of the copyright.

So far as 'know-how' licences are concerned, the position in Australia is much the same as in the United Kingdom. While there is no exemption from the provisions of the Trade Practices Act which specifically relates to know-how, such licences, if they relate to genuine 'know-how' of the trade secret kind concerning processes rather than goods produced by the processes, would appear to be outside the scope of the legislation to the same extent as patent, design and copyright licences. Any licence concerning know-how will be subject to the law of the relevant State or Territory, both in its interpretation and as relates to the substantive nature of the subject matter and, accordingly, may be treated in slightly differing ways depending upon the jurisdiction concerned.

Finally, there can be a licence under the good will of some business carried on within the jurisdiction by the licensor, or on behalf of the licensor. This situation often arises in the general area of franchising in which, initially, no intellectual property rights of any kind exist in Australia concerning the subject matter of the franchise agreement. However, if the franchise agreement which, let us suppose, relates to some kind of 'fast food' product provides that any good will in the business concerned is to become the property of the franchisor, it is possible for the good will to be generated by the franchisee for the benefit of the franchisor which can then license this good will to other franchisees, having acquired an intellectual property right. The purpose of mentioning this is merely to indicate that such a right exists and can be of very considerable commercial importance in a country such as Australia. The other side of the coin is that if the idea is imported into Australia independently of the franchisee, then the good will may well accrue to the importer and the franchisor may find that one less international market exists.

Like all jurisdictions, Australia has its own peculiar rules which in practice mitigate the difficulties which appear from the letter of the legislation. Obviously, before venturing into any agreements or contractual arrangements in that country it might be prudent to make specific enquiries to establish the most appropriate way in which to minimise the impact of the legislation on whatever business transaction is contemplated.

AUSTRIA

Convergence Versus Competition

DR FRIEDERICH SCHWANK

Introduction

The Austrian Background to Anti-trust

(i) The size of the country and its market

Austria is a rather small country[1] so its economy is to a great extent dependent on imports and exports. Accordingly on the one hand the Austrian market is subject to the influx of foreign products, and on the other the Austrian manufacturer has also to compete in foreign markets.

A small country will perhaps be more likely to allow the formation of cartels than a big country since a cartel stabilises the market, protects the existing economic structure and provides assistance to domestic industry competing with foreign products. The formation of cartels is welcomed as a means of fostering productivity and of increasing the ability of Austria's industry to compete in the international markets. Such cartels are economically justified as they further the national economy and Austria's international payment balance.

(ii) The economic system

Austria's economic system is influenced to a great extent by the size of its regulated and protected market. A considerable amount of industry is nationalised or held by nationalised banks. Moreover, important sectors of trade are strictly regulated and exempt from the supply and demand system of the free market. The regulated trade mainly concerns basic foodstuffs and energy. Together with the public sector and the co-operatives the regulated sector at present produces 31 per cent of net national product.

As a considerable portion of the market is so protected and regulated, protection rather than competition is the Austrian style. Protective refuge from the perils of the free market is sought by Austrian entrepreneurs in their cartels, in

---

1 An in-depth analysis of Austria's present economic situation and system seen as a result of policies pursued by the government and other institutions formed by organised labour and capital can be found in Hanns Abele *et al.*, *Handbuch der österreichischen Wirtschaftpolitik*, Vienna, 1982. Economic facts and figures referred to in the following chapters are also taken from this source if not indicated otherwise.

recommendations of prices, price limits and margins issued by entrepreneurial organisations and in the control of price increases.

(iii) The economic structure

The economic structure in Austria is dominated by the medium and small enterprise. The large number of these is the basis of the free market. The majority of large enterprises are nationalised. Their existence is often remote from the principles of the free market: to provide jobs is thought more important than to make profits. Accordingly the maintenance of existing enterprises is considered to be the economic justification for the formation of cartels. In particular during the last few years a number of cartels have been formed with a view to securing the survival of enterprises[2] which, without the protection granted by their cartels, would have gone into liquidation.

The economic structure of Austria is also to be characterised by a considerable share of foreign capital. At present about 30 per cent of the statutory capital of public companies (joint stock) is held by foreigners. In the trade sector 50 per cent and in the insurance business 65 per cent is owned by foreigners. The author is not sure about the impact of foreign capital on the Austrian anti-trust situation: his impression is that foreign capital is not usually involved in fierce competition – apart from a few aggressive multinationals. It appears to be rather conservative. For example, a few years ago the car rental business became very competitive in Austria. As a consequence, one of the multinational car rentals simply withdrew from the Austrian market.

The Political and Economic Philosophy

Austrian political and economic philosophies both tend towards compromise, to converge: arrangements with competitors are more often sought than aggressive competition with them – joining them rather than beating them.[3]

In Austria the understanding between labour and capital – the so-called 'Sozialpartnerschaft' – is the factual judge granting or denying the registration of cartels.[4] They decide whether or not a cartel is economically justified. As this is a political decision anyway there is no opportunity for the Cartel Court to make economic politics of its own, by way of rulings in cartel matters. The judgments and orders rendered by the Cartel Court are therefore not subject to hot political discussions. Such a system can of course only work if supported by a philosophy of convergence.

---

2   However, the Cartel Act has not adopted the concept of 'crisis cartel'.

3   The political and economic philosophy behind the Austrian Cartel Act and its historical development has been described in great detail in Gerhard Hoffmann, 'The Austrian Cartel Law: Principles and Background', (Spring 1969) *The Antitrust Bulletin*, Volume XIV, at 249 to 278.

4   Under the auspices of *Sozialpartnerschaft* a special commission has been installed, whose main function is to advise the Cartel Court whether the registration of a cartel is economically justified. See: Dr Viktor A. Straberger, 'Der Paritätische Ausschuss für Kartellangelegenheiten', *Zukunft des Wettbewerbs in Österreich*, Innsbruck, 1981.

The main field of activity of *Sozialpartnerschaft* is the control of the increase of prices of almost all goods and services offered on the Austrian market. They are subject to approval unless the prices concerned are already regulated by law. The application for an increase in prices is usually lodged by a group of market leaders through a section of the chamber of commerce representing the interests of that particular branch. This is followed by intensive negotiations in which the applicants have to prove that production costs have risen to the extent that they wish to increase their prices. If this can be proved, the proposed increase will be permitted. Usually the negotiations lead to a compromise.

Price control is administered by a commission set up as a result of an understanding between capital and labour. To a certain extent its task is the same as that of an administrative body set up under a cartel. Once a price increase has been allowed, the whole branch will increase its prices in a concerted action and once the market leaders wish to increase their prices again, they come together to file a new joint application: that is at least a group-effect.

Of course, this system impairs competition in the Austrian market. However, as a compromise reached in the commission is the result of serious negotiations and accepted by capital and labour, by producers and consumers, it does not create the adverse effects of an illicit cartel by way of which its members achieve profits due to the elimination of competition. I think the Austrian system of price control – despite the control – provides workable competition. Some of the market factors have been moved from the streets on to a round table. There the market conditions are more ideal.

Austria has close economic links with neighbouring large markets, in particular in Germany and Italy. Its membership of EFTA and its associate membership of EEC have a strong impact on the Austrian market.[5] Legislation has had to be changed in order to comply with the requirements of international conventions and agreements. In particular effective export cartels in EEC or EFTA countries are no longer economically justified, even if they would be beneficial to the domestic economy. The legal and economic links with other countries will force Austria to accept more competition than in the past and to exercise more restraint in the registration of cartels.

The State-Controlled Market

The Regulated Market

The legislation for the regulated market is very bulky and technically complicated.[6] The relevant statutes are often enacted for a limited period only and are repeatedly extended after much political discussion. These acts usually provide

---

5 See Michael Schweitzer, 'Barriers to a Common West European Economic Area: the Case of Austria', (1981) *Journal of Institutional and Theoretical Economics* 137 at 508 to 524.
6 See appendix A: legislation, under the heading market regulation legislation.

for the setting up of commissions composed of political and economic bodies to render orders under which the market is regulated, prices fixed and surcharges levied in order to increase or reduce production.

Goods subject to this regulated market are mainly basic foodstuffs and energy. The regulations are so sophisticated that the system actually works smoothly in the interest of both the producer and the consumer. The production, the processing and the marketing levels are either subsidised or surcharged by various percentages, thereby creating uniform prices at all levels and in all geographical areas concerned. The regulation of the market is effected by increasing or reducing any one or more of the components of the prices. Price regulation boards for the various products concerned have the authority to adjust the price components to regulate production, supply and consumption.[7]

The basis for the smooth working of the system is of course a convergent economic philosophy: producers on the various levels, wholesalers, retailers and consumers have to refrain from exercising their unrestrained power on the market in the common interest and find instead a reasonable distribution of the 'cake' by way of negotiation, compromise and package deals.

The Controlled Market

Under the auspices of *Sozialpartnerschaft* a system for controlling the prices on the market also has been created, known as Paritätische Kommission.[8] This commission comprises representatives of various bodies and associations representing the market powers. There is no constitutional or legal basis for this commission but its informal rule over the market is effective. It has discretion to claim or disclaim competence to assume control of the price of any product or service offered unless it is already otherwise subject to legal regulation.

Proposed increases in prices are submitted to the commission for approval. The submissions are supported by evidence of increased costs, particular needs of the trade, statistics from the whole branch, documentation on calculation of prices etc. If the proposed increase appears reasonable to every member of the commission it will be approved, otherwise negotiations are conducted until a result is found which is acceptable to everybody. As the commission is mainly concerned with the increases of prices of goods and services already offered on the market, the prices for new goods or new services introduced into the Austrian market do not need its approval.

---

7   For an example see appendix B: the regulation of the milk price.
8   See Johann Farnleitner, *Die Paritätische Kommission*, Eisenstadt, 1977, (2nd ed.). Farnleitner has served on the commission for many years: he gives in his book a first-hand account of the organization of this body and the procedures adopted. As there is neither a legal basis nor any official rules published, Farnleitner's book is considered as an authoritative source.

Anti-trust Law and Practice[9]

The Cartel Act

The main piece of legislation is the present Cartel Act from 1972, based on the Cartel Act of 1951.[10] The Act deals with cartels, recommendations issued by entrepreneurial organisations, market-dominating enterprises, mergers and acquisitions, the so-called net-price system and the respective procedures.

The Scope of Cartels

The Austrian Cartel Act is based on the principle of registration of economically justified cartels. At present 67 cartels are registered.[11] The most usual types of cartel concern conditions, prices, quotas, costing and discounts.

Some branches of trade or industry are regulated completely by a cartel, for instance cement, electric wiring, electric bulbs, vinegar, skis; others are regulated by a group of interlocking cartels, for example the paper industry starting with pulp, wood import and chip-wood cartels, through to the producers of envelopes and agreements between paper wholesalers.

Definitions of Cartels

Cartels are defined[12] as any agreements, understandings, harmonised conduct or recommendations or announcements of prices between or by entrepreneurs, which have an impact on competition. Accordingly there are the following types of cartel:

(1) cartels by way of agreements which are any agreements between economically independent entrepreneurs or associations of entrepreneurs which, in pursuance of the common interest, aim at controlling or restricting competition, in particular with regard to production, sales or prices;

(2) understandings between entrepreneurs to that effect;

(3) recommendations to observe fixed prices, price limits or costing directives if

  (a) economic or social pressure was to be applied for that purpose, or

  (b) such understandings or recommendations were not expressly and unambiguously designated as non-binding;

(4) harmonised conduct or concerted action that is action by entrepreneurs which is neither accidental nor incidental to the market situation and actu-

---

9 For further reference see Annual Reports on Austria in Annual Reports on Competition Policy in OECD Member Countries published by OECD, Paris.
10 Anti-trust legislation was already in force during the Austro-Hungarian Monarchy, for example in 1838 a decree declared all agreements controlling offers at public auctions null and void. In 1870 an Act was promulgated which made illegal all agreements of either employers or employees with an intention to control the labour market.
11 See appendix C: list of cartels registered at August 1982.
12 Section 1 Cartel Act.

ally creates the effect of controlling or restricting the market (thereby the Act considers actual behaviour on the market as a cartel, irrespective of any existing gentleman's agreement. Harmonised conduct has to be registered with the Cartel Court only if so required by it);

(5) cartels by way of announcement, in other words, any advertising of goods or services and quoting prices unless the prices quoted are expressly and unambiguously described as non-binding. In particular TV and radio commercials are concerned with this provision but also any advertisements, posters, price lists, information leaflets, prices printed or tagged on merchandise or its wrapping, unless such price information is supplied by the retailer or by the one who actually renders the services to the consumer.

Petty Cartels

Petty cartels[13] which do not supply more than five per cent of a national, and not more than 25 per cent of a local market, are valid without registration and can be registered without having to satisfy the test of economic justification. But if it is later discovered that it was not in fact economically justified at the time of its registration, such a petty cartel will be deregistered. They are subject to supervision in order to prevent abuses. If the share of the market is exceeded later on, the cartel will remain a petty cartel within the legal sense provided that no new member has joined this cartel.

Exemptions

Exempted from the Cartel Act are[14]

(1) cartels concerning forestry;

(2) cartels of banks, building societies and insurance companies, as their terms and conditions of business are under the control of the Ministry of Finance;

(3) cartels of all companies concerned with public transport and the transport of goods;

(4) generally also the commercial co-operatives, provided their cartel agreements are within the scope of their institutional terms;

(5) resale price maintenance for bookshops, art and music retailers and newsagents.

Foreign Cartels and Export Cartels

Foreign cartels are subject to the Austrian Cartel Act if they have an impact on the Austrian market.[15] However, the extraterritorial effect of the Austrian Cartel Act is limited in practice by the lack of means of enforcement available to a small country like Austria.

---

13   Section 2 Cartel Act.
14   Section 5 Cartel Act.
15   Section 4 Cartel Act.

Austrian cartels concerning foreign markets only are not subject to the Cartel Act unless the cartel impairs trade under the association agreement with the EEC, the EFTA agreement or the agreements of EFTA with Finland and Spain.[16]

There is no definition of what will be considered as 'economically justified'.[17] It is left to the persuasiveness of the facts and figures supplied by counsel representing the prospective members of the cartel. There are no established tests for economic justification. Usually the following factors are taken into account:

(1) situation of the particular industry or branch of trade;
(2) the smooth operation of the distribution of the goods on the market;
(3) the jobs concerned;
(4) the sufficient supply of goods and easy accessibility for the public;
(5) the interests of the end-consumer.

Only cartels which impair the smooth operation of the agreements with EEC and EFTA are in no instance economically justified.[18]

Procedure

The registration of cartels lies in the hands of the Cartel Court. Its decision can be appealed to the Superior Cartel Court organised as a special bench of the Supreme Court.[19]

An abuse of a cartel is subject to criminal proceedings against its members, officers and representatives with a maximum punishment of three years' imprisonment and heavy fines.[20]

Market Regulation for Skis

A cartel well known for its sophisticated terms and its scope of membership is the market regulation agreement for skis.[21] Members of this cartel are the Austrian ski-producers as well as almost all importers and distributors of foreign skis in Austria and the majority of retailers of skis. They all got into difficulties during the last few years due to overproduction caused by new production techniques, the market-power of powerful buyers, in particular chains, as well as fierce competition between sports shops.

In this cartel agreement the retail prices for skis are regulated and are bind-

---

16 Section 5(1)2 and (2) Cartel Act.
17 Section 24(1)6 Cartel Act.
18 Section 24(2) Cartel Act.
19 Sections 54 to 99 Cartel Act.
20 Sections 101 to 113 Cartel Act.
21 The market regulation for skis and a number of other cartels has been masterminded by Dr Viktor A. Straberger, who has also written the leading reference texts on Cartels and Antitrust in Austria. The author is indebted to Dr Straberger for material provided and valuable suggestions for this presentation.

ing. The producers and importers undertake to sell their products to those retailers only who are members of the cartel. They, in turn, have to sell the skis at fixed prices to consumers. The cartel also provides for sophisticated administrative machinery, *inter alia* an individual number on each pair of skis, recording of the names of buyers, etc.

However, despite the cartel one large ski-producer became insolvent or, one could say, thanks to the cartel not more than one became insolvent.

Dominant Positions

Market-dominating enterprises are defined by the Cartel Act[22] as follows:

(1) enterprises without or nearly without competitors in the market for their products or services; or

(2) enterprises having a market share of more than five per cent where

    (a) the whole market is supplied by two or three enterprises only; or

    (b) being one of the four biggest enterprises having together a market share of at least 80 per cent.

The relevant market is the whole national market including imports.[23] The Cartel Court can make an order forbidding the abuse of the dominant position by a market-leading enterprise. Extra profits made by such abuse can be forfeited.

At present there are about three hundred enterprises[24] registered as market-dominating. This low figure is surprising, as there are in fact a large number of other enterprises which do dominate the market but are not as yet registered. The reason for this lies in the policy of not strictly enforcing the relevant provisions of the Cartel Act. This policy is another result of *Sozialpartnerschaft* and it could be expected that the legal provisions would be strictly enforced only in circumstances under which the market leaders and mergers of enterprises could no longer be controlled by the informal means of *Sozialpartnerschaft*.

Mergers

Mergers, as defined by the Cartel Act,[25] can be any one of the following:

(1) acquisition of another enterprise, wholly or in the main part;

(2) purchase of shares of another enterprise exceeding 25 per cent of the capital;

(3) lease of factories or premises of another enterprise;

(4) obtaining at least half the positions on the board of directors or supervisory board of another company;

---

22 Sections 40 to 48 Cartel Act.
23 Products and services can be substituted by any others satisfying the same need under the given conditions of the market: section 41 Cartel Act.
24 In August 1982, a total number of 297 market-dominating enterprises was registered.
25 Sections 49 to 52 Cartel Act.

(5) every other link between enterprises enabling the one to dominate the other directly or indirectly.

All these mergers have to be registered with the cartel register within a month.[26] Non-compliance carries an administrative fine of up to A.S. 200,000 which is about £6,600.

Exempted from control and registration are mergers of enterprises which result in a market share of less than five per cent. The relevant market is the whole national market for the relevant goods or services including substitutes on the demand side at the present conditions of the market.

Vertical Restrictions

Vertical restrictions of competition by way of retail price maintenance are dealt with under the Cartel Act.[27] Recommendations to observe fixed prices, price limits or costing directives, by means of which competition is to be controlled or restricted, are considered as cartels, provided that

(1) economic or social pressure is to be applied for that purpose or
(2) such recommendations are not expressly and unambiguously described as non-binding.

Recommendations to observe prices, price limits or costing directives issued by professional bodies or societies furthering a particular industry or profession, provided such recommendations do not constitute a cartel, have to be notified to the cartel register and entered into the registry.[28] Thirty-nine such recommendations have been entered into the registry.[29] An example of such a recommendation is the schedule of fees for expert opinions on jewellery and watches issued by the professional body of gold and silversmiths.

The Market Power of the Trade

During the last few years the increasing market power of wholesalers and retailers, particularly those organised in chains, has become a danger to the smooth working of vertical competition. Producers have found themselves more and more at the mercy of the trade deciding which brand to buy and put into the supermarkets.

The response of Austrian legislation to this tendency was the Act concerning the improvement of consumer supply and conditions of competition (*Nahversorgungsgesetz*).[30] Under this Act practices of entrepreneurs can be forbidden if they impair workable competition. In particular the offering or claiming, the giving or accepting of moneys or other services, including rebates and special conditions granted between supplier and wholesaler, are considered

---

26 In August 1982, a total number of 107 mergers had been registered.
27 Section 1(1)4 Cartel Act.
28 Sections 36 to 39 Cartel Act.
29 As at August 1982.
30 [1977] *Federal Law Gazette* BGB1 at 392 as amended at [1980] 121.

to be such practices if there is no return for such additional payments or services. Also the supplier must not offer or grant differing conditions to particular retailers without reasonable justification.

The introduction of this Act in 1977 has in fact improved vertical competition and suppliers, wholesalers and retailers appear to comply with this voluntarily as they obviously do not wish to get involved in any proceedings under the Act.

Refusal to Supply

This Act also contains provisions concerning retailing and supply to retailers. Enterprises which normally supply retailers may be ordered by the Cartel Court to supply a given retailer if failure to supply – including refusal to supply – would either impair his ability to compete or result in gaps in the distribution system of everyday goods for the public. [31]

The retailer who was not supplied does not have the right to take the supplier to court. His remedy is to inform his branch of the Chamber of Commerce and they will lodge a complaint with the Cartel Court. As no case has yet been brought, up to date, it is assumed that the mere legal possibility is sufficient deterrent.

Tendencies of Forthcoming Legislation

The Cartel Act will be amended within the next few years. It is expected that the following topics will be included:

(1) a general time limit for all registered cartels, which means that the members of cartels will have to apply every three or five years for re-registration and again pass the test of economic justification for their cartel;

(2) the possible inclusion of co-operatives within the application of the Act as they have gained considerable market power due to their exemption from the Cartel Act;

(3) a new concept of dominant positions and merger control, based on a workable definition of the market and its concentration probably along the terms of Hirschman-Herfindahl-Index;

(4) a possible switch in the method of enforcement of the Cartel Act from criminal prosecution to heavy administrative fines comparable to EEC fines;

(5) exclusive distributorship agreements, giving clear terms within which they will comply with the law.

The general tendency of the amendment will be to introduce more competition into the Austrian market and to streamline it more with the European anti-trust policy.

---

31   In return the retailers must not conceal from the public their stocks of everyday goods and are obliged to sell those goods in usual quantities to the consumers.

The Foreigner and the Austrian Market

Starting Business Activities

The foreigner who wishes to sell on the Austrian market is well advised to take into account the specific characteristics of this market, which have been described above. In particular it is advisable to get in touch with the section of the Austrian chamber of commerce, which deals with the particular trade in which he is interested. Here he will be advised about any rules with which he must comply in his proposed activities. Unusual marketing practices, in particular with respect to wholesalers or commercial agents, should be checked with an Austrian counsel.

Distribution

Distribution agreements which provide for certain channels, for example authorised dealers, for the distribution of merchandise or exclusive distribution agreements became the concern of the Cartel Court only in the late 1970's.[32] In a number of cases agreements have been scrutinised and it has been held that these agreements can be cartels due to the effect they create on the market. Such cartels do not need registration unless the Cartel Court so requires.

As there is no established court practice and no legislation dealing with distribution, it is advisable to draft agreements very carefully and to refrain from adopting standard forms of contract used in other countries.

Licensing of Industrial Property Rights

The leading case was decided by the Austrian Supreme Court in 1964.[33] It was held that agreements which fall within the terms of the Cartel Act but concern the licensing of patents are not to be considered as cartels provided that the agreements and their restrictions in exercising the licence do not exceed the frame of the legal protection granted to the patent.

The Austrian practice appears to follow the 'essence doctrine' adopted in other jurisdictions.

The Use of Cartels

A foreigner should also check whether his business activities will be subject to any provisions of the Cartel Act. If his products are of particular value to the Austrian economy and if there are only a few competitors of his products on the market, the possibility of the registration of the cartel should be taken into consideration. After all, a cartel might not only be economically justified but also should work to the advantage of its members.

---

32 See Dr Viktor A. Straberger, 'Der Vertriebsbindungsvertrag in der österreichischen Praxis', [1980] GesRZ at 206 et seq.

33 Supreme Court, 24 November 1964, (4 Ob 346/64) ÖBl. 1965, 137.

Appendix A: Legislation on Anti-trust and Market Regulation
The legislation can be grouped as follows:

(1) anti-trust,
(2) restrictive practices,
(3) market regulation,
(4) external trade regulations.

It should be noted that these Acts are interlocking and should be considered as a complete set of legal rules governing the market. They are applied – and sometimes not applied – along the understanding of *Sozialpartnerschaft*.

Anti-trust Legislation

Kartellgesetz: Cartel Act

Nahversorgungsgesetz: Act concerning the improvement of consumer supply and conditions of competition

Restrictive Practices Legislation

Bundesgesetz gegen den unlauteren Wettbewerb: Unfair Competition Act

Rabattgesetz: Rebate Act

Zugabengesetz: Bonus Act (concerning the illegality of bonuses given in connection with goods and services)

Zuwendungsgesetz: Gift Act (concerning the illegality of gifts in the trade)

Einheitspreisgeschäfteverordnung: One-Price Shops Regulation (concerning the illegality of shops selling a collection of various goods for one price)

Ausverkaufsverordnung: Sales Regulation (concerning sales etc.)

Ladenschlussgesetz: Shop Closing Hour Act

Grundpreisauszeichnungsverordnung: Basic Price Regulation for Packed Consumer Goods

Market Regulation Legislation

Preisgesetz: Prices Act

Marktordnungsgesetz: Market Control Act (for milk and grain products)

Viehwirtschaftsgesetz: Livestock Trade Act (for controlling the livestock and meat market)

Weinwirtschaftsgesetz: Wine Trade Act

Geflügelwirtschaftsgesetz: Fowl Trade Act

Landwirtschaftsgesetz: Farming Act (containing measures to safeguard nutrition and to maintain an economically sound farming community)

Mühlengesetz: Mills Act

Versorgungssicherungsgesetz: Basic Supply Act (to ensure undisturbed production and supply generally to the people and other institutions with important economic and basic necessities)

Schrottlenkungsgesetz: Iron Scrap Control Act

Lebensmittelbewirtschaftungsgesetz: Victuals Control Act

Energielenkungsgesetz: Energy Control Act (containing measures to ensure the supply of energy)

Energieförderungsgesetz: Energy Support Act (containing support measures for energy supply industries)

Erdölbevorratungs- und Meldegesetz: Crude Storage and Information Act (concerning the keeping of emergency reserves for crude and oil products and information obligations in order to secure the supply of energy

Erdölbevorratungs-Förderungsgesetz: Crude reserves Support Act (concerning a federal guarantee for borrowings of the Crude Reserve Company)

External Trade Regulations

Außenhandelsgesetz: External Trade Act (concerning export and import of goods)

Antidumpinggesetz: Anti-Dumping Act (concerning measures for the import of goods subsidised abroad)

Antimarktstörungsgesetz: Act against interference with the market (containing measures to avoid damage to the Austrian economy by way of imports interfering with the market)

EGKS-Abkommen-Durchführungsgesetz: Act for performing Article 20 of the Agreement between Austria and the member states of the EEC

Ausfuhrförderungsgesetz: Export Supporting Act (concerning federal guarantees for export agreements)

Ausfuhrfinanzierungsförderungsgesetz: Export Financing Support Act (concerning the financing of export deals)

Außenhandelsförderungsbeitragsgesetz: Export Trade Supporting Contributions Act (levying contributions for the support of the export trade)

Appendix B: The Regulation of the Milk Price

Regulation of production level	*Austrian Schilling Currency*
The price the farmer is paid for one kilogramme of milk, including 8 per cent VAT, is	4.55

Further to 8 per cent VAT of   0.33
the farmer has to accept the following deductions
from this selling price for the purpose of market
regulations:

   (1) for furthering the sale of milk   0.09
   (2) for control of the milk-producing cattle   0.048
   (3) for advertising   0.015

leaving him with net proceeds of   4.067

Regulation of processing and marketing level

The dairy's buying price for one kilogramme of
milk is   4.55
less deductable 8 per cent VAT   0.33
Cost for one kilogramme raw milk   4.22
The following amounts are added before the milk
comes to the consumer:

   (1) contribution for compensation with the
       prices for butter and cheese (thereby
       subsidising butter and cheese)   2.10
   (2) transport cost balance contribution
       (therefore milk costs the same
       everywhere, irrespective of the costs of
       transport between producer and
       consumer)   0.34
   (3) for furthering the sale of milk   0.50
   (4) calculation adjustment for kilogramme
       into litre (one litre milk is slightly
       heavier than one kilogramme)   0.21
   (5) production, marketing and distribution
       costs of the dairy, including their profit 1.63
   (6) handling costs of the retailers, including
       their profit   0.99
   (7) 8 per cent VAT   0.80

Consumer's price for one litre milk   10.80

Appendix C: List of Cartels Registered at August 1982

This list shows only the cartels presently registered. Terminated cartels and cartels not required to be registered are not shown.

K5   *Altpapier Ein- und Verkaufsübereinkommen*: purchase and selling agreement concerning waste paper

K43   *Arbeitsgemeinschaft der Briefumschlaghersteller und Briefpapier-konfektionäre in Österreich*: joint venture of envelope and letter paper manufacturers in Austria

K40   *Autosammelladungskonferenz*: cargo collecting conference for the road

K41   *Bahnsammelladungskonferenz*: cargo collecting conference for the railway

K46   *Baustahlgitter*: steel-lattice for construction

K60   *Drahtseilverband*: wire cable association

K3   *Essigkartell*: vinegar cartel

K53   *Handpappenfabriken*: factories for hand-made cardboard

K23   *Holzfaserbau und Isolierplatten*: woodfibre and insulation panels

K34   *Kabel Evidenzbureau*: cable information bureau

K73   *Kartell des Großhandels mit elektrischen Leitungen*: cartel for wholesalers of electric wires

K68   *Kartellvertrag der österreichischen Zuckerindustrie*: cartel agreement of the Austrian sugar industry

K27   *Kartellvertrag der Zementindustrie*: cartel agreement of the cement industry

K2   *Montagekartell*: cartel for installations

K36   *Österreichische Glühlampenindustrie*: Austrian electric bulb industry

K35   *Österreichische Kleberollenerzeuger*: Austrian gummed-tape manufacturers

K54   *Österreichische Maschinenpappenfabriken*: Austrian machine-made cardboard factories

K62   *Österreichische Papierverkaufsgesellschaft (ÖPA)*: Austrian paper-selling company

K22   *Österreichische Scheideanstalten*: Austrian refineries

K39   *Österreichische Wellpappeeryeuger*: Austrian corrugated cardboard manufacturers

K11   *Preßhefekartell*: pressed yeast cartel

K15   *Sägen- und Maschinenmesserkonvention*: Saw and machine blades convention

K32   *Schulbücherkartell*: cartel for school books

K31   *Speiseölkartell*: cartel for edible oil

K17   *Spreißelholzvereinbarung*: agreement concerning chip wood

K51   *Sulfitzellstoffindustrie*: sulphite cellulose industry

K52   *Übereinkommen zum Verkauf von Hartplattenerzeugnissen in Österreich*: agreement on the sale of fibreboard products in Austria

K7   *Vereinbarung der österreichischen Kohlensäureindustrie*: agreement of the Austrian carbon dioxide industry

K48   *Vereinigung österreichischer Papiergroßhändler*: union of the Austrian paper wholesalers

K38   *Verkauf kaltgewalzten Bandstahles*: sale of cold rolled strip steel

K33   *Vertriebsgesellschaft für isolierte Leitungen*: marketing society for insulated cables

K61   *Werksübereinkommen Drahtindustrie*: working agreement concerning the wiring industry

K12   *Arbeitsgemeinschaft Veterinaria*: joint venture for veterinary goods

K37   *Arbeitsgemeinschaft Pharmazeutica*: joint venture for pharmaceuticals

K13   *Baumwollspinner Konditionenkartell*: cartel of conditions for cotton spinners

K14   *Baumwollweber Konditionenkartell*: cartel of conditions for cotton weavers

K45   *Konditionenkartell der Handelsmühlen Österreichs*: cartel of conditions for commercial mills in Austria

K8   *Lesezirkelkartell*: readers' circle cartel

K58   *Österreichische Zylinder-, Lager- und Kurbelwellenbearbeitungsbetriebe*: Austrian cylinder, bearings and crankshaft works

K56   *Pharmig Interessengemeinschaft pharmazeutischer Erzeuger in Österreich*: Pharmig venture of manufacturers of pharmaceuticals in Austria

K47   *Photoartikel*: photographic articles

K19   *Sonderausschuß Walzstahl*: special commission concerning rolled steel

K42   *Tegu Interessengemeinschaft technischer Gummi- und Asbestwarengroßhändler*: Tegu venture of technical wholesalers of rubber and asbestos wares

K30   *Textillohnveredelungsindustrie*: commissioned finishing industry for textiles

K18   *Übereinkommen der Seidenweber*: agreement of silk weavers

K81   *Bagatellkartell Morak-Jordan*: petty cartel Morak-Jordan

K82   *Bagatellkartel Schmidt-Miba*: petty cartel Schmidt-Miba

K26   *Bagatellkartell der Opeldirekhändler Österreichs*: petty cartel of Opel direkt dealers in Austria

K76   *Bagatellkartell 'VÖM' Verband österreichischer Motoreninstandsetzungsbetriebe, Konditionenvereinbarung*: petty cartel 'VÖM' (Union of Austrian motor repair works)

K21   *Daimler-Benz AG – Steyr-Daimler-Puch*: Daimler-Benz AG – Steyr-Daimler-Puch

K80   *Grundig (Vertriebsbindung)*: Grundig (restrictive distribution agreement)

K15   *Hamol kosmetische Produkte AG*: Hamol cosmetic products company

K74   *Sortenbereinigungskartell österreichischer Papiererzeuger*: cartel for settling the varieties of Austrian paper producers

K67   *Vertriebs- und Rationalisierungsvertrag Backerbsen und Frittaten*: marketing and rationalisation agreement for fried batter peas and pancake noodles

K78   *Wirkungskartell der Coca Cola GesmbH*: cartel by effect of Coca Cola GesmbH

K64   *Sondervereinbarung Sonnberger*: special agreement Sonnberger

K65   *Wiener Neustädter Pappenfabrik*: cardboard manufacturer of Wiener Neustadt

K75   *Bagatellkartell Oö. Brennstoffhändler*: petty cartel of fuel dealers in Upper Austria

K79   *Erzeugung und Großhandel Isolierte Leitungen*: production and wholesale of insulated wiring

K83   *Gipskartonplattenerzeuger*: manufacturers of plaster panels

K84   *BMW-Steyr*: BMW-Steyr

K85   *Marktregelungsvertrag Ski*: market regulation agreement for skis

K86   *Kooperationsvertrag TWU-Stubai*: cooperation agreement TWU-Stubai

K88   *Ingelen, Figer & Co. (Vertriebsbindung)*: Ingelen, Figer & Co. (restrictive distribution agreement)

K89   *Hartplattenindustrie*: fibre boards industry

K90   *Körting (Vertriebsbindung)*: Körting (restrictive distribution agreement)

K91   *Hartplattenindustrie*: fibre boards industry

BELGIUM

Vertical Price Fixing in Belgium

EMIL PAULIS

Introduction

Vertical price fixing in Belgium is regulated mainly by general civil law provisions contained in the *Code Civil Belge* of 1803 (*Code Napoléon*). The analysis of these provisions will be the subject of the first section of this article. There are however a number of specific laws which limit the freedom of price fixing, sometimes to a considerable extent. These specific laws will be explained in the second part. The present article will not deal with the application by the Belgian courts of Articles 85 and 86 of the EEC Treaty which are of course complementary to the Belgian legislation but can only apply where the anti-competitive restrictions resulting from vertical price fixing affect trade between the EEC Member States.

General Civil Law Provisions

In the analysis of the general civil law provisions, a distinction will be drawn between, on the one hand, the effects of vertical price fixing agreements between the contracting parties, and on the other hand the effects of such agreements on third parties who are not parties to these agreements. Following this distinction between the contractual and extra-contractual aspects of vertical price fixing, the following topics will next be examined:

   (1) the question of validity of vertical price fixing agreements
   (2) the question of *Lückenlosigkeit* (watertightness) of these agreements and
   (3) the consequences of a breach of a price fixing contract.

Then, the next section of the article will principally deal with the theory of *tierce complicité* which was developed by doctrine and jurisprudence to establish a third party liability in connection with violations of restrictive contracts.

Contractual Aspects

(i) Validity of vertical price fixing agreements

Based on the principal of freedom to contract (*principe de l'autonomie de la volonté*) vertical price fixing agreements are generally accepted as lawful, both by the courts and authoritative legal literature. There are however two exceptions to this freedom. Price fixing agreements are illegal

(1) if they are specifically prohibited by law or

(2) if their object is contrary to good morals or to public policy. [1]

Derogations from price fixing freedom by specific laws will be treated in the second part of the article. An agreement would be contrary to good morals and public policy if its object was to create abnormal price increases or to assure to dealers abnormal profits. [2] On the contrary, price agreements are valid if they have for instance as their objective one or more of the following:

(1) to ensure a fair recovery of costs and to assure a fair profit,

(2) to maintain the quality and reputation of a branded product,

(3) to treat equally small dealers and big department stores, or

(4) to protect the market against price cutting.

The validity of price fixing agreements therefore depends on the objective(s) pursued. This makes it necessary to analyse in each case the economic justification underlying the price agreement. This does not however alter the exceptional application of Articles 6 and 1133 and leaves untouched the general principle of validity of vertical price fixing agreements.

(ii) 'Lückenlosigkeit' of the vertical price fixing system

The practising of vertical price fixing raises the question of whether the manufacturer, importer or distributor is obliged to impose its fixed price on all Belgian dealers ('close' or 'watertight' system of distribution). The Court and the legal writers [3] require for the validity of a vertical price fixing system that it fulfills the criteria of *Lückenlosigkeit*. This is based on the general principle of equal treatment, and on article 1134 *Code Civil* which provides that agreements must be executed in good faith (*de bonne foi*). It follows that a manufacturer applying fixed prices has a positive obligation to ensure:

(1) that all dealers or intermediaries are bound by contract to apply the fixed price (with an obligation upon all wholesalers to impose the same obligation on their retailers),

---

1 Articles 6 and 1133 Code Civil.

2 See cases quoted in Robert Kruithof, *De Verticale Prijsbinding van Merkartikelen*, at 85, Note 17.

3 See R. Kruithof, *op.cit*, at 86, Notes 18 and 19; L. Van Bunnen, *Droits intellectuels et problèmes de concurrence*, UCL at 95; and Van Rijn and Heenen, *Principes de droit commercial*, 1976, No. 220 at 229.

(2) that the contracting parties actually observe the fixed price, which may require the installing of regular controls and the prosecution in court of any violation of the price system.

Kruithof defends the view that a price fixing system need not be uniform for the whole country.[4] According to that writer, a manufacturer is under an obligation to impose the same fixed price only on those dealers who are in competition with each other. A manufacturer may therefore charge different prices in different cities or different regions and he may even decide not to apply a fixed price system in a particular part of the country while he does so in the rest of Belgium.

(iii) Breach of price fixing contracts

It follows from the principle of *Lückenlosigkeit* analysed above and from the application of the adage *exceptio non adimpleti contractus*, recognised in civil law, that if one dealer fails to apply the fixed price, the other dealers are no longer bound to sell at that price. There are basically three possible courses of action open to the manufacturer in order to remedy such a failure to comply with the fixed price obligation:

(1) Action of annulment of the contract (*action en résolution*) with a claim for damages against the defaulting party. Such action would be based on Article 1184 *Code Civil*. If the contract contains no stipulated liquidated damages, the Court will assess the damages *ex aequo et bono*.
(2) An action for specific performance with periodic penalty payments (*astreintes*) in order to compel the defaulting party to put an end to its breach of contract. Such action would be based on Article 1184 *Code Civil* and Article 1385 *bis* of the Belgian *Code Judiciaire*.
(3) A refusal to supply the defaulting party. An individual refusal to supply is in principle acceptable.[5] Such refusal becomes however unlawful if it is abusive. In that case it becomes an act contrary to honest commercial practice, for instance if a distributor suddenly stops supplying one of his long-established dealers without legitimate justification.[6] Collective boycott measures, on the contrary, are in principle illegal.[7] Collective boycotts can however be lawful if their object is the protection of legitimate professional and trading interests such as the prevention of an undue fall in prices, the guarantee of the quality of a product and the securing of a fair remuneration to the trade or profession.[8]

The manufacturer may not bring an application for a cease and desist order

---

4   R. Kruithof, *op.cit.*, at 87.
5   See L. Van Bunnen, *op.cit.*, at 95 and 100.
6   See Trib. Comm. Bruxelles, 16 December 1974, JCB 1975, III, 186; see also certain limitations resulting from the law on price control, discussed in the second half of this paper.
7   See *Fedetab* case, Court of Appeal, Brux., 27 May 1968, JT 1968, at 646 and Trib. Comm. Nivelles, 1 March 1973, JCB III at 484.
8   See the pharmaceuticals case *Union Spepha*, Cass. 2 June 1960, Pas. 1960, I, at 1133.

(an injunction of cessation) under Articles 54 and 55 of the Law of 14 July 1971 on commercial practices.[9] Such action is not possible because the Law of 1971 does not apply to a breach of contract but applies only to extra-contractual acts contrary to honest commercial practice within the meaning of that law. An application for an injunction of cessation would however be admissible if a breach of contract was at the same time an act contrary to honest commercial practice. This would require illegal conduct, such as:

(1) an abusive refusal to supply,
(2) a violation of public policy,
(3) an act of *tierce complicité*,[10]
(4) selling at a loss contrary to Article 22 of the Law of 14 July 1971,
(5) illegal advertising contrary to Article 20 of the same law,
(6) defacing of control numbers inscribed on branded goods to render controls by the manufacturer impossible.

The above acts are more usually those of third parties not bound by a vertical price fixing contract. The liability of third parties in connection with vertical price fixing is dealt with in the following section.

Extracontractual Aspects

Can a third party be bound by a price fixing contract concluded between a manufacturer and his dealers? If not, can such third party incur a liability towards the manufacturer if he participates with a contracting party in the violation of a price fixing contract? If so, in what circumstances? These are the questions that will be examined under this section.

Article 1165 Code civil stipulates:

> Les conventions n'ont d'effet qu'entre les parties contractantes: elles ne nuisent point au tiers, et elles ne lui profitent que dans le cas prévu par l'article 1121 (stipulation in favour of a third party).

This Article in essence stipulates that contracts create rights and obligations only as between the contracting parties. As a consequence, third parties are not bound by contracts concluded between other parties. This principle is also valid for vertical price fixing contracts. Such contracts are not normally enforceable against third parties, in other words third parties do not have to respect the fixed price when reselling products subject to a price fixing contract.

However, in a decision of 27 May 1909, the Belgian Supreme Court (Cour de Cassation) made a distinction between the internal effects of a contract and the existence of the contract as such.[11] The Court held that the existence of the contract as a matter of fact had to be recognised by third parties. This opened

---

9 For a commentary on that law, see E. Paulis, 'An Introduction to Belgian Anti-trust Law', [1980] ECLR at 413.
10 See under *Extracontractual Aspects* below.
11 Cass. 27 May 1909, Pas. 1909, I, 272.

the way to an action for damages against third parties who participate with a contracting party in the violation of a restrictive contract such as a vertical price fixing agreement. Following this decision, doctrine and jurisprudence have developed the *théorie de la tierce complicité*. This theory concerns the liability of a third party who participates in the violation of another party's contract. This new liability is an extracontractual liability which has given rise to several applications and to the development of two separate doctrines.

The first doctrine on *tierce complicité* is based on a decision of the Supreme Court of 24 November 1932. [12] The case concerned an exclusive purchase contract between a brewery and a guest-house whereby the latter was to purchase all its drinks from the brewery. A second brewery knew about the existence of this exclusive purchase contract but nevertheless supplied the guest-house with its drinks. The Court held:

> . . . la seule connaissance d'une convention n'engage pas la responsabilité du tiers qui a participé avec le débiteur à son inexécution; qu'il faut en outre et nécessairement qu'il ait agi en vue d'aider celui-ci à violer ses engagements; attendu que, dans l'espèce, l'arrêt entrepris constate en fait et souverainement qu'il n'est point établi à suffisance de droit qu'il y avait eu, chez l'intimé Rigaux, une intention doleuse ou une véritable mauvaise foi lorsqu'il a exécuté les commandes qui lui étaient passées par Lambert.

Following this decision, there are two conditions required for the application of the liability of third parties:

(1) knowledge of the existence of the exclusive contract and
(2) an act of bad faith, that is an intention to assist the other party in the violation of its contractual obligation. [13]

This would for instance be the situation where a third party induced a contracting party of the manufacturer to violate its price maintenance obligation, defaced the numbers on the goods to render any control by the manufacturer impossible or refused to indicate the name of its supplier.

The second doctrine on *tierce complicité* differs from the first in that it does not require an act of bad faith; the mere knowledge and direct participation in the violation of a contract is sufficient to make the third party liable towards the manufacturer. In other words, the knowledge of the existence of the contract as such imposes on third parties a positive obligation to refrain from helping another party to violate its contractual obligations.

Kruithof has submitted that these two different doctrines could be reconciled by the application of the theory of *abus de droit*. [14] *Abus de droit* arises in cases of abuses of rights to cause prejudice to somebody else, or, more generally, in

---

12　Cass. 24 November 1932, Pas. 1933, I, 19; see also Cass. 9 November 1973, Pas. 1974, I, 270; Comm. Brux. 30 June 1972, JCB, 1973 III, 44.
13　See cases quoted by R. Kruithof, *op.cit.*, at 98, Note 53.
14　R. Kruithof, *op.cit.*, at 102 and 103.

cases of fault in the exercise of a right which defeats the purpose of a law. This includes cases where the exercise of a right goes manifestly beyond the limits of the normal exercise of that right by a prudent and careful person.[15] Kruithof submits that there would always be an *abus de droit* where a third party knows of the existence of a price fixing contract and participates directly with a contracting party in the violation of a contract, if such violation had not been possible without the help of that third party. The intention of the third party and the seriousness of his fault would however be irrelevant.

In relation to the third parties' liability based on *tierce complicité*, it need hardly be noted that proof of either the act of bad faith (intention to help the other party violate its obligations) or of fault in the exercise of a right (*abus de droit*) will be difficult in most cases. As an alternative, a manufacturer could sue a third party for having committed an act contrary to honest commercial practices within the meaning of Articles 54 and 55 of the Law of 14 July 1971. This requires proof of illegal conduct on the part of a third party (such as those acts mentioned in the section on the breach of price fixing contracts above). The mere fact that a third party resells below a fixed price is not in itself an act contrary to honest commercial practices. This would be otherwise where such third party had committed an act such as the defacing of control numbers on branded goods. There are cases in which, while there is no *tierce complicité*, there is nevertheless an act contrary to honest commercial practices. This would be the case where a retailer, having been himself supplied by a third party, had not participated directly in the violation of a price fixing contract, but had none the less committed an act qualifying under Articles 54 and 55 of the Law of 14 July 1971 by defacing the control numbers of the goods resold below the fixed price.

In that case the manufacturer and other retailers concerned could be allowed to file an application for a cease and desist order requesting the retailer concerned to cease committing the act contrary to honest commercial practices, but they could not request that retailer to stop selling below the fixed price. For the course of such an action, the judge would not be empowered to grant damages, which requires a separate action and proof of *tierce complicité*. An action for damages is usually only possible against a third party who has been supplied directly by a contracting party bound by a vertical price agreement.

Specific Legislation Limiting Vertical Price Fixing

The specific laws which limit the freedom of price fixing pursuant to Article 1133 *Code Civil*[16] are examined in the section below. This analysis will relate to:

(1) the Law of 14 July 1971 on commercial practices,

---

15   See Cass. 10 September 1971, RW 1971 to 1972, K.321.
16   See above under *Validity of Vertical Price Fixing Contracts*.

(2) the Law of 27 May 1960 on abuse of economic power, and
(3) the Law of 30 July 1971 on price control.

Only those legal provisions which have a direct bearing on vertical price fixing will be dealt with below.

Law of 14 July 1971 on Commercial Practices

Article 22 of the Law on commercial practices stipulates:

> Il est interdit à tout commercant d'offrir en vente ou de vendre au consommateur un produit à perte.
>
> Est considerée comme une vente à perte, toute vente à un prix qui n'est pas au moins égal au prix auquel le produit a été facturé lors de l'approvisionnement ou auquel il serait facturé en cas de réapprovisionnement. Est assimilée à une vente à perte, toute vente qui, compte tenu de ces prix ainsi que des frais généraux, ne procure au vendeur qu'une marge bénéficiaire exceptionnellement réduite.

This provision which prohibits sales at below cost or with only an exceptionally low profit margin, applies only at consumer level. The manufacturer remains free to sell at a loss to his wholesalers or retailers. Article 22 therefore affects only the freedom to fix retail prices below cost price or with only an exceptionally small profit margin. Article 23 allows for certain exceptions to the application of Article 22. One of these exceptions concerns the case where, due to competition, the sale price can be reduced to stay in line with the price generally charged by competitors for the same goods, for example where a small retail shop aligns its price with that of a big department store[17]. Article 23 further provides that if a party is prohibited by contract from selling at a loss, such contract is not enforceable against that party if, having to react to the competition of others, it notifies the manufacturer or its supplier by registered letter of its intention to sell at a loss and of the price it will apply, unless the notified party offers within fifteen days of receipt of the notification to repurchase the goods concerned at the price indicated in the notification. In fact, Article 23 provides a means by which the manufacturer can keep control over its pricing policy.

Law of 27 May 1960 on Abuse of Economic Power

Article 1 of this Law defines economic power as being:

> . . . le pouvoir que possède une personne physique ou morale agissant isolément ou un groupe de ces personnes agissant de concert d'exercer sur le territoire du Royaume, par des activités industrielles, commerciales,

---

17   See Pres.Comm.Brux. 4 June 1973, JCB 1973, 477; Pres.Comm.Charleroi 11 February 1975, BRC No. 11, 12, at 72.

agricoles ou financières, une influence prépondérante sur l'approvisionne-
ment du marché de marchandises ou de capitaux, sur le prix ou la qualité
d'une marchandise ou d'un service déterminé.

The holding of such economic power is not in itself illegal, but an abuse of that
power may be illegal. There will be abuse if one or more persons holding
economic power cause prejudice to the general interest by practices which
distort or restrict the rules of fair competition, or which hinder either the
economic freedom of producers, distributors or consumers or the development
of production or exchange (Article 2).

Under this Law of 1960 individual or collective vertical price fixing agreements and refusals to supply in connection with the enforcement of fixed prices,
may be abusive and be made subject to fines if they are carried out by an enterprise or a group of enterprises which has economic power on the Belgian
market. The enforcement of this law is ensured by an administrative body
(Conseil du Contentieux Economique), to the exclusion of ordinary courts.
However, the complicated procedure of enforcement and the length of the procedure have so far hindered an effective application of this law. [18]

Although the ordinary courts have in principle no jurisdiction in respect of
the Law of 1960, they may take account of that Law in the application of the
Law of 1971 on commercial practices. In a case decided by the Supreme Court
involving the 'Groupement des fabricants de papiers peints (wall paper) de
Belgique', [19] the applicant, Societé Anonyme Rath and Doodeheefver, who had
left the groupement, brought an action against this association based on the
Law of 1960 alleging abuse of economic power on the ground that this association had concluded an agreement with the customers of all its members granting a special rebate of two per cent if the customers undertook to place all their
purchases effected in Belgium with a member of the association. The applicant
claimed that this rebate amounted in fact to a boycott against his enterprise,
since almost all companies producing wall paper were members of the association concluding this agreement. The Court dismissed the application based on
the Law of 1960 because of lack of jurisdiction. However, the Court held that
a violation of the Law of 1960 could constitute in itself a practice contrary to
honest commercial practices within the meaning of the Law of 1971 on
Commercial Practices. On the basis of the facts of this case, the Court found
that the agreement concluded between the association and its customers was de-
liberately aimed at the elimination of one of their members who had left the association and could not be justified by a legitimate interest. Therefore, the
Court declared that the granting of this rebate constituted an act contrary to
honest commercial practices.

---

18 See E. Paulis, *op. cit.*, [1980] ECLR at 413.
19 Cass., 18 February 1965, RCJB, 1967 at 245.

Law of 30 July 1971 on Price Control

In this paragraph, the following price regimes will be examined:

(1) normal price,
(2) maximum prices,
(3) price regulating contracts and
(4) notification of price increases.

(i) Normal price

Article 1 section 2 of the law on price control provides the following:

> . . . . il est interdit de pratiquer des prix supérieurs aux prix normaux. Les
> Cours et tribunaux apprécient souverainement le caractère anormal des
> prix. Il tiennent compte, à cet egard, notamment des bénéfices réalisés, de
> l'état du marché et des frais d'exploitation du commerce ou de l'industrie,
> tels que les frais de production, de fabrication, de mise en oeuvre et de
> transport.

This means in particular that any fixed price will be illegal if it is not a normal
price. The Courts will determine in each case what an 'abnormal' price is by
taking into account, *inter alia*, the realised profit, the fixed and variable costs
and the market situation. The latter element, that is the general price level in the
market, seems to be the determining criterion in the eyes of most courts.[20]

(ii) Maximum prices

Article 2 of the same law empowers the Minister of Economic Affairs to fix
maximum prices for any products or services (excluding services rendered
under an employment contract) and to fix maximum profit margins for any ven-
dor or intermediary. It is forbidden by law to sell or purchase goods or services
at prices exceeding maximum prices fixed by the Minister. It follows that the
parties may not agree on a fixed price which would exceed a maximum price
fixed by the Minister. It is possible that in respect of a particular manufacturer
and a particular product the maximum price fixed by ministerial decree exceeds
the normal price. In that case, the parties may apply only the normal price, not
the maximum price. If the normal price is below the maximum price, the normal price has priority over the maximum price.[21]

(iii) Price regulating contracts

The Minister of Economic Affairs also has the right to conclude price regulating
contracts (called *contrats de programme*) with individual or grouped enterprises for a fixed period of time.[22] These contracts lay down specific criteria
according to which the price may fluctuate. They provide for specific sanctions

---

20   See Tribunal Correctionnel Bruxelles, 27 April 1978, JT 1978 at 512 and Van Bunnen,
op.cit., at 13.
21   See Van Bunnen, *op.cit.*, at 14 and 15.
22   Article 1 section 3.

in case of breach of the contract. Such contracts have for instance been concluded for the following products: animals feed stuffs, margarines, chocolates, coffee, imported timber, non-ferrous metals, electrical household appliances and petroleum products. Where such contracts have been concluded, the enterprises concerned are no longer free to fix by individual contracts the sales prices applicable to their products.

At this point it should be noted that, in derogation of the general principle authorising individual refusals to supply with the aim to enforce a price fixing agreement,[23], Article 2 section 3 of the Law of 1971 makes it unlawful for manufacturers or distributors to refuse to sell with the intention of defeating the application of maximum prices or price regulating contracts, provided the demand for the products concerned is not abnormal and originates from bona fide purchasers. Article 4 of the same law further empowers the Minister to designate specific products which it is in all circumstances illegal to refuse to sell. In this latter case, the Minister is entitled to determine the conditions of sale and supply[24]. A Ministerial Decree of 10 July 1945 has applied the prohibition of Article 4 on refusal to supply to all products of which the production, processing, consumption, sale, offer on sale, purchase, storage, or transport are regulated by the Minister or for which a maximum price has been fixed. This constitutes an important limitation of the principle of freedom of contract, since almost all products are in one way or another regulated by the Minister.[25] Article 4 could have a wide scope of application at the moment because, following the devaluation of the Belgian franc, the Government introduced a general freeze on prices on 22 February 1982.[26]

(iv) Notification of price increases
Pursuant to Article 2 section 4 of the Law of 1971, a ministerial decree of 22 December 1971 provides that any price increase of goods or services not the subject of maximum prices (services rendered under an employment contract excepted) must be notified at least three months in advance to the Ministry of Economic Affairs. If the Minister opposes or limits the price increase, the applicant must make a second notification. The price increase can then be applied two months following this second notification; where a price increase notification has been made, the Minister has the right to fix a maximum price for a period of six months for an individual enterprise and a particular product.

The price increase notification and its possible consequence (maximum price for six months) are naturally a preliminary condition to any vertical price fixing contract. The price fixed by agreement must first have been notified and authorised by the Minister following the procedure explained above.

---

23   See under *Breach of Price Fixing Contract* above.
24   See Cass. 24 May 1965, Pas. 1965, I, 1030 and P. Van Ommeslaghe *Droit des obligations*, 1976 to 1977, at 11 and 118.
25   See M. A. Flamme, *Législation industrielle ou Droit Administratif de L'Economie*, 1979 to 1980 at 170 Note 2.
26   Ministerial decree of 22 February 1982, *Moniteur belge* 23-2. 1982.

The obligation to make the price increase notification applies principally at production level and in particular to the following persons:

(1) manufacturers and importers;
(2) non-manufacturing enterprises selling products to which they have added a label or trademark; sales agencies;
(3) distributors who establish between themselves or for several enterprises collective tariffs.

The obligation does not in principle apply to enterprises whose annual turnover (excluding VAT) does not exceed B. Fr. 7.5 million.

Article 9 of the ministerial decree of 1971 contains specific provisions on price fixing by distribution:

> Les distributeurs ne peuvent augmenter les prix des produits, matières, denrées, marchandises ou prestations que dans la mesure où leurs fournisseurs, producteurs, importateurs ou distributeurs ont appliqué une hausse de prix permise par la réglementation.
>
> Au surplus, ils ne peuvent appliquer, pour la détermination des nouveaux prix de vente, une marge commerciale en pourcentage supérieure à la marge commerciale anterieure.
>
> De même, lorsque les distributeurs obtiennent de leurs fournisseurs des prix ou conditions inférieures à ceux ayant donné lieu à la détermination de leurs prix de vente, la marge commerciale en pourcentage ne peut être augmentée.
>
> Lorsque les producteurs et importateurs établissent des prix de revente pour les distributeurs, le Ministre des Affaires economiques peut, en conclusion de leurs déclarations de hausse, limiter les marges commerciales de distribution dont il est fait usage pour les établir.

Article 9 limits price increases at the distribution level up to the end-consumer. The first paragraph prohibits any price increase by distributors which would not be strictly identical to the increase in price applied by their suppliers in accordance with the price notification procedure. Therefore, price increases by distributors depend on increases by their suppliers, having been lawfully obtained.

The second and third paragraph add the obligation on distributors not to increase the profit margin applied to their previous price, even if they obtain better conditions from their suppliers. This effectively constitutes a positive obligation to reduce the selling price following a reduction of the purchase price.

The fourth paragraph gives the Minister an explicit right to determine the profit margin used by manufacturers in case they establish a fixed retail price for their distributors.

The provisions of the Law of 1971 on price control as explained above apply in principle to all products and services. However, there are a number of exceptions:

(1) Exceptions resulting from international treaties:

(a) Articles 60 and 61 of the Treaty establishing the European Coal and Steel Community which grant to the Commission exclusive authority to fix prices for coal and steel products;

(b) Articles 67, 68 and 69 of the Treaty establishing the European Atomic Energy Community which grant exclusive authority to the Commission and Council in respect of prices of uranium and plutonium;

(c) the exclusive authority of the EEC Council to fix prices for agricultural products which are the subject of a common agricultural organisation;[27]

(d) the fixing by the EEC Council of transport tariffs.[28]

(2) Exceptions resulting from specific national legislation:

(a) a number of products and services are not subject to the Law of 1971 on price control but are regulated by specific laws. This is for instance the case for pharmaceutical products and for wine and alcoholic drinks. This is further the case for the whole of the financial, banking and insurance sector and for services provided by professions such as doctors, dentists and lawyers. This is not a complete list of all specific price régimes, some of which are only regulated by ministerial circulars.

(b) Article 57 of the Law of 30 March 1976 which limits the application of price revision clauses contained in industrial and commercial contracts.

Conclusion

In summary, the above analysis shows that vertical price fixing agreements are in principle valid under Belgian law. There are however two exceptions to this validity:

(1) limitations resulting from specific laws, in particular the Law of 14 July 1971 on commercial practices restricting the freedom to sell below cost to end-consumers, the Law of 27 May 1960 on abuse of economic power authorising an administrative body to fine abuses on pricing which affect the general interest and the Law of 30 July 1971 on price control with pro-

---

27 See however *Dechmann* case 154/77, [1978] ECR, 1573; see also *Danis* case 16 to 20/79 [1979] ECR, 3327 discussed by Waelbroek, 'La Compatibilité de la procédure de déclaration préalable de hausse de prix avec les règles du Traité de Rome', in [1981] RCJB at 12 and by E. Paulis, 'The Danis case' in [1980] ECLR at 163.

28 See Council Regulation (EEC) 2831/77 of 12 December 1977 on the fixing of rates for the carriage of goods by road between Member States, [1977] OJ L334/22.

visions on normal prices, maximum prices, price regulating contracts and notification of price increases;

(2) limitations resulting from Article 1133 of the Belgian *Code Civil* prohibiting contracts contrary to good morals and public policy.

We have further seen that a vertical price fixing system requires a watertight application (*Lückenlosigkeit*). This requirement applies however only between dealers in direct competition.

The possible remedies in case of breach of a vertical price fixing contract can be either an action for annulment of the contract with damages, or an action for specific performance with periodic penalty payments or a straightforward refusal to supply the defaulting party. This latter measure however is extremely dangerous in particular if it is a collective boycott measure or if it concerns products or services regulated by the Law of 1971 on price control (Article 2 section 3 and Article 4). An injunction procedure based on the Law of 14 July 1971 on commercial practices is in principle not possible because such law does not apply to a breach of contract, but only to extracontractual acts contrary to honest commercial practices.

The third party liability is confined by Article 1165 of the Belgian Code Civil. Third parties can be held liable for damages if they knowingly and with the intention of assisting another party, participate directly in the violation of a vertical price fixing contract. This is at least the situation based on the decision of the Supreme Court of 24 December 1932. There are however other opinions which are less restrictive in the application of this third party liability. Third parties may also be pursued on the basis of the Law of 14 July 1971 for committing acts contrary to honest commercial practices. That law does not however permit the judge to grant damages.

On the whole, Belgian law and jurisprudence have taken a fairly liberal approach to questions of price fixing and refusal to supply as a measure of enforcement of price fixing contracts. This approach is however tempered by some specific laws and in particular by the Law on price control of 1971 and by the possible application by the Belgian Courts of Articles 85 and 86 of the EEC Treaty, to the extent that a vertical price fixing practice would affect trade between Member States of the Common Market.

CANADA

Civil Jurisdictions and Remedies Under Canadian Competition Law

TIMOTHY KENNISH

Introduction

The particular aspect of Canadian competition law which forms the subject-matter of these remarks, namely civil jurisdictions and remedies, has a relatively short history. Until 1976, when the Combines Investigation Act (Canada) (the Act) was amended to provide for the recovery of civil damages by private litigants able to demonstrate having sustained loss or damage as a consequence of a violation of the criminal prohibitions in the Act and the inclusion of the variety of civil law-based 'reviewable trade practices' (both of which will be discussed in some detail below), Canadian anti-trust or competition law has had an exclusively criminal law basis. Although there have been several previous attempts by the Federal Government to create civil jurisdictions in this field, such as the Board of Commerce Act of 1919 and the Dominion Trade and Industry Commission Act in the 1930's, such efforts have consistently been held to be beyond its constitutional authority.

As a consequence, the only constitutionally assured basis for such legislation to date (which was confirmed by the Judicial Committee of the Privy Council in *Proprietary Articles Trade Association v The Attorney-General for Canada* (1931) AC 310 has been the Federal Government's authority to make laws in relation to criminal matters. The 1976 amendments are clearly not yet safe from constitutional challenge and it remains to be seen whether they will be sustained.

In addition, the Supreme Court of Canada in *Direct Lumber Co. Ltd v Western Plywood Co. Ltd* (1962) SCR 646 held that, at least as regards the price discrimination provisions of the law, the Canadian Parliament did not intend to confer private rights of action and thus denied relief to a plaintiff seeking damages alleged to have been sustained by the discriminatory pricing activities of the defendant. There has been a more recent development suggesting that, at least in the context of a common law conspiracy claim, it may be possible to bring an action based on a violation of the Act without the necessity of relying upon a particular provision in the Act providing for the recovery of damages. This will also be discussed in somewhat greater detail below.

Although the emergence of civil jurisdictions and remedies in the competition law field in Canada is, as mentioned, of relatively recent origin, these matters have been a principal focus of the debate which has raged over competition law reform in Canada since the Economic Council of Canada, in the late 1960's, following its review of inadequacies in the existing law first recommended their inclusion in the legislation.

There is very little doubt that the development of Canadian competition law generally and the enforcement of the existing laws have been greatly hampered by the lack of a clear authority on the part of the Federal Government to legislate in this area on other than a criminal law basis and the need, in terms of enforcing the law which we do have, of demonstrating violations of its provisions according to the criminal law standard of proof beyond a reasonable doubt.

The enforcement problem has been particularly obvious in relation to such matters as mergers and monopoly which the Act at present purports to regulate through criminal law. As evidence of this, it need only be mentioned that, to date, the Government has yet to be successful in a contested merger prosecution and its record in relation to monopoly offences is similarly dismal. The contrast between the Canadian experience and the development of the law in these areas in the United States could not be more obvious. This has undoubtedly led to frustration on the part of Candian competition (or anti-combines as they are called) law enforcement officials and has created pressure for reform proposals which in some cases have been quite extreme.

Constitutional Law Issues

The extent to which Canadian law is successful in expanding beyond its historical limitations will depend on the outcome of a number of cases which are just now beginning to probe the more constitutionally sensitive provisions of the 1976 amendments. To date litigation has focused on two principal constitutional issues relating firstly to the provision for the recovery of civil damages under section 31.1 of the Combines Investigation Act; and secondly to the authority (purportedly established by the 1976 amendments) of Federal combines officials to institute and conduct prosecutions and proceedings under the Act. Although the Supreme Court of Canada has yet to rule on these issues, it appears that there are now several cases which will be considered by that court in the near future.

There are three principal theories of federal legislative authority under which the provisions of the 1976 amendments mentioned above have been sought to be upheld. The first and most obvious is the long-acknowledged jurisdiction of the Federal Government to deal with matters relating to criminal law, including procedure in relation to criminal matters. Secondly there is the federal authority to regulate trade and commerce, insofar as such authority may apply to matters affecting Canada as a whole. The third basis of constitutionality for this type of legislation is the 'national concern' doctrine under the general residual authority of Parliament 'to make laws for the Peace, Order and Good Government of Canada' (POGG). On the other hand, persons who contest the validity of such legislation do so principally on the basis that it trenches on the provinces' exclusive jurisdiction either to make laws in respect of property and civil rights, or to establish and administer courts of both civil and criminal jurisdiction. There is also an argument based on the provincial authority to legislate in respect of all matters of a merely local or private nature in a province.

Section 31.1 of the Combines Investigation Act provides for the recovery of damages and costs by a plaintiff who is able to demonstrate having suffered loss or damage as a result of conduct that would constitute an offence under the Act or a breach of an order of the Restrictive Trade Practices Commission (RTPC) or of any court. There is no requirement that the defendant should have been convicted of such an offence under the Act nor indeed that any criminal proceedings should have been undertaken with respect thereto.

The first case in which the constitutionality of this provision was fully considered arose in *Rocois Construction Inc. v Quebec Ready Mix Inc. et al.* (1980) 1 FC 184 (Federal Court of Canada). The court ruled that the civil damage action remedy was unconstitutional on the basis that it related to matters of property and civil rights and was not supportable under the trade and commerce or POGG authorities or as being properly ancillary to the Federal Government's powers to legislate in respect of criminal law. This case is at present on appeal.

A similar conclusion was reached in an Ontario case, *Seiko Time Canada Ltd v Consumers Distributing Co. Ltd* (1980) 50 CPR (2d) 147 (Ontario Supreme Court) where the plaintiff, suing the defendant principally in a passing-off action, also sought to recover damages under section 31.1 on the basis that the defendant had violated the misleading advertising provisions of the Combines Investigation Act. While the plaintiff was successful in its common law passing-off action, the court dismissed the claim under section 31.1 on the grounds that the provision was *ultra vires* the Canadian Parliament. Although the decision was affirmed on appeal by the Ontario Court of Appeal, the Court of Appeal expressly stated that, in upholding the lower court decision, it was not to be considered as having agreed with the trial judge that the private damage action provision was invalid.

A contrary conclusion was reached in an Alberta case, *Henuset Bros Ltd v Syncrude Canada et al.* (1980) 114 DLR (3d) 300 (Alberta Queen's Bench). In that case, the plaintiff sought damages alleged to have been suffered by it as a result of the rejection by the defendants of its low bids to carry out certain pipeline construction projects, it being further alleged that the reason for such rejection was that the defendants had conspired to restrain competition unduly in the pipeline construction industry. Counsel for the Crown argued that the legislation could be upheld under the Federal Government's authority to make laws in respect of trade and commerce, criminal law and peace, order and good government. In the result the trial judge held section 31.1 to be constitutionally valid under the trade and commerce authority on the grounds that it was part of an overall legislative scheme for the general regulation of trade and commerce throughout Canada. Although it affected property and civil rights in the province to some degree, it was nevertheless within the legislative competence of the Federal Government.

While less directly relevant to the matter of the Federal Government's competence to provide civil remedies and to legislate generally on a civil law basis, the cases dealing with the Federal Government's authority to authorise federal officials to conduct prosecutions under the Act seems destined to reach the Supreme Court of Canada first. There are two opposing lines of authority. One is represented by the judgment of the Ontario Court of Appeal in *R. v Hoffman-LaRoche* (1982) 125 DLR (3d) 607 and suggests that the Federal Government has a fairly comprehensive authority to enact laws in relation to competition on the basis of its jurisdiction in respect of trade and commerce on the basis of its jurisdiction in respect of trade and commerce and its residual authority under the POGG clause. The opposing viewpoint, which denies such a capacity, has been most recently articulated by the Alberta Court of Appeal in the *Canadian Pacific Transport Company* case decided earlier this year. While the Ontario case has not been further appealed, the Alberta court's decision is now on appeal before the Supreme Court of Canada.

The constitutional issue has also been raised in a pending case brought under one of the reviewable trade practice provisions established by the 1976 amendments: *Petrofina Canada Inc. and Attorney General for Canada et al.* (1980) 4 CPR (2d) 201 (Federal Court). In that case Petrofina, against whom a refusal to deal order had been sought, brought a motion to restrain the Restrictive Trade Practices Commission and the Director of Investigation and Research under the Act from proceeding with the case pending a final adjudication on the constitutional validity of the law there sought to be enforced. However, the same judge who held section 31(2) to be unconstitutional in the *Rocois Construction* case declined to rule on the issue before a decision had been made by the RTPC, holding that the fact that the constitutionality of a statute is called into question does not affect the mandatory force of its enactments, since a statute is presumed to be valid until a final determination to the contrary is made.

Until such time as the constitutionality or otherwise of these provisions is finally determined, it is doubtful whether there will be much in the way of case authority dealing with their meaning and intended scope. In addition, the implementation of a number of further proposed legislative initiatives will undoubtedly be affected by the Supreme Court's resolution of these issues. For example, the Federal Government has most recently proposed that mergers and monopolies should be dealt with wholly on a civil law basis. In addition, in several previous legislative reform proposals, which have not been proceeded with (but which have probably not been forgotten), amendments were contemplated to provide for class and substitute actions and the obtaining of injunctive relief as an aid to private damage actions. Proposals have also been advanced from time to time to deal with shared monopoly, price differentiation (volume pricing), intellectual and industrial property rights, inter-locking directorates, specialisation agreements, and export/import restrictions on a civil law basis. A good deal therefore hangs on the outcome of the currently pending constitutional litigation arising out of the 1976 amendments.

In the meantime, pending a conclusive determination regarding the constitutional validity or otherwise of the civil law-based amendments passed in 1976, it is pertinent to consider their actual provisions.

Reviewable Trade Practices

The 1976 amendments created a new type of provision which was neither criminal law nor enforceable by private action. Such provisions, commonly referred to as 'reviewable trade practice' provisions, typically deal with practices encountered in the vertical distribution of goods which, depending on the circumstances, may or may not have substantial adverse competitive effects warranting remedial orders of a prohibitory or modifying character. Such provisions have been enacted with respect to exclusive dealing, tied selling, refusals to deal, consignment selling, market restriction, and refusals to supply by foreign suppliers. There are also provisions designed to nullify the influence of foreign laws and directives and to deny the effect of foreign judgments.

The only person having status to call such provisions in aid is the Director of Investigation and Research, who is the chief enforcement official under the Combines Investigation Act. Under the Act, the Director is empowered to apply to the Restrictive Trade Practices Commission for remedial orders in respect of such practices and the Commission, if it is satisfied that the factual prerequisites of the exercise of its jurisdiction in this regard exist, is authorised to make an order directed at terminating or neutralising the competitive adverse effects of the practice, most commonly of the cease and desist type.

Two points should be borne in mind in particular with respect to the Commission's jurisdiction to deal with reviewable trade practices:

(1) The Commission is empowered, but not obliged, to make an order in circumstances where all the factual prerequisites of the exercise of its jurisdiction exist. It would appear that the Commission is still expected to exercise its judgment concerning the qualitative impact on competition of the practice sought to be prohibited or modified. This is particularly important in relation to such matters as exclusive dealing and tied selling which are not necessarily so detrimental to the public interest as to warrant their outright prohibition. If there was not the case, Parliament would undoubtedly have opted to proscribe such practices altogether instead of conferring the discretionary jurisdiction on the Commission which it has.

(2) A second point is that the orders made by the Commission may only have a prospective operation. No adverse consequences attach to a supplier engaging in such a practice (assuming it does not also violate one of the

specific criminal provisions such as the offence of monopoly) prior to an order being made against it by the Commission. Once an order is made, contravention of such an order is a criminal offence and private damage liability exposure arises under section 31.1 at the instance of any plaintiff who can establish that it suffered damage as a consequence of the violation of such an order.

Refusals to Deal

Perhaps the most controversial of the reviewable trade practice provisions is section 31(2) which authorises the Commission to make orders arising out of refusals to deal by suppliers. Under that section (which has yet to receive consideration by a court in any decided case), the Commission is authorised to make an order where it finds that:

(1) a person is substantially affected in his business or is precluded from carrying on business due to his inability to obtain adequate supplies of a product anywhere in a market on usual trade terms;

(2) such person is unable to obtain adequate supplies of the product because of insufficient competition among suppliers thereof in the market;

(3) such person is willing and able to meet the usual trade terms of the supplier; and

(4) the product is in ample supply.

In such a case the Commission may, where the product in question is an article, make a recommendation for the reduction or removal of customs duties so as to equalise the position of the complainant with other persons who are able to obtain supplies in Canada. Alternatively, the Commission may require that one or more suppliers of the product accept the person as a customer within a specified time on usual trade terms. The section purports to specify the circumstances in which an article may be regarded as a separate product for this purpose. It also defines 'trade terms' for the purposes of the provision. With regard to the former point, the provision states that an article is not a separate product by reason only of its differentiation by trade mark or proprietary name unless the article so differentiated occupies such a dominant position in the market as to affect substantially the ability of a person to carry on business who is denied access to the article in question. 'Trade terms' is defined as meaning terms in respect of payment, units of purchase and reasonable technical and servicing requirements.

The provision is of undoubted significance since it deals both with discontinuance of supply and refusal to supply and may be said to interfere with the supplier's traditional freedom to select its own channels of distribution. However, there have as yet been only a few cases initiated under it and in each of these the applications have been discontinued when, during the course of the proceedings, either the denying supplier agreed to terms with the complainant or the complainant was able to obtain an alternative source of supply. In the *Director of Investigation and Research and National Rubber Company Limited* case an order was sought under section 31(2). The complainant, Federal Industries, was a customer for other products of National Rubber against whom the order was sought but had been refused distribution rights with respect to masticated rubber. Ultimately, in response to the Director's application under the section, National Rubber put Federal Industries on supply and the case was withdrawn. In *Director of Investigation and Research and Imperial Oil Limited et al.* (1980) an application was made on behalf of Perrette Dairy Products Limited to require the respondents to accept Perrette as a customer on usual trade terms in the Eastern Canadian market. The case was withdrawn in mid-hearing because Perrette had received supplies from another source and was no long substantially affected in its business due to its inability to obtain adequate supplies.

Exclusive Dealing

There have been two principal cases decided by the Commission under the reviewable trade practice provisions, one relating to exclusive dealing, *Director of Investigation and Research v Bombardier Ltd* (1981) 56 CPR 216, and the other dealing with tied selling, the *Bureau of Broadcast Measurement* case.

The *Bombardier* case was the first proceeding to go the full distance through to a decision of the Commission. An order was sought from the Commission to restrain Bombardier, a snowmobile manufacturer, from continuing to engage in the practice of exclusive dealing and to require it to resupply those dealers whose franchises it had cancelled by reason of their non-observance of the exclusive dealing requirement in Bombardier's dealer franchise agreement. The case arose under subsection 31(4)(2) of the Act which authorises the Commission, on application by the Director, to make such orders where it finds that exclusive dealing, because it is engaged in by a major supplier of a product in a market, is likely to impede entry into or expansion of a firm in the market with the result that competition is or is likely to be lessened substantially.

In this case there was no question that these were exclusive dealerships and that Bombardier had enforced the exclusivity provisions in the dealer agreements. In addition, Bombardier was considered to be a 'major supplier' of snowmobile equipment in Canada with approximately 60 per cent of all sales by manufacturers in the Province of Quebec and the Maritime Provinces and 40 per cent in the Province of Ontario. The Commission, however, was not satisfied that there was evidence of any substantial lessening of competition. There was no evidence of Bombardier's exclusive dealing policy having any impact on competition at the manufacturing level or of competition at the wholesale or retail levels being substantially adversely affected by such practice. During the period in question, there was a reduction in the number of manufacturers with a consequent turnover of dealer organisations. The evidence was, however, that these organisations tended to fall to the remaining competitors rather than to Bombardier. It is an interesting footnote to this case that it consumed some 32 days of hearings.

Tied Selling

In the *Bureau of Broadcast Measurement* (tied selling) case it was established in evidence that the Bureau of Broadcast Measurement (BBM) held a monopoly position in the provision of radio audience survey data. It was also a supplier of television audience survey data, a field in which A.C. Neilson was a competitor. The evidence established that BBM's price for the sale of both radio and TV audience survey data together was not only considerably less than that of the two surveys purchased separately but also that it was much less than the price a customer would have to pay to purchase radio survey data from BBM and television survey data from A.C. Neilson.

The RTPC's jurisdiction to make an order against the practice of tied selling is similar to its jurisdiction in respect of exclusive dealing. That is, it could make such an order where the supplier in question was a 'major supplier' and where the effect of the practice would be to create barriers to entry or expansion in the market in question and thereby cause a substantial lessening of competition. However, in the case of tied selling there is a defence where it can be established that there is a technological necessity for the two products to be sold together.

It was established that BBM had 100 per cent of the relevant national market for radio audience survey data and upwards of 80 per cent of the corresponding survey data relating to television broadcasting. It was accordingly held to be a major supplier of both products. The technological necessity defence was rejected as being inapplicable on the ground that it was to be confined to cases in which the reputation of the tying product would be destroyed if the other product was not sold in conjunction with it. The Commission further concluded that there would be, or was, a substantial lessening of competition as a consequence of this practice. In this regard it observed that there had been no new entrants in the radio measurement business for 18 years and there were no perceived potential entrants at the time of the application. A.C. Neilson was the only competitor on the TV side of the business and its sales had fallen substantially in the preceding ten years. The order of the Commission has been appealed to the Federal Court of Appeal.

Market Restriction

The Act defines 'market restriction' (also a reviewable trade practice within the jurisdiction of the RTPC) as meaning any practice whereby a supplier of a product, as a condition of supplying the product to a customer, requires that customer to supply such product only in a defined market or exacts a penalty of any kind from the customer if he supplies the product outside a defined market. In order for the Commission to have jurisdiction to order the cessation of a market restriction practice it must find that it is engaged in by a major supplier or that it is wide-spread in relation to a product and that the result of the practice is likely substantially to lessen competition in relation to the product. However, the Commission is directed not to make an order where in its opinion the market restriction is or will be engaged in only for a reasonable period of time to facilitate the entry of a new supplier of a product into a market or of a new product into a market. There is also an exception for intra-corporate dealings including a special provision apparently designed to permit the continuance of established distribution practices by suppliers of ingredients in the food and beverage industry.

Other Reviewable Trade Practices

There are also provisions dealing with the adverse effects of consignment selling (sometimes resorted to in order to facilitate effective price discrimination or price maintenance), foreign laws, judgments and directives (concern has frequently been expressed over the degree to which Canadian subsidiaries of multinational corporations have been induced to act as a result of influences from outside Canada) and refusals to supply by foreign suppliers (designed to prevent Canadian purchasers from being unduly affected by wrongful competition originating from abroad). Unfortunately limitations of time do not permit of a full discussion of these provisions.

Specialised Tribunal Versus Courts

Possibly as a consequence of the Federal Government's frustration with both the procedural delays and the decision in the *Bombardier* case, in its 1981 *Framework for Discussion* paper proposing reforms to the competition legislation the Government suggested that the reviewable trade practice jurisdictions at present exercised by the RTPC should be transferred to the courts. The position originally taken by the Government with respect to these matters was that since they involve more difficult economic judgments which are not considered to be appropriate subjects for continued regulation on a criminal law basis, they should be dealt with under the jurisdiction of a specialised tribunal having appropriate expertise to deal with these more complex situations. However, having advocated a transfer of these and other civil law jurisdictions to the courts in the *Framework* paper, it now appears that it may once again have changed its position in this matter.

Such vacillation on the issue of whether such jurisdictions ought to be exercised by a specialised administrative tribunal or by the courts reflects the debate which has been going on for a considerable period. The principal argument in favour of a body such as the RTPC exercising a civil jurisdiction in respect of these kinds of matters is that it would enable the focusing of greater economic expertise than is possessed by the courts on the more legal/economic issues on a case-by-case basis and that such a body would be better able to evaluate the impact on competition of particular restrictive conduct. While there is considerable sentiment (particularly in the business community) favouring the type of adjudication which occurs in a court of law through the operation of the adversarial process and which is subject to the normal appeal opportunities, it should also be borne in mind that the courts might have been less hide-bound in some of their competition law decisions had they not been dealing with the criminal law burden of proof beyond a reasonable doubt, a standard which is not particularly amenable to the evaluation of complex economic issues of fact. Finally the point is also made, in support of conferring such a jurisdiction upon the courts, that they frequently hear and decide cases on the basis of expert evidence, including expert economic evidence.

Private Damage Action

The other significant civil law provision introduced by the 1976 amendments was the private damage action provision (section 31.1) previously alluded to. Apart from cases in which the constitutional validity of this provision has been challenged (which have been referred to above) there is as yet no judicial authority concerning its scope of application. Perhaps one reason for this, apart from the constitutional uncertainty, has to do with the fact that under the Canadian court system unsuccessful plaintiffs are frequently required to pay the costs of their legal adversaries.

As mentioned above, the present combines law has been interpreted as not giving rise to private rights of action. (There is one somewhat anomalous Quebec case, *Beaubien et Cie Ltee v Canadian General Electric et al.* (1976) 30 CPR (2d) 100 in which a bankrupt distributor was held entitled to recover for damages suffered as a consequence of a conspiracy among suppliers on the basis of their violation of the conspiracy provisions of the Act in an action brought at a time when there was no specific provision for the recovery of damages in the statute.) Section 31.1 now provides for the recovery of single damages by private action at the instance of any person who suffered loss or damage as a result of a violation of a specific prohibition in the Act or by reason of the failure of any person to comply with an order of the Restrictive Trade Practices Commission made under its authority with respect to reviewable trade practices. In any such action, the court hearing the matter may also award to the injured party an additional amount not exceeding the full cost to the plaintiff of any investigation in connection with the matter and of proceedings under the section.

Subsection 31.1(2) provides that in any private action commenced under subsection (1) the record of proceedings in any court in which the defendant was convicted of an offence under the Act or a failure to comply with an order of the Restrictive Trade Practices Commission is, in the absence of evidence to the contrary, proof that the person against whom the action was brought engaged in conduct contrary to the Act or failed to comply with such order. Also any evidence given in such proceedings as to the effect on the plaintiff of any act or omission constitutes evidence of such effect in the private action. Obviously in the absence of any mechanism such as there is under the United

States anti-trust law practice for entering a plea of *nolo contendere* whereby an accused may plead guilty in a criminal proceeding without thereby admitting liability in a subsequent civil action with respect to the same matter, there is considerably less inclination on the part of an accused to enter pleas of guilty in proceedings brought under the Combines Investigation Act where there is some possibility of the recovery of damages against the accused by an injured party.

Subsection (4) provides that no action may be brought under the section based on conduct which is contrary to the criminal prohibitions in the Act after two years from the day on which the conduct was engaged in or the day on which any criminal proceedings related thereto were finally disposed of, whichever is later. If an action is brought based on a failure of a person to comply with an RTPC order, the action must be brought within two years from the day on which the order of the Commission was violated or the day on which any criminal proceedings relating thereto were finally disposed of, whichever is later.

It was established in an early case, *Eli Lilly and Co. v Marzone Chemicals Ltd* (1976) 29 CPR (2d) 253, that a plaintiff may invoke the provisions of section 31.1 whether or not an offence has previously been found to exist in criminal proceedings and notwithstanding that such criminal proceedings have not even been instituted. This judgment was recently followed in *Bell Canada v Intra Canada Telecommunications* (1982) 62 CPR (2d) 21. Theoretically the possibility exists (since the record in the criminal action is only relevant to the civil action to the extent that there are determinations made therein against the accused which would be of assistance to the plaintiff in the civil action) of an accused being acquitted in a criminal case and yet being found liable in the corresponding private damage suit.

A number of substantial questions concerning the nature and scope of the remedy provided by the section remain to be considered. These include whether or not the relevant standard of proof for success in a private damage action based upon alleged violation of a criminal provision of the statute is proof beyond a reasonable doubt or only the ordinary civil law burden of the balance of probabilities. While the latter would appear to be the case, the matter is not entirely free from doubt. Then there are questions of the type which have been extensively litigated in the United States concerning what parties have standing to sue under the section and how a court should go about quantifying or measuring the damage sustained by the injured party. It is not clear from a reading of the section ('any person who has suffered loss or damage as a result of . . . conduct which is contrary to any provision . . .') whether this section would support actions by potential plaintiffs who are only consequentially affected by the offending act, as for example a remote customer in a chain of distribution where the first sale violated the price discrimination provisions of the law. Nor is it clear whether the disfavoured customer in a price discrimination case would automatically receive compensation for the price differential as his measure of damage or whether he must demonstrate that he actually lost out in the competition for the resale of the products as a consequence of his having to pay a higher price than his competitor.

Unquestionably should section 31.1 withstand its current constitutional challenge it is a potentially significant remedial provision. At the present time, however, that potential is largely untapped. Two additional points should be mentioned before leaving the discussion of this provision. The first is that the Act does not contain any authority for a plaintiff proceeding under this section to obtain injunctive relief to preclude or forestall the sustaining of injury for which damages may be recovered. In addition it would not appear that the right to such injunctive relief may be obtained in the absence of a specific provision in the Act. A second point is that, since under most existing provincial laws governing the constitution of class actions it is a requirement that all members of the class should have quantitatively similar amounts of damages recoverable, class actions would not appear to be available to broad groups of potential litigants who may individually have suffered relatively modest amounts of damages but who on a collective basis may have a claim for a large absolute amount. Both injunctive relief in aid of private damage action suits and provision for class actions were contained in proposed amendments to the legislation which have since been withdrawn.

Although as mentioned above, the Supreme Court of Canada had held in the *Direct Lumber* case that the Act did not confer private rights of action, the court in that case left open the possibility of damages being recovered where the offence is one of conspiracy to violate the provisions of the Act. In a recent decision of the courts in British Columbia in *B.C. Lightweight Aggregate Ltd v Canada Cement* (1979 B.C. Supreme Court, 1982 B.C. Court of Appeal), it has been held that a plaintiff may succeed in a common law conspiracy action and recover damages, to the extent in that case of Canadian $750,000, from defendants who have been convicted of offences under section 32 of the Combines Investigation Act where it could be shown that the damage suffered by the plaintiff was as a consequence of the illegal activities which constituted a violation of the Combines Act. In that case the court characterised the action as being one of common law conspiracy founded upon unlawful means where the unlawful means were a violation of the Combines Investigation Act. This case is now on appeal to the Supreme Court of Canada. In its consideration of the appeal the court will undoubtedly consider the House of Lords decision in *Lonrho Ltd and others v Shell Petroleum Co. and others* (1981) 2 All ER 459 which denied recovery to plaintiffs who were injured by a conspiracy entered into to protect the defendants' interest rather than to cause injury to the plaintiffs. In the *Lightweight* case there is evidence to support the view that it was not the purpose of the conspirators to cause injury to the plaintiff but to the defendant's customers through charging higher prices.

Current Proposals for Reform

In the Spring of 1981, the Government set out, in what was ostensibly a discussion paper designed to elicit the views of interested business groups concerning possible reforms of the Combines Investigation Act, a number of suggestions which would involve the creation of new civil jurisdictions in respect of matters which have heretofore been subject only to criminal law regulation.

Monopoly

In the paper (customarily described as the *Framework for Discussion*) the Government proposed that monopoly should not be treated on a solely civil law basis. Under the proposals, a monopoly would be considered to exist where one or more firms account for a dominant share of any market in Canada. The proposals further contemplate that firms would be deemed to have such a dominant share if a given percentage (suggestions range from 33 to 75 per cent) is accounted for by any firm or group of firms. In addition, in the case of joint monopolies, where four or fewer firms have together in excess of a prescribed aggregate market share (again the suggestions range from 33 to 75 per cent), they would be deemed to constitute firms having such a dominant share. Such firms would be prohibited from engaging in anti-competitive conduct of an exclusionary, restrictive or predatory nature. The *Framework* paper includes a non-exhaustive list of conduct considered to be 'anti-competitive', including such conduct as the pre-emptive acquisition of scarce facilities or resources, full-line forcing and market saturation advertising.

It would appear that a principal motivation of the Government in advancing these proposals is to assist in easing problems of enforcement which have been encountered in prosecutions under the criminal monopoly provision. However, one can certainly question the desirability of automatic liability resulting simply from a combination of certain identified conduct and the possession of a presumptively dominant market position without any requirement for measuring the impact of such conduct on competition generally. In terms of identifying 'joint monopolies' no collusive conduct would apparently be required. Rather, if it could be shown that a number of large firms in a highly concentrated industry recognise that they will all benefit by pursuing the same lines of conduct and acted accordingly, they would be considered to be joint monopolists and, if they engaged in 'anti-competitive' conduct, they would be held to be in violation of the law. Given the concentrated nature of many Canadian businesses, particularly in the manufacturing sectors, it can be expected that these provisions would structurally at least be applicable to the leading firms. That being the case, there would be difficult judgments for many companies in initiating actions (which competitors might follow), or in following a competitor's lead in taking action which might be regarded as exclusionary or restrictive.

Mergers

The matter of mergers has been a central issue in the continuing debate over competition law reform, in particular because it is the area in which the deficiencies of the criminal law regulatory approach have been so demonstrable. As mentioned no convictions have ever been obtained in a contested Canadian merger case. Notwithstanding that the civil regulation of mergers would appear to be desirable, the proposed handling of mergers under the *Framework* proposals is among the more controversial aspects of that paper. In terms of the application of the law to mergers, it is proposed that mergers involving a significant lessening of competition would be held to be unlawful (the previous reform proposals having suggested a standard of 'substantial lessening of competition' and the present law making mergers unlawful only where competition is or is likely to be lessened 'to the detriment or against the interest of the public'). This change, if adopted, would appear to eliminate any need for judicial evaluation of the degree to which actual detriment has been suffered by the public as a consequence of the reduction in competition. The legality of the merger would be determined solely on the basis of whether there has been a significant lessening of competition.

In the case of vertical mergers the matter would be assessed on the basis of the degree of market foreclosure involved. However, the proposal with respect to horizontal mergers adopts a more structuralist approach. The legality of a horizontal merger, at least initially, would be judged solely by reference to whether or not the merged enterprise constituted in excess of a prescribed percentage of the relevant market (just what that threshold percentage ought to be was a matter on which the *Framework* paper invited comments). If the combined enterprise exceeded that threshold, the merger would be presumptively unlawful, subject to court approval being given by a specific order tailored to modify the presumed adverse effects of the merger. The *Framework* proposals also contemplate a pre-merger notification requirement which evidently will only be required in the case of mergers either which are large in themselves or which involve large corporations. Advance notice of any merger which involves enterprises having sales or assets exceeding certain dollar thresholds (anywhere from Canadian $100 million to Canadian $500 million has been suggested for consideration - or possibly the top 50 or 300 largest companies) would have to be given to the Director under the Act who would then have a period of time (60 days has been suggested) to indicate whether or not he intends to proceed against it.

Finally, amendments are proposed to the Foreign Investment Review Act (FIRA) which are designed to make it clear that FIRA approved mergers may nevertheless subsequently be challenged under the Combines Act where the Director has previously certified his intention to proceed against the merger. In such cases, no consideration of the competition law aspects of the proposed merger will be given by Cabinet in connection with a FIRA review. Although this may be a practical solution of sorts, it is nevertheless somewhat anomalous to consider that the merger judged by the Cabinet to be of 'significant benefit to Canada' could be restrained or dissolved on the basis of its contravention of Canadian competition laws.

Export/Import Restrictions

Another new civil jurisdiction contemplated in the *Framework* paper relates to export/import restrictions. The paper proposes to deal with certain perceived adverse effects of multinational business structures. Under the proposed legislation a court exercising civil jurisdiction would be empowered to issue orders requiring Canadian subsidiaries to withdraw from agreements or arrangements with affiliates or to refrain from implementing or enforcing such agreements or arrangements which either restrict exports from Canada or imports into Canada for the purpose of protecting price levels in Canada or abroad. The jurisdiction could only be exercised where the Canadian corporation accounted for some prescribed percentage of the market.

Conclusion

In conclusion, it may be stated that while the future development of Canadian competition law would seem to lie in the direction of new civil jurisdictions which are being created to overcome deficiencies in the existing law, a great deal depends on the outcome of the constitutional litigation to determine the extent to which the Federal Government does in fact have the necessary authority to legislate in this area.

FRANCE

French Competition Law and the Law of 19 July 1977

PHILIPPE NOUEL

The Pre-1977 Position

Until the Competition Law of 19 July 1977 (the 1977 Law) was enacted, French competition law was fairly limited in scope. With the exception of Article 419 of the Criminal Code which made certain unfair market practices a criminal offence,[1] competition law was originally introduced in France by way of an amendment to a Law enacted in 1945. The Ordinance of 30 June 1945 empowered the authorities to prosecute certain anti-competitive acts. The Law was primarily introduced as a means of controlling the black market and for this reason was primarily concerned with prices and supplies to the civilian population.

Subsequently the Law was amended to make it a criminal offence to refuse to sell to any person who wished to purchase, and further modifications were made in 1953, 1958 and 1967.

It was not until the Law of 1977, however, that a comprehensive Competition Law was introduced into France, and like its predecessors this law reflects the economic and social conditions of the time and the Government's policy to liberalise the national economy and stimulate competition by eliminating restrictive practices.

In addition to its much broader scope, the 1977 Law is also important in that its objective is to restore competition rather than to punish anti-competitive acts. Accordingly the emphasis is on administrative rather than criminal sanctions for anti-competitive conduct. This change in emphasis has made the authorities less reluctant to interfere in situations which clearly do not show any criminal intent, and has led to the competition rules being applied much more vigorously than was the case before the Law of 1977 was brought into effect.

---

1   See below.

The Law of 19 July 1977

The Competent Authorities

The central authority for the enforcement of competition matters is the 'Commission de la Concurrence' (the Commission) which was established by the 1977 Law to replace the former 'Commission Technique des Ententes et des Positions Dominantes'.

The Commission is larger than its predecessor and has considerably greater powers and duties. Investigations into anti-competitive practices may be initiated by the Commission on its own initiative, or on the initiative of the Minister of Economic Affairs, or on the initiative of regional authorities such as the municipalities, trade unions, professional organisations and consumer associations. In addition, the national courts themselves have power to request an opinion of the Commission where it is appropriate to do so.

The Commission publishes a report annually and the report for the year ended November 1981 indicates that since the 1977 Law was brought into effect, 158 investigations had been started, 70 of these on the initiative of the Minister of Economic Affairs, 41 at the request of regional authorities, professional organisations and consumer associations, 22 at the request of the courts, 17 by the Commission itself and six at the request of Parliament.

The Simplified Procedure *(Article 55)*

This is a special shortened form of procedure which may be adopted by the authorities in cases which are not considered serious. Following an investigation, the President of the Commission reports his decision to the Minister of Economic Affairs and the latter may under Article 55 of the 1977 Law impose a fine not exceeding F.Fr. 200,000. The number of cases involving this procedure is not substantial and seems to be decreasing (ten cases in 1979, six cases in 1980, no case in 1981). Its principal disadvantage is that the Minister is not required to give detailed reasons for his finding so that no general principles of law can be established from cases dealt with in this way.

The Normal Procedure

The normal procedure calls for a complete investigation of the case by the Commission's staff and a hearing of the various parties involved. The Commission then gives its opinion *(avis)*, and pursuant to this the Minister will give a formal decision (the Commission has no power of decision).

The Commission opinion may make recommendations as to the level of fines to be imposed or other action which it feels the Minister ought to take. Any fine ordered by the Minister must not exceed that recommended by the Commission, but subject to that, the Minister is not bound to follow the advice of the Commission, although in practice he will usually do so.

The Minister also has extremely wide powers to require undertakings to take such action as may be necessary to bring to an end the practices complained of. Failure to comply with the ministerial decision can lead to further fines being imposed.

Companies or persons to whom a decision is addressed have the right of appeal to the Supreme Administrative Court (Conseil d'état).

In more serious cases, rather than making a decision himself, the Minister may decide on the opinion of the Commission to order the case to be transferred to a Criminal Court which will then decide whether a criminal offence has been committed, and in an appropriate case sentence the person in charge of the undertaking to a fine or imprisonment. Thus under the 1977 Law the Minister now has a wide discretion in the form of sanctions available to him. In practice, the number of cases which are referred to the criminal court under the new Law is small. The 1978 Commission Report mentions two cases and the 1979 Report four, the 1980 Report one case and the 1981 Report none.

It is interesting to note that the criminal courts do not invariably follow the advice of the Commission. In two recent cases, the very old *Whisky* case[2] and the *Water Meter* case[3] for example, the courts took a decision contrary to the findings of the Commission.

Penalties

The number of cases in which fines of an administrative nature have been inflicted is increasing. The 1979 Commission Report indicates that fines were imposed in only two cases of one million francs and forty thousand francs respectively. The 1980 Report indicates that fines were imposed in four cases (F.Fr. 25,000 to F.Fr. 2.5 million). The 1981 Report indicates that fines were imposed in ten cases F.Fr. 20,000 to F.Fr. 1.5 million.

However it seems that in general the Commission prefers to ask the Minister to issue requests to undertakings to cease and desist from restrictive practices and where necessary to dismantle anti-competitive combinations with the possibility of fines only introduced in the event of the undertakings concerned not complying with the ministerial decision.

This tendency to encourage competition rather than punish anti-competitive practices has continued since the last Commission Report. In the *Electro Acoustic Equipment* case,[4] the Commission recommended fines totalling twenty million French francs; this was reduced to eight million francs by the Minister in his decision.

In the Fertilizer Case[5] the Commission recommended a fine up to F.Fr. 3 millions. It was reduced to F.Fr. 1.5 million by the Minister in his decision.

The legality of imposing a double administrative and criminal penalty has

2 The *Whisky* case, Rapport de la Commission Technique des Ententes, JO 1193.72.
3 The *Water Meter* case, BOSP 25 July 1979 No.16.
4 The *Electro Acoustic Equipment* case, BOSP 9 February 1980 No.4.
5 BOCC 12 December 1981 No.23.

also been raised in a recent case, the *Secteur de l'Assainissement en région Parisienne*.[6] In its opinion in that case the Commission took the unusual step of asking for both an administrative fine and for a criminal prosecution. The Minister decided against inflicting a fine but in favour of referring the matter to the Criminal Court. The generally held view amongst practitioners is that although not prohibited by the legislation, it is not possible to order two different penalties in respect of the same offence. This could give rise to an extremely complex situation if, for example, the 'Conseil d'état', on appeal from the decision of the Minister and the Criminal Court, gave conflicting judgments. Indeed, the Criminal Court in the *Schlumberger* case,[7] suggested that such a double penalty would be impossible, but it was not required to decide the issue.

The Rights of the Defence

The procedure begins with the Commission appointing one of its officers, the investigator, to carry out an investigation into the alleged infringement of the competition rules and the undertaking concerned. The investigator has full power to request documents and is also entitled to interrogate witnesses.

When his investigation is complete, the inspector provides a report to the Commission and a copy of the report is delivered to 'interested parties', who are invited to present their comments. The Commission then submits its opinion, but it is obliged to respect the rights of the defence, and before making its opinion it must give all interested parties the opportunity to be heard.

The Commission, like its EEC equivalent in Brussels, takes a fairly narrow view of the rights of the defence to material collected in the investigation. In its 1978 Report the Commission stated that it was not compelled to give interested parties anything other than the report itself. It has however declared that it is giving consideration to the possibility of disclosing to interested parties in a more systematic way the report of the investigator and the various documents in which the investigator has recorded the facts, but so far this has not been correctly done. In the *Carboxyque* case, for example,[8] the Commission has reaffirmed that the only documents which interested parties may have are the reports and documents expressly mentioned in the investigator's report. The complaint need not be disclosed when the report does not rely on it, even though the whole case was started as a result of the complaint. The *Carboxyque* case was the subject of an appeal before the Conseil d'état but the appeal was withdrawn so that a definitive ruling on the point was not given.

Until recently 'interested parties' were also a fairly narrowly defined group according to the Commission and comprised only those parties against whom the investigation is made and those whose complaint set in motion the Commission investigation pursuant to Article 52.4 of the 1977 Law. The latter are those regional authorities, trade unions, professional organisations and con-

---

6 *Secteur de l'Assainissement en région Parisienne*, BOSP 15 May 1980 No.10.
7 *Schlumberger* case—see Note 6 above.
8 *Carboxyque* case, BOSP 13 July 1979 No.15.

sumer groups who have lodged complaints. Individuals or enterprises lodging such complaints were not considered by the Commission to be interested parties. They may in some cases be heard as witnesses by the Commission or by the inspector in charge of the report, but they are never allowed to have a copy of the documents or of the report. This narrow attitude changed in 1981. The Commission now accepts that it should communicate the Report to plaintiffs and to other 'interested parties'.[9]

It must be emphasised that in the *Schlumberger* case[10] the Court decided that where an interested party has not been given a copy of the report, however, no criminal proceedings may be instituted against him.

Article 16 of the Law of July 1977 provides that the proceeding before the Commission de la Concurrence must be fully contradictory (*pleinement contradictoire*). A long discussion was opened between the advocates and the Commission on the meaning of this Article.

The Conseil d'Etat in a decision of 13 March 1981[11] admitted that since the Commission is not a jurisdiction but an administrative commission the proceeding need not be organized as before a criminal court. As long as the 'interested parties' have received all documents on which the recommendation is based the rights of the defence have been respected. Many lawyers have strongly protested against this decision.

Third Party Rights

Parties claiming to have suffered damage as a result of an anti-competitive practice may not be parties to proceedings before the Commission. They may however intervene in criminal proceedings where they are allowed to claim damages. An alternative option open to injured third parties is to start a civil action in a commercial or civil court based on the provisions of the 1977 Law and this may be done even though the Commission has not rendered a decision. In such circumstances the court concerned may refer the matter to the Commission for an opinion on the legality of the acts which are complained of, but the courts are not bound in any way by the findings of the Commission.

Injured parties may also themselves start an action in accordance with Article 419 of the Penal Code, and as with criminal cases initiated by the Minister under the 1977 Law, they may claim damages.

Publication

The opinion of the Commission and the decision taken by the Minister are published shortly after the decision has been notified to the parties concerned, except where the opinion was rendered at the request of a court in connection with current proceedings.

---

9   Report for 1981 at 21.
10   As Note 7 above.
11   [1982] Gaz.Pal. 21/22 May.

The Application of Article 419 of the Criminal Code

The French Criminal Code has always contained a provision against restrictive practices in the form of Article 419 which has been modified at various times. In its present form it makes it a criminal offence for anyone either alone or with others to act or to attempt to act on the market in such a way as to obtain a benefit which would not result from the application of the law of supply and demand, and therefore cause or attempt to cause an artificial increase or reduction in the prices of goods or negotiable instruments.

There is therefore a very clear overlap between the functions of Article 419 and the 1977 Law. When the 1977 Law was before Parliament, the possibility of repealing Article 419 was considered but no decision to do so was ever taken.

This issue has become important in certain cases and was considered in detail in the so-called *Ententes Pétrolières* case,[12] in that particular case, which was brought under the pre-1977 Law, a consent decree had been entered into between the Minister and the oil company. Despite this consent decree various criminal actions brought by individuals and local authorities on identical facts are still under way after various decisions of the Court of Appeal and of the Supreme Court (Cour de Cassation).

At the present time, therefore, it appears that the two procedures could exist side by side, one under Article 419 in which the intervention of the Commission is not necessary and one under the 1977 Law under which no prosecution may take place unless the Commission has given its prior opinion. Another important and perhaps anomalous feature of this situation is that a case terminated by a fine or without a penalty on the report of the Commission under the 1977 Law may be reopened if Article 419 is invoked.

The Prohibition of Anti-Competitive Agreements and Dominant Positions

Applications for Special Exemption

Article 50 of 1977 Law prohibits all agreements restricting competition and dominant positions distorting the 'normal functioning of the market'. Article 51 of the 1977 Law states that:

> Article 50 [which prohibits restrictive practices and abuses of dominant positions] will not be applicable when the practices are a direct consequence of Government legislation or when the parties can show that their effect is to achieve economic progress through [*inter alia*] improved productivity.

Essentially, therefore, it is the French law equivalent of Article 85 of the EEC Treaty.

One of the important differences between French and EEC competition law,

---

12   *Ententes Pétrolières*, JO (Documents Administratifs) 66, 19 July 1974.

however, is that whereas the benefit of Article 85(3) is only obtained as a consequence of a notification to the EEC Commission, French law provides for no such notification. The Commission has however construed the 1977 Law as meaning that the benefit of Article 51 will not be granted to any party who has not expressly admitted being guilty of a concerted practice or an abuse of a dominant position. Most of the opinions given by the Commission state that 'The undertakings claimed that no unlawful restrictive practice had been committed; consequently they may not claim the benefit of Article 51.'

This approach adopted by the Commission has been much criticised by lawyers representing undertakings. They claim that the Commission has added to Article 51 a condition which was never intended by the legislation. Furthermore, the right of defendants to plead in the alternative is well recognised in other areas of law and it is argued that there is no reason why a similar latitude should not be available to defendants prosecuted under the Competition Law. The Commission has so far remained adamant and refused to examine whether the benefit of Article 51 can be claimed unless the parties have expressly admitted an infringement of Article 50.

It seems that the courts may not be wholeheartedly in support of the Commission's attitude in this respect. In the judgment of the Court of Nanterre in the *Water Meter* case[13] the Court seems implicitly to have applied Article 51, but without stating expressly that it was doing so. This issue is therefore not entirely free from doubt.

The Substantive Law

As mentioned above, the Commission has, in addition to its duties to initiate general investigations in matters of competition, the duty to deal with specific cases, and more particularly cases concerning mergers and concentrations, restrictive practices and dominant positions.

Mergers and Concentrations

The control of mergers and concentrations is an entirely new feature of French law introduced by the 1977 legislation.

The Commission has no power to investigate a merger on its own initiative, but may only do so at the request of the Minister himself moved *motu proprio* or by a notification made by the undertaking concerned. A notification by the undertaking must be made within three months of the effective date of the concentration and a decision rendered within eight months. Otherwise there is no specific time limit within which the Minister is required to act.

In order to trigger an investigation, four conditions must be satisfied:

---

13   As Note 3 above.

— an operation has taken place which has legal consequences such as a purchase of shares, transfer of assets etc.;
— the operation must result in a concentration in which the undertakings involved control together 40 per cent of national consumption of the particular product or when one of them controls 25 per cent of national consumption of the product;
— the operation must have a sufficient effect on competition;
— the adverse effect on competition caused by the concentration must override the economic advantages to be obtained from it.

If the Commission concludes that the concentration is undesirable, it may report to the Minister accordingly, and the Minister may make such decisions as are necessary to restore the balance of competition, and in an extreme case has power to order that the concentration should be undone.

The only case referred to in the 1979 Commission Report concerns the merger between Vallourec and Tubes de la Providence,[14] these two companies had decided to merge their activities in the manufacture and sale of certain tubes. Following the Commission recommendations, the Minister decided that the merger could be approved, although such approval was granted subject to certain conditions imposed under Article 8 of the 1977 Law, which gives to the Commission and the Minister powers to take steps to restore the balance of competition following a merger. The merged company was ordered to refrain from increasing its control and influence over the trade of tubes in France, and was obliged to waive all provisions of exclusivity in its present and future contracts with persons engaged in the trade of tubes, before the merger could be approved.

An opinion has also been rendered in the *Segma* case[15] in which the parties notified the Commission of the purchase by the group Generale Occidentale of the shares of a company called Segma. As a consequence of the purchase, Generale Occidentale would have a 77 per cent share of the market of mustards, 52 per cent of vinegars and 50 per cent of pickles, and thus well above the limits provided by the Law.

After examining the market, the Commission found that the concentration could have serious effects on competition, in particular because competing undertakings in the relevant markets were considerably smaller. Another important factor noted by the Commission was the strength of Generale Occidentale and Segma's trade marks, which enabled them to obtain much higher margins than identical products sold without such marks to institutions or under distributors' 'house' marks—a similar situation to that found by the EEC Commission and the European Court of Justice in the *United Brands* case.[16]

Despite these factors, the Commission decided to approve the concentration because of the economic advantages which could result from it, and in particu-

14   *Vallourec/Tubes de la Providence* merger, BOSP 19 May 1979 No.10.
15   *Segma*, BOSP 1 December 1979 No.24.
16   *United Brands v the Commission* [1978] ECR 207; [1978] 1 CMLR 429.

lar, a reduction of the costs of production for Segma and the improvement of its financial position.

In order to safeguard competition in the market, however, approval was subject to the following conditions:

— the specialised subsidiary of Generale Occidientale was barred from exercising any influence over Segma;
— the marketing networks of each company were to be kept separate;
— no discriminatory provision should exist within the group between the various companies;
— no commercial exclusivity would be established on contracts with customers;
— the exports of Segma should be developed.

In 1981, the Commission rendered only one opinion on merger: IWKA and Cie Générale des Eaux/Société Grange Frères.[17] IWKA and Cie Générale des Eaux had acquired 35 per cent of the shares of Grange Frères whose activity was in a competing sector. The Minister approved this acquisition on condition that competition continued at product distribution level.

Thus it can be seen that the aim pursued by the Commission, as in other aspects of the application of the 1977 Law, is to compel the parties involved to maintain or restore competition rather than prohibit the particular market conduct in question. If no measures are adequate to achieve this objective, then the Commission will order the concentration to be dismantled, but so far the Commission has not opted for this extreme solution and it is not known whether they have so far contemplated it.

It appears that the new Law on mergers and concentrations has developed very little.

Restrictive Practices

The principal work of the Commission, as with its pre-1977 predecessor, is in the field of restrictive practices, including the abuse of monopoly power.

The Commission usually opens a case on the initiative of the Minister. Both its investigation and its ultimate finding is however wholly independent of the Minister of Economic Affairs.

Before 1977 the Commission dealt mostly, if not exclusively, with industrial companies; since 1977 however the new Commission's sphere of influence is much broader and has covered companies operating in the services sector, and in particular funeral companies, insurance companies etc.

The 1977 Law contains a definition of restrictive practices which is similar to the one found in Article 85(1) EEC Treaty.

The Commission has made it clear that the legal form adopted for the restrictive practice is irrelevant. There are no particular legal structures, even though

---

17   BOCC, 11 March 1981 No.4.

the Government may encourage their use, which could justify a restrictive practice. Thus the '*Groupement d'Intérêts Economiques*', the form of joint venture which has been specially created by Parliament to facilitate co-operation between companies, would never protect undertakings from prosecution. The important point is the objective of the practice, not the form which has been adopted.[18]

As to the independence of undertakings, the Commission reaffirmed in the *Water Meter* case[18] the principle that no competition is to be expected between companies belonging to the same group. Subsidiaries were defined in that particular case as companies in which the main shareholder owns at least 50 per cent of the share capital. It is not yet known to what extent effective management and control might give rise to a parent/subsidiary relationship where there is less than 50 per cent ownership.

In general, the Commission approach towards restrictive practices is little different from that adopted by the EEC Commission. Agreements on price fixing, divisions of markets, concerted bids for public works as well as measures taken to prevent other undertakings from manufacturing or selling have been the main practices which have been examined by the Commission, and any conduct likely to lessen competition or interfere with technical or economic progress is likely to be declared illegal.

The following are examples of practices which have been found to be illegal:

(1) Joint price lists are *per se* illegal—the Commission announced that it has departed from the view taken some years ago by its predecessor that the legality of joint price lists was to be judged according to the use which the parties made of them. The establishment of the joint price list by employers' or manufacturers' associations is considered *per se* illegal, even though the price list might not be compulsory or indeed applied at all. Such a price list is regarded as an incentive for the members of the association to fix the same prices or the same margin of commission. The Commission stated in its 1979 Report that such lists encouraged producers or distributors to establish their prices or commissions on a basis other than that resulting from an examination of their own costs, and there was therefore no incentive to reduce the manufacturing or distribution costs involved. In its 1981 Report, the Commission mentions several cases.[20]

(2) Practices under which competitors inform themselves of their prices are not *per se* illegal if the level of prices is different. Such information will be illegal, in all cases where the public authorities have asked for bids for public works[21] or where it appears that the similarity of prices is the consequence of a mutual information.[22]

---

18   The Commission has recalled this principle in the *Explosives* case, BOSP 20 April 1979 No.8 and in the *Triponnet/Transgroup* case, BOCC 8 May 1982 No.12.
19   See Note 3 above.
20   *Baker Association*, BOCC 24 July 1981 No.14; *Fertilizer* case, BOCC 12 December 1981 No.15.
21   *Greenspaces* case, BOCC 17 October 1981 No.19.
22   *Fertilizer* case, BOCC 12 December 1981 No.15.

(3) Agreements not to compete are illegal when their provisions give a protection disproportionate to their objective.

(4) Exclusive dealing may be lawful. One of the main tests is that the product should be a new one. Exclusivity can then be justified as a legitimate guarantee of a return on investment for a distributor who is required to undertake substantial promotional or marketing expenses. If the product is well established on the market, then exclusive dealing would be harder to justify, and in the *Feudor* case[23] exclusive dealing contracts were declared illegal in view of the large share of the market enjoyed by the product.

(5) Joint purchasing organisations have been declared illegal, but it is necessary to strike a balance between the adverse effects on competition and the possible improvements in distribution and marketing which may arise from them.

(6) Joint selling organisations have been declared illegal, unless the balance between adverse effects and possible improvements makes Article 51 applicable.[24]

(7) Restriction to the entry of competitors on the market has been condemned in several cases concerning refusal to grant a trade mark,[25] boycott[26] and refusal to supply.

(8) Global rebates (*Remises cartellisées*) which are calculated on the basis of total purchases made from all the producers will always be illegal.

(9) Although manufacturers' and traders' associations will not of themselves constitute restrictive practices, the Commission has issued strict warnings to such associations that if they are found to operate or participate in concerted practices, there are likely to be personal prosecutions and fines, because the Commission considers the existence of such associations a serious aggravating circumstance.

(10) The Commission is also particularly sensitive with regard to concerted practices in bids for public works and has issued a warning that any such concerted practices will be dealt with severely. The 1981 Report mentions two cases.

Market Dominance

(1) Definition of a dominant position

As with other forms of restrictive practices, the approach adopted by the Commission follows very closely that adopted by the EEC Commission in the application of Article 86 of the EEC Treaty.

The first priority is market definition. The Commission has stated that products or services which have between themselves a significant degree of substi-

---

23 *Feudor* case, BOSP 1 June 1978.
24 *Superphosphate* case, BOCC 12 December 1981 No.23.
25 *Products for Wood Preservation* case, BOCC 2 July 1980 No.14.
26 *'Generiques' Drugs* case, BOCC 17 July 1981 No.13.
27 *Pieces of Furniture* case, BOCC 16 January 1981 No.1.

tution for a particular type of consumer sharing the same characteristics will form a single market. An illustration of the importance of consumer characteristics can be seen in the *Records* case[29] in which the Commission identified a market for records sold in specialised shops as quite distinct from that for records sold in supermarkets. See also *Insurance Construction* case and *Water Distribution* case.[30]

The geographical market must also be determined, and it should be stressed that the Commission has found market dominance to exist even in very small areas, for example a small village community in the case of funeral directors.

Market share is obviously a very important factor and gives rise to a presumption of dominance. Market share alone will not be sufficient, however, and other factors must be present. In the *Feudor* case,[31] for example, Feudor was not found to be dominant even though it had 46 per cent of the market. This was because the distributors in the market were also highly concentrated and enjoyed substantial market powers, so that Feudor was not in a position to dominate the market. In contrast, Pont à Mousson[32] was found to be dominant with only 20 per cent of the relevant market. In that case the Commission found that it was the only company in the market able to offer a complete range of products, its technology was far in advance of competitors, and Pont à Mousson had a strong position in associated products. (For the definition of dominant position, see also *Vaccins Antiaphteux* case and *Water Distribution* case.)

In determining market share, the production of associated undertakings may be taken into account, but interestingly products consumed by the producer for its own needs are not included.

In its 1979 Annual Report the Commission defined a dominant position as follows:

> It allows an undertaking or a group of undertakings to act without regard to the exigencies of external competitive pressures but also to impose its own will on competitors or its own conditions on suppliers or customers who are not in a position to find adequate alternative sources of supply.[33]

In its 1980 Report, the Commission has given a similar definition. Although the wording may be slightly different, the concept is very much the same as that adopted both by the EEC Commission and the European Court of Justice.

(2) *Abuse of a dominant position*

The mere holding of a dominant position does not in itself constitute an abuse.[34] Indeed, the Commission does not speak of abuse of a dominant

---

29   Records JO (*Documents Administratifs*) 62, 8 July 1978.
30   BOCE 14 June 1980 No.13 and BOCC 16 January 1981 No.1.
31   See Note 23 above.
32   *Pont à Mousson*, JO (Documents Administratifs) 62, 7 July 1978.
33   Ref. to 1979 Annual Report—JO (Documents Administratifs) 10, 6 February 1980.
34   See for example the European Court of Justice's definition of market dominance in *United Brands v the Commission* (Note 16 above).

position but of '*entrave au fonctionnement normal du marché*' (restrictions on the normal functioning of the market). As a result, conduct which in normal circumstances would not be considered anti-competitive may well be so where dominance exists, and in dealing with such cases, the Commission again adopts the approach of trying to restore objective conditions of competition rather than to impose penalties for abuse.

The *Water Meter* case[35] which is currently before the courts is important since it represents the first test of the validity of the Commission's policy in relation to the control of abuse of a dominant position. The Minister, on the advice of the Commission, brought prosecutions on five instances of abuse. It seems, however, that the Criminal Court is applying a rather stricter interpretation of the Law. Three of the alleged offences have been dismissed and the Court has ordered further investigations into the remaining two. The Minister has appealed against the judgment of the Criminal Court, but in the meantime the decision does illustrate that the Court is imposing a much greater burden of proof than was thought to be necessary by the Commission.

Obtaining an Exemption under Article 51

As mentioned earlier, Article 51 allows the Commission to grant a special exemption to restrictive practices where they contribute to the development of economic progress, in particular by the increase of productivity.

The advantages of the new exemption are to some extent compromised by the current view of the Commission that undertakings may only benefit if they first admit that the conduct under review infringes the 1977 Law. Nevertheless, as we have seen there is judicial doubt as to the validity of this approach.

(i) Article 51.1
This article exempts unlawful acts which are the result of a law or decree, but to qualify, the legislation must have been enacted after 1 November 1967.

Not surprisingly, the Commission has interpreted Article 51.1 strictly. There must exist a direct relationship between the particular law or decree and the practices which are complained of. A mere approval by public authorities of concerted practices does not make the act lawful, although it may well be considered by the Commission to constitute an extenuating circumstance. The Commission takes the view in all cases that if the administration intends to permit conduct which will reduce competition, it must do so unequivocally by enacting laws or decrees with mandatory effect.

(ii) Article 51.2
This procedure was first used in 1979 in the *Zinc* case,[36] in which agreement was reached between competitors for the closing of a rolling mill to allow for

---

35   See Note 3 above.
36   *Zinc* case, BOSP 19 May 1979 No.10.

the modernisation of other installations and to avoid the existence of excessive capacity. The Commission has stressed the point that this decision would not be applied in all cases where a recession exists. In the *Zinc* case, the extent of the investment to modernise the plants was such that excessive capacities would be inevitable.

In examining the application of Article 51.2, the Commission is required to strike an economic balance between the advantages and disadvantages of the concerted practices. Gains in productivity must be found and they must be a direct result of the existence of a concerted practice. Furthermore, the advantages resulting from the concerted practice must be divided in an equitable manner between all people concerned, and particularly consumers. [37]

---

37   *Vins de Cahors* case, BOCC 9 December 1981 No.22.

GERMANY: Federal Republic

The Impact of Recent Amendments to German Cartel Law

JOCHIM SEDEMUND

On 1 May 1980 the fourth amendment of the German Law against Restraints on Competition (GWB) came into effect. The main emphasis of the new amendment is focused on a tightening up of merger control (the relevant provisions taking effect retroactively from 28 February 1980), improvement of the supervision of abusive practices by market dominating enterprises, and measures aimed at the protection of efficient competition. Particular attention has been given to the problems created by the intrusion of large enterprises into markets previously characterised by small or medium-sized businesses. The new Law makes further provision in respect of the exemptions accorded to banks, insurance companies, and public utilities, and the supervision of abusive practices in the field of export cartels has been tightened up. The maximum fine which may be imposed under section 38 for infringements of the Law has been raised from DM 100,000 to DM 1 million.[1]

Merger Control – Presumptions of Market Dominance

The Federal Cartel Office (FCA) must prohibit a 'merger'[2] under section 24 if

---

1 Under both the old and the new law a fine which can be increased to up to three times the amount of the proceeds realised by virtue of the violation may be imposed; the new law provides however, that the amount of the proceeds realised may be estimated, which was not previously possible.
2 The transactions constituting a 'merger' within the meaning of the Law are defined by section 23(2 & 3) and include, among others, the acquisition of shares of 25 per cent or more, or of a substantial part of, the assets of another enterprise.

it is to be anticipated that the merger will result in or reinforce a market dominating position.[3]

'Big' Enterprises: Protection of Small Business

While certain presumptions of a market-dominating position had already been introduced in 1973 for horizontal mergers in the form of market shares,[4] no such presumptions existed until now with regard to an increase in (financial) resources. In this respect the amendment has brought changes which are of great importance, particularly for 'big' business.

The new section 23(a)(1) No. 1 provides rebuttable presumptions of the creation or strengthening of a superior market position: where an enterprise with an annual turnover of at least DM 2 billion merges into another enterprise which:

(1) is either active in a market where small and medium-sized firms have a total market share of at least two-thirds and where the merging firms reach a share of five per cent[5] or

(2) is in a dominant position in one or more markets where sales of at least DM 150 million were made during the previous fiscal year.[6]

While the specific goal of this provision is the protection of small and medium-sized enterprises, section 23(1) No. 2 concerns 'largeness as such'; this provision introduces a corresponding presumption where the enterprises participating in the merger together had sales of at least DM 12 billion during the preceding fiscal year, and at least two of the participating enterprises had sales of at least DM one billion each (so-called 'elephants' marriage). The section is aimed particularly at 'vertical' and conglomerate mergers; in other words, forms of merger which, unlike so-called 'horizontal' mergers, lead not to an enlargement of market shares, but to an increase or strengthening of reserves. The new presumptions effect a certain easing of the burden of proof in the case of vertical and conglomerate mergers, in the same way as section 22(3) has done since 1973 in the case of horizontal mergers.

The statutory provision of these new presumptions does not exclude the possibility that a superior market position may be created or strengthened without the requirements of the presumptions having been satisfied; similarly it is possible that in particular cases the presumptions may be rebutted despite all the requirements having been met. One is concerned here – at least theoretically – not with presumptions in the forensic sense, but rather with what the legislature refers to as 'leading indicators' ('*Aufgreiftatbestande*')[7] which merely

---

3 Market dominance is defined in section 22(1) as the absence of substantial competition or the existence of a superior market position in relation to competitors.

4 Cf. section on exemptions below.

5 Section 23(a)(1) No. 1(a).

6 Section 23(a)(1) No. 1(b).

7 Cf. the Report of the Economics Committee of the Bundestag-Drucksache 8/3690, at 26.

indicate the creation or strengthening of a superior market position within the framework of the FCA's duty to undertake an *ex officio* investigation. The presumptions do not, therefore, reverse the legal burden of proof, or do away with the FCA's duty to investigate on its own initiative the question of whether a position of market superiority has arisen or been strengthened, but rather place a certain explanatory burden on the enterprise which, when fulfilled, compels the Authority to undertake a full *ex officio* investigation and rebuttal of the objections raised by the enterprise.

The total turnover of the participating enterprise plays a central role in the new presumptions. The size of the enterprise as reflected in its turnover does not, of course, necessarily correspond to an internal financial strength, but can in fact lead to a lessening of the risk of competition and to the deterrence and discouragement of substantially smaller enterprises. The Federal Supreme Court had already recognised in the *GKN/Sachs* case[8] for example, that this would certainly be the case where a widely diversified and financially powerful combine took over a market-dominating company in its competitive vicinity (that is, in a 'proximate market', this type of merger being called a '*Markterweiterungszusammenschluss*') whereupon competitors would feel that they had more reason than before to desist from entering the market or pursuing a competitive price policy. It is not necessary that there should be objective grounds for expecting an actual deployment of financial strength at the time of the merger. The qualification made by the Federal Supreme Court regarding market proximity has been dropped by the amendment. Accordingly, the presumptions are not limited to *Markterweiterungszusammenschlusse*.

Oligopolies

Under section 22(2) two or more enterprises are deemed to be market-dominating if substantial competition for a particular type of goods or commercial services generally or in particular markets does not exist between them, and if together they fulfil the requirements of the definition of market dominance contained in section 22(1). Under section 22(3) No. 2 it is presumed that the conditions of section 22(2) are fulfilled if, for a particular type of goods or commercial services:

(1) three or fewer enterprises have a combined market share of 50 per cent or more, or

(2) five or fewer enterprises have a combined market share of two-thirds or more, this presumption not applying if the enterprises involved had sales of less than DM 100 million during the preceding fiscal year.

These presumptions listed in section 22(3) — like those of section 23(a)(1)

---

8   WuW/E BGH 1501.

No. 1 above – are to be viewed merely as 'leading indicators' and are not intended to reverse the burden of proof.[9]

Under section 23(a)(2), however, and for the purposes of merger control only, the new amendment does reverse the burden of proof by means of a rebuttable presumption of law. As with section 22(3) the presumption will arise where three or fewer enterprises have a market share of 50 per cent or more, or five or fewer enterprises have a market share of two-thirds. The presumption may be rebutted where the enterprises involved show that the circumstances are such that substantial competition may still be expected between them after the merger or the aggregate of enterprises does not have a superior market position in relation to other competitors. The section does not apply where the enterprises involved had sales of less than DM 150 million in the preceding fiscal year, or if the enterprises participating in the merger together have a market share not exceeding 15 per cent.

It is made clear that the new presumption only applies to enterprises with a leading market share; insofar as the group contains an enterprise with an annual turnover of less than DM 150 million (parent, subsidiary, and associated companies being taken into account in the computation of turnover), such enterprise will escape the presumption, without the presumption ceasing to apply to the other members of the group. Section 22(3) No. 2 contains no corresponding provision.

The Economics Committee of the Bundestag anticipated that the presumption would be rebutted if it could be proved that, by means of the merger, the balance of power within the oligopoly could be made more equal, without this involving a substantial narrowing of the oligopoly. This might be the case, for example, where the weaker oligopolist in an 'asymmetrical' oligopoly strengthens his position by merging with an outsider. The 15 per cent market share limit will serve to exclude such mergers from the operation of the presumption. According to the Committee, the DM 150 million turnover limit should also ensure that small and medium-sized enterprises are not subject to the presumption. Thus, for the first time in the GWB a reference point may be found for the application of the concept of 'small' or 'medium-sized' enterprises, where the relative market and size factors do not suffice in an individual case.

Exemptions from Merger Control

Under section 24(8) No. 1 mergers in which the participating enterprises together with their affiliates and associated enterprises had combined sales of less than DM 500 million during the preceding fiscal year are not subject to merger control, even if it is anticipated that the merger will result in or strengthen a position of market dominance. Under section 24(8) No. 2 merger control is also excluded, even where the DM 500 million limit is exceeded, where an

---

9   Cf. Economics Committee's Report of 1973, Drucksache 7/765, at 6.

independent enterprise with sales of less than DM 50 million during the previous fiscal year merges with another enterprise. This limit is lowered by the amendment to DM 4 million in cases where the acquiring enterprise had sales of at least DM 1 billion in the previous fiscal year.

Under the old law only mergers which could be expected to affect the whole Federal Republic or a substantial part of it were subject to merger control. This limitation has been dropped in the amendment.

The 'bagatelle market' provision of the old law has been somewhat modified by the amendment. As before prohibition of a merger is excluded where the market affected by the merger is one where the total volume of sales in the previous fiscal year amounted to less than DM 10 million. This produced the effect, however, that new expanding markets were not subject to merger control until the DM 10 million mark was passed, which meant that new, potentially important markets could be dominated while still in the early developmental stage. In order to prevent this, therefore, the amendment has added the proviso that the market in question must have existed for at least five years.[10]

Pre-Merger Control

The area of 'preventive' merger control has been widened in the new section 24(a)(1), according to which (*inter alia*) pre-merger notification of a merger must be given to the Federal Cartel Office if one of the participating enterprises had sales of at least DM 2 billion in the preceding fiscal year or at least two of the enterprises participating in the merger had sales of DM 1 million or more each. The DM 2 billion sales criterion has been specifically chosen so that the enterprises covered by the new presumptions of market dominance in section 23 are made fully aware of the Federal Cartel Office's evaluation of the merger before the merger takes place. The Federal Government was of the opinion[11], that preventive control was necessary here on the grounds that once such a merger has taken place, the original pre-merger competitive conditions often cannot be restored by a subsequent dissolution order.

Under the previous Law the enterprises proposing to participate in a merger requiring compulsory pre-merger notification had to wait until the expiry of the four months' period specified in section 24(a)(2) before they could validly complete the merger. The new Law provides under section 24(4) that the waiting period may be shortened by the Federal Cartel Office giving notice in writing that the proposed merger does not fulfil the conditions justifying a prohibition. This provision shall apply particularly to mergers consummated in foreign countries; it may be interesting to note that on this occasion the Federal Cartel Office's opinion has been confirmed[12] that in principle mergers of foreign enter-

---

10   Section 24(8) No. 3.
11   Cf. the Federal Government's draft Bill Drucksache 82136 at 23.
12   Cf. Report of the Economics Committee at 28 above.

prises in foreign countries which have an effect on German markets are also subject to German merger control, including the obligation of pre-merger notification.

'Participation' in a Merger

Under section 23(2) Nos 1 and 2 a merger may be constituted *inter alia* by the acquisition of shares in an enterprise or of a substantial part of its assets. Where shares in an enterprise are acquired, only the acquiring enterprise and the enterprise in which the shares are acquired 'participate' in the merger. The seller does not 'participate' insofar as he either transfers all the shares, or retains less than 25 per cent of them.[13] The concept of 'participation' is of importance in determining the criteria for notification of a merger,[14] compulsory pre-merger notification[15] and merger control.[16] The Bundesgerichtshof (Federal Supreme Court) at one time took the view that an enterprise selling off a significant portion of its assets would be considered a 'participating enterprise', but subsequently abandoned this interpretation. This development has been confirmed in the amendment: as far as acquisition of the assets of another enterprise wholly or to a significant extent is concerned, only the acquired part of the assets is relevant for the purposes of computing market shares, number of employees, and turnover of the seller.[17] This applies correspondingly with regard to the acquisition of shares, insofar as less than 25 per cent of the shares remain with the seller, and the seller does not retain a controlling influence on the enterprise.[18]

The 'Enterprise' Concept

Basically the Law only applies to 'enterprises' as opposed to private persons. However, section 23(1) also provides that a person or association of persons with a majority holding in an enterprise, and acquiring shares in another enterprise, shall be deemed to be an 'enterprise' for the purposes of the statute. The corresponding provision in the old Law applied only to mergers accomplished by acquisition of shares, and only then when the majority shareholder himself acquired shares in another enterprise. These limitations have been removed by the new amendment.

---

13 Consequently the seller 'participates' if he retains 25 per cent of the shares or more; in this case, a joint 'venture' is deemed to be created which then constitutes a separate merger.
14 Section 23.
15 Section 24(a).
16 Section 24.
17 Section 23(1) sentence 8.
18 Section 23(1) sentence 9.

Acquisition of Minority Interests of Less Than 25 Per Cent

Under section 23(2) No. 2(a) and (b) the acquisition of shares in another enterprise amounting to 25 per cent or 50 per cent of the voting capital of the other enterprise is deemed to be a merger. In order to prevent circumvention of the 25 per cent limit the new amendment provides that the acquisition of shares will also be deemed to be a merger insofar as the purchaser by contract, articles of association (or partnership agreement) or resolution acquires a legal position equivalent to the position of a shareholder in a joint-stock company with more than a 25 per cent interest in the voting capital. As may be seen, the requirements of section 23(2) No. 2 (a) and (b) presume that the enterprise in which the shares are acquired has a voting capital. With joint-stock companies this will always be the case, but as far as partnerships are concerned, this will only be so where there is a direct link between the partners' participation in capital and their voting rights. The amendment therefore provides that voting rights shall be deemed to be equivalent to shares in an enterprise.

Supervision of Abusive and Discriminatory Practices by Market-Dominating Enterprises

Definition of Abusive Practices under Section 22

The German Cartel Authority has power under section 22 GWB to prohibit abusive practices by market-dominating enterprises. The new amendment provides three concrete examples of such abuses, so as to facilitate the application of the section. These examples are to be viewed merely as providing concrete illustrations of the concept of an abuse within the meaning of the section, and do not provide an exhaustive interpretation, or in any way limit the application of the general concept. According to section 22(4), an abuse exists where a market-dominating enterprise as seller or purchaser of a special type of goods or commercial services:

(1) unjustifiably restricts the competitive opportunities of other enterprises to such a degree that competition in the market is substantially affected;
(2) demands terms which could with a high degree of probability not be charged under effective competition (taking into consideration the behaviour of enterprises on comparable markets with effective competition) or
(3) unjustifiably imposes terms less favourable than those imposed by the market-dominating enterprise itself in comparable markets on similar enterprises.

Sanctions for Violations of Section 22

Under the previous Law it was possible for an enterprise to persist in an abusive practice during the time between the initial issuing of a prohibition order under section 22(4) by the Federal Cartel Authority and the giving of final judgment in the matter by the relevant appellate court, without incurring liability in damages in respect of the continued abuse during this period.[19] The new Law closes this gap by providing section 35(2) that a claim for damages incurred during this period by competitors or purchasers will lie against the enterprise concerned, provided that the order in question was issued with the purpose not merely of safeguarding competitive conditions generally, but also of protecting the respective competitors or purchasers. This will usually be the case. Furthermore, section 37(b) GWB empowers the Federal Cartel Authority to confiscate the revenues obtained by means of an abusive practice which has been continued after the issue of a prohibition order. So as to avoid imposing a double burden, however, the section provides relief from confiscation to the extent that the enterprise concerned has already paid damages under section 35(2). Moreover, the Authority is obliged to reimburse revenues confiscated to the extent that the enterprise concerned subsequently proves payment of damages pursuant to a final judgment under section 35(2).

Supervision of Power of Demand

The provisions of section 22 GWB, which empower the FCA to prohibit abusive exploitation by market-dominating enterprises of their position of market dominance, and the provisions of section 26(2) GWB, which prohibit market dominating enterprises and enterprises occupying a position of relative market strength from unfairly hindering other enterprises or engaging in discriminatory market behaviour, apply equally to both the supply and the demand sides of the market. The federal Government took the view, however, that experience had shown that the criterion of high market shares, while providing a suitable reference point for the investigation of market dominance on the supply side of the market, had proved inadequate for the establishment of a position of relative market strength on the demand side.[20] Accordingly, for the purposes of prohibition proceedings initiated by the Federal Cartel Authority under section 37(a), section 26(2) now provides a 'presumption' that a purchaser occupies a position of relative market strength *vis-à-vis* a supplier within the meaning of the section, if this purchaser, in addition to usual price discounts or other normal considerations, regularly receives particularly favourable terms not granted to other purchasers of a comparable type – for example, retailers, wholesalers, industrial purchasers, etc. This 'presumption', like those contained in the new section 23(a), is not a presumption of law, but rather a 'leading indicator' ('*Aufgreiftatbestand*'), and therefore does not work to reverse the legal burden of proof. For

---

19 Abusive practices in the field of hindrance of competitors or discrimination against customers, however, will often also constitute a violation of section 26(2), which is self-executing, and may give rise to claims for damages without any prior order of the Cartel Authority.

20 See the Federal Government's draft Bill at 24.

a discussion of this distinction the reader is referred to the comments on section 23(a) above.

Under the new section 26(3) market-dominating enterprises, enterprises occupying a position of relative market power, and cartels are forbidden to exploit their market position so as to induce other enterprises in the course of business to grant them preferential terms, in the absence of facts justifying the granting of such terms – in other words, differences in the terms granted to different purchasers or suppliers must relate to differences in their respective performances. It is true that in many cases a purchaser who compels a supplier to grant him preferential terms will in any case thereby unfairly hinder within the meaning of section 26(2) other less powerful purchasers competing with him. Experience has shown, however, that such hindrance is difficult to prove.[21] Moreover, it was not previously clear whether the prohibition against discrimination in section 26(2) covered cases of 'indirect discrimination' (*mittelbare Diskriminierung*). The new section 26(3) therefore makes it absolutely clear that discriminatory conduct induced by enterprises on the demand side is subject to the prohibition against discrimination.

Improved Protection for Small and Medium-Sized Business

The new section 37(a)(3) GWB empowers the Federal Cartel Authority to prohibit an enterprise, which by reason of its superior market power in relation to small and medium-sized competitors is able substantially to influence market conditions, from engaging in a practice which directly or indirectly unfairly hinders such competitors, and is liable to affect competition with lasting effect. The section is distinguished from other provisions dealing with the hindrance of competition through the abuse of market power (sections 22(4) and 26(2)) primarily by the different formulation of the concept of market power which it contains. While section 22(4) depends for its operation on the 'absolute' concept of market power represented by the 'absence of any substantial competition'[22] and section 26(2) sentence 2 is based on the criterion of 'relative' market superiority in 'vertical' relationships between enterprises on different market levels, section 37(a)(3) introduces for the first time a concept of relative market power applying to 'horizontal' relationships between competitors on the same market level. The new provision is intended to provide for the situation where an unfair hindrance of competitors is based not so much on the exploitation of an absolute superiority of an enterprise over all its competitors, or on a relative market power *vis-à-vis* dependent enterprises within the meaning of section 26(2) sentence 2, but rather on the abuse by an enterprise of a relative position of power *vis-à-vis* some of its competitors (that is, small and medium-sized competitors).

---

21   See the Federal Government's draft Bill at 25.
22   Section 22(1) No. 2.

GREECE

The Greek Anti-trust Law

COSTAS VAINANIDIS

I General Introduction

1. The legal background

Until 1977 the need to protect free competition and to confront anti-competitive behaviour, was basically covered by Articles 178 and 179 of the Greek Civil Code and by Law 146/1914 on 'unfair competition'. A few provisions of a quasi-anti-trust law nature can also be found in the market police control legislation which traditionally has been used as a means of depressing prices and profits when free competition was considered unable to play its role as a price regulator.

Articles 178 and 179 of the Greek Civil Code render void an agreement which restricts excessively the freedom of a person, economic freedom included, as being *contra bonos mores*; similarly Article 281 of the same Code prohibits the exercise of a right, if such an exercise exceeds manifestly the limits laid down by good faith or *bonos mores* or by the social and economic purpose of the right in question.

Law 146/1914 on 'unfair competition' has offered quite a lot to individual traders who suffered damages from 'unfair' commercial practices of their competitors (passing off, misleading advertisements, disclosure of industrial secrets etc.), but it has very rarely been used for the protection of free competition; inversely, it was sometimes used in order to enforce rights whose exercise could have anti-competitive results in the market (there exist court decisions which by using Law 146/1914 offered absolute territorial protection to exclusive dealers;[1] more recent court decisions, by referring to the free competition principles, refused a Law 146/1914 protection to exclusive dealers thus approaching the issue differently).[2]

---

1 Athens Court of First Instance judgments No. 23241/1964, 929/1967, 13310/1967 and Athens Court of Appeal judgment No. 9/1968.
2 Athens Court of Appeal judgment No. 3805/1978, Lamia Court of First Instance judgment No. 501/1980, and Athens Court of First Instance judgment No. 8660/1981.

2. Introduction and Development of Greek Anti-trust Law

In 1977 when Greece was looking forward to acceding as a full member of the European Community, the introduction of a Greek anti-trust law in conjunction with the EEC competition law had been considered as a step towards harmonisation of the Greek legal system with that of the European Community; at the same time such a law could serve as a positive reaction of the conservative Government to the increasing demand of the opposition for a law to cope with monopolies and oligopolies; therefore, on 26 September 1977 the Greek Parliament passed Law 703/77 to control monopolies and oligopolies and to protect free competition[3] (the Law).

Although the Law came into effect on 27 March 1978, it was more than eighteen months later that it turned from paper into practice. Not without reason, the Ministry of Commerce found it very difficult to cope with the Law itself. There was no former law to be used as a guide, there was no Greek anti-trust case law, there was no Greek bibliography dealing with the subject; the existing staff had to be trained and experts employed. It is indeed true that some of the resolutions of the then existing Competition Protection Committee, especially the first ones, seem to reflect a lack of adequate knowledge on the subject.

Following the accession of Greece as a full member to the EEC[4] more attention was focused on competition law. The references to EEC competition law became more frequent and they were most often followed by references to the national anti-trust law. By the beginning of 1981 it had become evident that industry and commerce were finding it very difficult to digest some of the first unfortunate resolutions of the Competition Protection Committee; at the same time the anti-trust department of the Ministry of Commerce, known as the Competition Protection Service, had come to trace the drawbacks of the Law, using the experience gained through its day to day practice.

These circumstances incited the Minister of Commerce in the former conservative Government to announce twice within the first semester of 1981 that he intended to amend the Law, although he did not finally do so until the 'New Democracy' conservative party passed into opposition following the general elections of October 1981.

It was expected that the Socialist PASOK party of Dr Andreas Papandreou, which took over from the Conservatives, would investigate anti-competitive practices vigorously, and immediately after the elections the pro-Government press were heralding a 'war' against monopolies using Law 703/77.

Instead followed a long period of dormancy (January 1982 to December 1982) which may have been responsible for two noteworthy events:

(1) the Competition Protection Committee (an administrative organ with decisive powers to a great extent independent of governmental influences)

---

3   Published in issue No. 278/26 September 1977 of the *Greek Government Gazette*.
4   1 January 1981.

was tacitly inactivated from January 1982 and then officially abolished in April 1982 by Ministerial Decree, all its decisive powers having been taken over by the Minister of Commerce; and

(2) the then Minister of Commerce and his deputy, following a major reshuffle of the Cabinet, resigned from their posts in July 1982.

It took five months from the resignation of the former Minister before the present Minister of Commerce announced in December 1982 that he was to reactivate Law 703/77. Indeed, on 26 January 1983, the Minister had issued the long expected 'Code of Rules' for the operation of the Competition Committee (a mere advisory organ cited with the Minister, set up by the Socialist Government in April 1982 to replace the former Competition Protection Committee), and on 9 March 1983 the new Competition Committee held its first session.

Since this paper was written, another seven sessions of the Competition Committee have been held, and six anti-trust cases have been considered so far, but no advisory opinion on any of them has yet been passed to the Minister for his formal Decision.

It remains to be seen to what extent the advisory opinions of the Competition Committee and the Ministerial Decisions expected will enlighten practitioners and traders after 20 months of obscurity and confusion as to what our new anti-trust authorities deem as permissible and what as violations of Greek anti-trust laws.

II The Law

1. *The Construction of the Law*

The Law is divided into seven chapters:

Chapter 1 (Subject of Control)

This contains the core of the Law. Articles 1 (prohibited collaboration), 2 (abusive exploitation of dominant position), 3 (general provision), 4 (permitted merger between undertakings), 5 (exceptions and special regulations) and 6 (collaboration between exporters) specify under what circumstances and to whom the Law might apply (Articles 1 to 6).

Chapter 2 (Organs)[5]

The second chapter refers to the decision making and executive organs entrusted with the application and enforcement of the Law (Articles 7 to 13).

---

5 Chapters 2 and 3 should be read in the light of ministerial decision No. B3/395 by which the Competition Protection Committee was abolished.

Chapter 3 (Judicial Protection)

Chapter three prescribes the judicial remedies available to the parties involved in anti-trust proceedings (Articles 14 to 18).

Chapter 4 (Register - Notification)

This deals with the registration of notifications, resolutions and court decisions. It also deals with the 'notifications' and their effects (Articles 19 to 23).

Chapter 5 (Complaints and Investigations)

Chapter five refers to the right to complain, the collection of evidence and the power given to the cartel authorities to carry out on the spot investigations (Articles 24 to 27).

Chapter 6 (Sanctions - Charges)

Chapter six provides for criminal sanctions (Articles 28 to 31).

Chapter 7 (Final Provisions)

The last chapter enunciates in Article 32 the 'effects doctrine' as regards the applicability of the Law to all restrictions of competition which might affect free competition in Greece. It also contains certain provisions of a transitional character and procedural nature (Articles 32 to 37).

2. Scope of Application of the Law

Contrary to the normal practice which places the articles concerning the application of the law in its preamble, the relevant Article of Law 703/77 is placed among the final provisions of the Law. Thus Article 32 of chapter seven enunciates the 'effects doctrine' in the Greek anti-trust legislation, providing that the Law applies to all restrictions of competition which can actually or potentially affect competition in Greece regardless of the nationality and place of establishment of the undertakings involved and the place where the agreements, decisions or concerted practices materialised.

3. What is Prohibited

(a) Restrictive Agreements

Article 1(1)[6] of Law 703/77 prohibits all agreements between undertakings, decisions by associations of undertakings and concerted practices which restrict

---

6   For full text of Article 1 see Appendix A.

competition; it should be said that Article 1 of the Law is nothing more than the Greek translation of Article 85 of the EEC Treaty amended as follows:

(1) The words '. . . as incompatible with the Common Market . . .' '. . . which may affect trade between Member States . . .' and the words '. . . within the Common Market . . .' contained in Article 85(1) of the EEC Treaty have been, for self-explanatory reasons, deleted. Although distortion of competition can only be seen within a certain geographic framework, there is no such reference in Article 1 of the Law. Contrarily, there exists such a reference in Article 2 of the Law (abusive exploitation of dominant position). Since Article 32 of the Law confirms that the Law deals with distortions of competition 'in the home market', the omission of such a reference in Article 1 can only be attributed to an oversight.

(2) The word 'markets' contained in Article 85(1)b of the EEC Treaty has been replaced in Article 1(1)b of the Law by the world 'disposition'. There is no apparent justification for this replacement, nor is it expected to have any impact on the interpretation of the Law.

(3) Article 1(1)d of Law 703/77 appears slightly different from the corresponding Article 85(1)d of the EEC Treaty. The 'unjustifiable refusal to sell, purchase, or engage in other transactions' has been added on Article 1(1)d of Law 703/77 as a characteristic example of applying dissimilar conditions to equivalent transactions, whereas the words 'thereby placing them at a competitive disadvantage', which appear in Article 85(1)d of the EEC Treaty, have been replaced by the words 'in a manner raising difficulties over the operation of competition'.

All agreements falling within the scope of Article 1(1) are rendered null and void by the second paragraph of the same Article.

(b) Abusive exploitation of dominant position

Article 2[7] of Law 703/77 which prohibits the abusive conduct of dominant firms in the Greek market is also the Greek version of Article 86 of the EEC Treaty. Apart from the self-explanatory replacement of the words 'Common Market' by the words 'home market' and the addition of the words 'unjustifiable refusal to sell, purchase or engage in other transactions' as a characteristic example of applying dissimilar conditions to equivalent transactions, Article 2 of Law 703/77 is a copy of Article 86 of the EEC Treaty.

The fact that the Law refers explicitly in both Articles 1 and 2 to the refusal to sell as a prohibited practice explains the sensitivity shown by the Greek anti-trust authorities on this issue; moreover, it should be noted that 'refusal to sell', even as an individual practice of a non-dominant undertaking, violates the existing Market Police control legislation and in particular Article 31(2) of the Market Police Code[8] when it refers to goods satisfying necessities of life.

---

7 For full text of Article 2 see Appendix B.
8 Legislative Decree 136/30-30 September 1946 as amended by Article 10 of Legislative Decree 218/1973.

(c) Automatic nullity

Article 3 of the Law makes clear that no prior resolution of any authority whatsoever is required for the conduct proscribed by Articles 1 and 2 to be prohibited.

4. Who Escapes the Application of the Law

(a) Granting of exemption

Under Article 1(3) agreements or categories of agreements, decisions and concerted practices falling within the scope of Article 1(1) may qualify for a full or partial exemption, provided that they are duly notified (Article 10) to an executive organ called the Competition Protection Service and that they meet certain cumulative requirements explicitly stipulated in Article 1(3) of the Law, which coincide absolutely with the ones listed in Article 85(3) of the EEC Treaty.

(b) Negative clearance

Undertakings which have concluded an agreement or are contemplating coming to an agreement, or dominant undertakings which have taken or are planning to take certain measures which could be caught by Article 2 of the Law, may seek a 'negative clearance' before or after they conclude the agreement in question or they act in a way which could be deemed to be an abuse of dominancy.

Following the abolition of the Competition Protection Committee by Ministerial Decision No. B3/395, the Minister of Commerce alone is now competent to grant an Article 1(3) exemption or an Article 11(1) negative clearance.

(c) Mergers

In Article 4(1) the drafters of the Law made clear that mergers, as such, do not fall within the scope of Article 1(1).

Under Article 4(2) the notion of 'merger' includes

(1) establishment of a new undertaking
(2) absorption of one or more undertakings into another and
(3) purchase of one or more undertakings by another

(d) Exemption to undertakings serving Common Benefit

Since Article 4(1) of the Law makes no reference to Article 2 (abusive exploitation of dominant position), a merger which allows the independent firm which arises from the merger, or allows the purchaser of his competitors to become dominant, might be caught by Article 2 of Law 703/77. There is no doubt that Article 4 is placed in the Law for the purpose of allowing Greek firms to merge with others in order to enable them to confront effectively their strong competitors in the European markets.

Article 5(1) provides that the Law applies equally to public corporations and undertakings engaged in activities destined to serve the 'common benefit', (undertakings engaged in activities of a social character as water supply, electricity supply, telecommunications etc. are usually considered to be such), but allows the Ministers of National Economy (formerly Minister of Co-ordination) and Commerce by common accord to exempt any of them, individually or by category, from the application of the Law, provided they are of general importance to the national economy.

Exemptions under Article 5 of the Law have been granted to the War Industry S.A., a company mainly owned by the state, engaged in the manu-facture of armaments, and to the Greek Aircraft Industry S.A., an undertaking whose activities are of considerable importance to national defence.

The same article, in paragraph 2, provides that the Law also applies to undertakings or associations of undertakings engaged in the production, processing, conversion or trade of agricultural products, products of animal husbandry, forest produce and fisheries but similarly the application of the Law to categories of such undertakings or certain sectors of their activities might be exempted by joint resolutions of the Ministers of National Economy, Commerce and Agriculture.

Moreover, the Law applies to land, air and sea transport, but the competent Ministers, namely, the Ministers of National Economy, Commerce and Communication in the case of land and air transport, and the Ministers of National Economy, Commerce and Merchant Marine, in the case of sea transport, are empowered to introduce new regulations and exemptions from the provisions of the Law (Article 5(3)).

No exemptions have been granted under Article 5(2) and (3) yet.

(e) Export Promoting Agreements
Article 6 of the Law under the heading 'collaboration between exporters' provides that the Law does not apply to agreements, decisions and concerted practices which aim 'exclusively' at securing, promoting and supporting exports, provided they do not prejudice the international obligations of the state. The Ministers of National Economy and Commerce are, however, empowered to resolve (by joint decision) that the Law applies even to export promoting agreements concerning specific categories of undertakings or products. The reference to the 'international obligations of the state', which is obviously destined to serve as a reminder of the prohibition to establish export cartels under the EEC Treaty, together with the word 'exclusively' which excludes from the application of the Law agreements, decisions of undertakings or concerted practices having additional aims, limits considerably the scope of Article 6 of the Law.

5. Organs Entrusted with the Application of the Law

(a) The Competition Protection Service (CPS)
The application and enforcement of the Law is entrusted to a Department of the

Ministry of Commerce called the Competition Protection Service (CPS).

The CPS is an executive organ having the following main powers and responsibilities:

(1) to keep a permanent public registry of collaboration between undertakings where all relevant irrevocable resolutions of the Minister of Commerce as well as the relevant judgments of the lower administrative courts and the Council of State (Conseil d'Etat) are recorded;

(2) to keep a confidential temporary register of collaboration between enterprises, where all notifications made according to the relevant provisions of the Law are recorded;

(3) to carry out investigations in order to ascertain infringements of the Law;

(4) to bring cases before the Minister of Commerce;

(5) to observe the application and enforcement of the resolutions of the Minister of Commerce;

(6) to refer any infringements of the Law to the Public Prosecutor and finally

(7) to perform any act in general destined to serve the application and observance of the Law.

(b) The Competition Committee (CC)

By joint ministerial decision No. B3/395 taken by the Ministers of Government Presidency and Commerce by virtue of legislative authorisation[9] the then existing Competition Protection Committee (CPC), which under the Law was the decision making administrative body entrusted with the application of the Law, has been replaced by a merely advisory organ called the Competition Committee, sited at the Ministry of Commerce and consisting of a chairman, six members, the director of the Competition Protection Service as general spokesman without voting rights and an official of the same as Secretary of the Committee.[10]

The six members of the Competition Committee come one each from the following official bodies:

(1) Ministry of Finance,

(2) Bank of Greece,

(3) Athens Traders Association,

(4) Greek Industries Association,

(5) General Federation of Greek Workers and

(6) the most representative organisation of the small and medium-sized undertakings.

Under Article 7 of the Ministerial Decision the new Competition Committee is restricted to merely advisory duties. By Ministerial Decision No

---

9   The|legislative|authorisation|has been given by Article 4 section 2 of Law 1232/1982 'to bring back, amend and complete the provisions of Legislative Decree 4352/1964 and other provisions'.

10   The head of the Competition Protection Service was one of the seven members of the Competition Protection Committee who had voting rights.

K6-50/26.1.83 taken by the Minister of Commerce and Code of Rules for the operation of the CC have been laid down. (For an analysis of the Code see: [1983] ECLR 145.).

(c) The Minister of Commerce

Until 26 April 1982, when Joint Ministerial Decision No. B3/395 was taken, the competence to make decisions of the Minister of Commerce was limited to those of a rather general character, which had to be taken jointly with other Ministers under Articles 5 (possibility of exempting public corporations etc. from the application of the Law) and 6 (possibility of exempting export promoting agreements from the benefits of article 6) of Law 703/77.

The Minister of Commerce, apart from his general power to lodge an appeal before the administrative courts against resolutions of the Competition Protection Committee, could influence only indirectly and to a very limited extent the decision-making powers of the Competition Protection Committee, mainly through the vote of the Head of the Competition Protection Service cast during the meetings of the CPC before it delivered its formal resolutions.

From 26 April 1983 onwards all decisive competences provided by Law 703/77 are now vested in the Minister of Commerce and are exercised by the latter even without the concurrent opinion of the new Competition Committee and without following the procedural rules laid down by Law 703/77.[11] Consequently the Minister of Commerce is now exclusively competent, either on his own initiative or following a formal complaint lodged with the CPS, to decide in a given case whether the Law has been violated or not.

Whenever he ascertains that an infringement of Articles 1(1) (prohibited collaboration) or 2 (abusive exploitation of dominant position) has taken place, the following courses are open to him:

(1) to address a recommendation to the undertakings concerned requiring them to bring to an end the infringement in question;

(2) to order them to cease the violation in the future;

(3) to threaten fines for future violations of the Law;

(4) to render the above threatened fines due and payable when he ascertains by resolution the continuation or repetition of the infringement and

(5) to impose fines to a maximum of ten per cent of the total turnover of the undertaking concerned in the year when the infringement took place or the year before.

The Minister of Commerce became also exclusively competent to grant an Article 1(3) exemption from the application of the Law and he may also grant an Article 11(1) 'negative clearance' by certifying that on the basis of the facts known to him there is no infringement of Articles 1(1) and 2 of the Law.

6. Register - Notification

The Law in Article 20 provides that all decisions, agreements and concerted

---

11   Article 7 of joint ministerial decision No. B3/395.

practices in existence when the Law came into effect had to be notified to the CPS within four months of the Law coming into effect, that is by 28 July 1978 at the latest. Surprisingly, and contrary to the corresponding provisions of the EEC Law, fines may be imposed even for duly notified agreements if the Minister of Commerce finds that a duly notified agreement infringes Article 1(1) of the Law and does not qualify for an Article 1(3) exemption.

Lack of notification within the fixed four month period deprived interested parties of the opportunity to seek an Article 1(3) exemption and subjected them to a fine ranging from Dr. 100,000 to Dr. 200,000 each. Taking into consideration that at that time there was ignorance and confusion among traders as to the existence, interpretation and the implications of the Law (something which still exists today, although to a lesser extent), it is not surprising that less than a handful of notifications of old agreements were made within the four month term. The result now is that no one dares to notify an old agreement. Instead, its cancellation and the signing of a fresh agreement, bearing a new date, is preferred. Such a practice allows the parties to seek a negative clearance or an Article 1(3) exemption and to avoid the fines mentioned above; this is certainly not always easy for practical reasons.

'New' agreements, decisions and concerted practices have to be notified to the CPS within one month of their conclusion. Again, failure to notify in time deprives the parties of the possibility to obtain an Article 1(3) exemption and renders them liable to fines of not less than Dr. 100,000 and not more than Dr. 500,000.

It is interesting to note that although 'mergers' are not caught by Article 1(1) pursuant to Article 4 (permitted merger of undertakings), they have to be notified as well; the same fine, Dr. 100,000 to Dr. 500,000, may be imposed for failure to notify a 'merger' in time. The only reasonable explanation of this need for notification seems to be the wish of the CPS to have the opportunity to ascertain whether the merger in question amounts to an 'abuse of a dominant position', that is whether it falls within the scope of Article 2.

Curiously enough, the CPC in one of its last formal resolutions [12] resolved by majority that notification of all mergers to the Competition Protection Service was obligatory in order for the latter to be offered the opportunity to examine, not only whether the merger as such amounted to an abuse of dominancy, but also to investigate whether, apart from a merger which was not caught as such by Article 1(1) of the Law, there were other terms in the takeover agreement which might fall foul of Article 1(1).

Under Article 23 of the Law, duly notified agreements, decisions and concerted practices are provisionally valid until the Minister of Commerce passes a resolution. In case the Minister resolves that the notified agreement, decision or concerted practice violates the Law and does not qualify for an exemption, the nullity dates back to the day on which the term for its notification expired.

---

12   CPC Resolution No. 17/8 January 82 N. *Karabelas Bros-Conversion of Timber Industry SA.*

7. Complaints and Investigations

Any physical or legal person is entitled by law to file a formal complaint for violation of the Law. All civil servants and servants of public undertakings are obliged to notify the CPS immediately of any violations of the Law brought to their attention. Failure to do so exposes them to the risk of imprisonment for up to six months or a fine of Dr. 20,000 to Dr. 200,000.

It is unfortunate that the Law threatens such unrealistic fines although in practice it is absolutely clear that there is no public prosecutor who would prosecute, nor penal court which would impose even a one Drachma fine on a civil servant for such a failure. It is certain that these penal provisions will follow the fate of similar provisions in other Greek laws; they will merely be ignored both by the people and the courts.

The Law also contains detailed provisions on the wide powers of investigation granted to the CPS, either by requesting written answers or by carrying out investigations on the spot. Heavy fines, which might reach Dr. one million, are intended to make anyone subject to investigation more eager to furnish information to the CPS.

8. Penal Provisions - Fines

Apart from the various fines of a non-criminal nature which are contained in the Law, there is a special chapter dealing with the penal sanctions reserved for the infringers of the Law.

Thus the following are threatened with imprisonment of not less than three months and not more than five years, and with a fine of not less than Dr. 100,000 and not more than Dr. 200,000:

(1) the physical persons or representatives of legal persons who violate Article 1(1) and 2 of the Law;

(2) anyone who obstructs the investigations carried out by the competent anti-trust authorities;

(3) anyone who refuses to supply information requested by the CPS;

(4) anyone who knowingly supplies false information or withholds the truth;

(5) anyone who refuses to give a sworn statement or refuses to give an unsworn statement although he has been requested to do so by the CPS as well as anyone who during such a deposition knowingly tells lies or refuses to disclose or conceals the truth.

Regardless of whether the respective agreements or decisions were put into practice, the following persons are liable to the above-mentioned penal sanctions in cases where the agreements, decisions or concerted practices in question were found to violate Article 1(1) or Article 2 of the Law:

(1) entrepreneurs, in the cases of personal undertakings;

(2) partners who have unlimited liability, in the cases of partnerships;

(3) administrators, in the cases of companies of limited liability and in the cases of cooperatives;

(4) each individual member of the boards of directors in the cases of *sociétés anonymes*.

Moreover, the same people are jointly and severally liable, with the legal entities they represent, for the payment of any fines imposed upon the legal entities in question. Consequently payment of the fines can be enforced upon their personal properties and, if they refuse or are unable to settle the fine imposed upon the company they represent, they may be detained until such payment is effected.

It is noteworthy that there is no other example in Greek company law where the members of the board of directors are by law jointly and severally liable with the *société anonyme* for debts of the latter; before Law 703/77 came into effect it was only the managing director of a *société anonyme* who was jointly and severally liable with the latter to pay the debts of the company due to the state.

III Judicial Remedies

1. Before the Administrative Courts

Under Article 14 of the Law the resolutions of the now abolished CPC were subject to appeal before the Athens three-member Administrative Court of First Instance. An appeal had to be lodged before the competent Court within 20 days after the CPC resolution was served on the party concerned. The CPC resolutions were immediately enforceable but the enforcement could be suspended until a judgment was issued on appeal by order of the Head of the Athens Administrative Court.

Decisions of the Athens Administrative Court of First Instance were open to appeal before the Athens Administrative Court of Appeal and decisions of the latter were further open to an appeal before the Council of State (Conseil d'Etat). Apart from the party immediately involved, the complainant and the Minister of Commerce were also entitled to lodge an appeal.

The above mentioned judicial remedies were available until 26 April 1982 when Joint Ministerial Decision No.B3/395 was issued; it is now very obscure whether the same judicial remedies are still available against the formal resolutions of the Minister of Commerce who has taken over the decision making powers of the abolished CPC. It appears that two different views could be supported, but none has been tested yet, since no ministerial decision which might give rise to an appeal before the courts has so far been issued.

According to the first view which seems to reflect the opinion of those who drafted the joint ministerial decision No.B3/395 (as far as Law 703/77 is concerned), Articles 1 of the joint ministerial decision by abolishing the CPC, 7 by releasing the Minister of Commerce from the obligation to follow the procedures laid down by Law 703/77 and 8 by releasing the new Competition Committee from the obligation to follow the juridical procedures of Law 703/77 which are contrary to the mere advisory role of the same, have deprived the undertakings concerned of the right of appeal to the Athens Administrative Court of First Instance and to the Athens Administrative Court of Appeal. Therefore only the Council of State, it is said is competent to annul ministerial decisions under Law 703/77 according to the general rules for annulment of administrative acts on questions of law, on the following four grounds:

(1) lack of competence

(2) infringement of an essential procedural requirement

(3) infringement of rule of law

(4) misuse of powers.

According to the second view, which seems to us to be the correct one, since the joint ministerial decision did not explicitly renounce the judicial remedies available, it would be onerous for those subjected to the Law to be deprived of the first and second stage of appeal, the more so since they are also deprived of their right to challenge the ministerial decision on the facts. This view is also supported by the recent tendency to widen the jurisdiction of the lower administrative courts in order to offer citizens as many judicial remedies as possible.

It should be mentioned that anyone who has lodged a complaint under Article 24(1) of Law 703/77 with the CPC is entitled to seek interim measures against the alleged infringer of the Law before the local civil court.

2. Before the Civil Courts

Under Article 18 of the Law ordinary civil courts are entitled to examine the validity of agreements in cases pending before them allegedly violating Articles 1 (restrictive agreements etc.) or 2 (abuse of dominant position), but their verdicts thereon are not binding upon the Minister or the Administrative Courts. Moreover, under the same Article, anyone who has a legitimate interest and has already lodged a formal complaint with the CPS for an alleged violation of the Law may apply for interim measures before the competent single-member civil court; such measures might be adopted in order to offer preliminary relief pending the issue of the formal Ministerial Decision to be taken as a result of the complaint lodged with the CPS.

An interesting question, to which the answer is yet far from clear, is whether there are any other civil remedies available to those who have suffered damages caused by agreements, decisions, concerted practices and by the abusive exploitation of dominancy infringing Articles 1 and 2 of the Law.

Two opposing views are supported by commentators, but there is no case law on this issue yet.

Under the first,[13] the civil remedies are exhausted in those explicitly stated in Law 703/77. Consequently no action for damages under Article 914 of the

---

13   For example A. Georgiadis – M. Stathopoulos, *Civil Code* Athens, 1980, Law of Contract (Article 532, page 107).

Greek Civil Code may be brought before the civil courts.[14] This view is supported by the fact that the Law contains detailed administrative proceedings and involves the Administrative and Criminal Courts directly, whereas there is no hint even in the Law that private parties may sue infringers for damages sustained or that they may request the civil courts to order infringers to refrain from violating the Law.[15] Moreover, it is said that the primary purpose of the Law is to serve the public interest and not to confer individual rights on the undertakings concerned.

According to the second viewpoint,[16] for a finding that an individual may claim damages under Article 914 of the Greek Civil Code, it first has to be established whether Law 703/77 was enacted in order also to protect 'individual interests'; if that is the case, then an action for damages is permissible. The same view finds that Articles 1 and 2 of Law 703/77 are undoubtedly destined to protect individual interests as well.

Certainly, Law 703/77 is primarily and predominantly intended to regulate competitive market powers in order to protect the public interest. However, although it is practically impossible to predict how Greek case law will eventually settle the issue, the Law also seems designed to protect individual interests, therefore an action for damages under Article 914 of the Greek Civil Code should be allowed against infringers.

It would be a severe drawback to the Law's main aim of serving the public interest if its secondary purpose of protecting individual interests is denied, as the interests of individual undertakings are seriously affected by violations of Articles 1 and 2 of the Law. An individual's right to claim damages would serve as an incentive to oppose anti-competitive behaviour and as a deterrent to potential infringers, thus furthering the Law's primary objective of protecting the public interest.

IV Relation Between Greek and EEC Competition Law

From 1 January 1981 onwards, following the accession of Greece as a full member to the EEC, Article 85(1) and 86 of the EEC Treaty, both having according to the well established case law of the European Court of Justice 'direct effect' for individual citizens, have been incorporated into the legal order of the Hellenic Republic and apply in parallel with the provisions of Law 703/77.

In 1980 the CPS, in a printed advisory leaflet addressed to Greek traders,

---

14   Article 914 of the Greek Civil Code reads as follows:
He who in violation of the Law causes damages to another (intentionally or negligently) is obliged to pay damages.
15   It should be noted that in Articles 1 and 3 of Law 146/14 on 'unfair competition' it is explicitly stated that infringers may be sued 'for refraining from acting and for damages sustained by the plaintiffs'.
16   For example A. Liakopoulos, *Economic Freedom as an Object of Protection by Competition Law*, Athens, 1981.

forecast that Law 703/77 and the EEC rules on competition were to apply 'in parallel' and 'independently' of each other after the accession of the Hellenic Republic to the Community, and it elucidated the word 'independently' by saying that Law 703/77 applies whenever competition is prevented, restricted or distorted in the home market, whereas EEC competition law applies whenever competition is prevented, restricted or distorted in a way affecting trade between Member States.

In the same leaflet the CPS has also mentioned that both legal systems might well apply simultaneously and cumulatively, but it has carefully abstained from giving guidelines as to what would happen in a case of conflict between the two legal systems, as for example in a case where the EEC Commission grants an Article 85(3) exemption and at the same time it is found that the agreement exempted by the Commission is caught by Article 1 of the Law 703/77 and does not qualify for an Article 1(3) exemption, or similarly in a case where an exclusive distribution agreement falls within the scope of EEC Regulation 67/67 but at the same time infringes Article 1 of the Law 703/77.

Two years later, in 1983, there is still no official pronouncement or case law as to the solution to be given by the Greek anti-trust authorities in a case of conflict between EEC competition law and national law. Nevertheless, it is expected that, since Law 703/77 contains no provisions dealing expressly with the relationship between EEC competition law and national law in case of conflict, the Greek anti-trust authorities will have no practical difficulty in following the principles laid down by the European Court of Justice in *Wilholm v Bundeskartellamt*; this expectation is corroborated by the few decisions of Greek courts already reported[17] issued by single member courts in interim measures proceedings where, although not faced with cases of conflict between Articles 85 and 86 of the EEC Treaty and Law 703/77, they did not hesitate to proclaim that Articles 85(1) and 86 of the EEC Treaty are part of the Greek legal order and in one case[18] to elaborate further by saying that

> . . . besides, Articles 85 and 86 EEC Treaty have been characterised by the European Court of Justice in *Bosch* (13/1961), ERT-*Sabam* (127/1973) and *Sacchi* (155/1973) as immediately and directly applicable, namely they apply immediately and even without the interference of the national legislator or any other internal procedure whatsoever . . . and the national judge is obliged to apply national law as amended by Community Law . . .

thus showing remarkable loyalty to the pronouncements of the European Court of Justice. In another decision of the Athens Court of Appeal reported in 1983,[19] there is also a reference to the direct applicability of Articles 85 and 86 of the EEC Treaty.

Moreover, it is interesting to note that so far the Greek anti-trust authorities in interpreting Articles 1(1) and 2 of Law 703/77 follow very closely the

---

17   Athens Court of First Instance judgments No. 556/1981, 8660/1981, 1841/1982.
18   Athens Court of First Instance judgment No. 556/1981.
19   Athens Court of Appeal 7964/1982.

interpretation developed by the EEC Commission and the dicta of the European Court of Justice which refer to the corresponding Article 85(1) and 86 of the EEC Treaty, and that six out of the 26 Resolutions issued by the CPC before it was abolished include explicit references to EEC competition law, cases and bibliography.

Although it is not yet known whether the new Competition Committee and the Minister will align their opinions/decisions with the interpretations and *dicta* of the EEC authorities and Court, it is expected that the Greek courts will be the ones to establish the supremacy of the EEC rules vis-à-vis national anti-trust legislation and to harmonise the interpretation and application of Law 703/77 with the corresponding provisions of EEC competition law.

V Conclusions

As explicitly stated in an advisory pamphlet issued by the Competition Protection Service in 1980, Law 703/77 'to control monopolies and oligopolies and to protect free competition' was intended to enhance competition between undertakings within the framework of free competition principles, to improve the quality of products, to obtain lower prices and better trading terms, to make undertakings internationally competitive in view of Greece's forthcoming accession to the EEC, having as its ultimate aim the benefit of consumers and the people generally.

Six years later, the contribution of Law 703/77 to achieving any of the above aims is disappointing. It appears that responsibility for the Law's extremely poor performance lies primarily with its drafters, although the organs entrusted with its application are not devoid of responsibility for the time which has been wasted.

As has been demonstrated, Law 703/77 is a model of the EEC competition rules transferred into Greek national territory; slavish copying of EEC competition law – although an easy solution – was certainly not appropriate since it prevented the creation of an anti-trust law developed in harmony with the structure and peculiarities of the Greek economy. Certainly the performance of the Law would have been much better if the drafters, instead of translating into Greek Articles 85 and 86 EEC, had proceeded before drafting with a comparative analysis of national anti-trust systems, in particular of those European countries whose social, political and economic characteristics are more similar to those of Greece. Any information on the efficiency of such national systems could have been used as a guide as far as Greece was concerned.

In Greece, a small country with no anti-trust law tradition, the Law should have been much more precise, detailed and clear. Although it is accepted that this would have limited the scope and interpretation of the Law by the administration and the courts, it is believed that such clarity and precision would have helped traders, manufacturers – even judges, lawyers and economists who might not be conversant with such a new subject – to be aware of the rights and duties that the anti-trust legislation grants or devolves on undertakings operating in the Greek market.

Moreover, the Law is extremely strict without apparent justification. The provisions of a criminal nature are far stricter than similar provisions in other European countries, and even more so than the corresponding provisions in the American anti-trust laws! Destructive criminal penalties punishing behaviour which, before the Law was enacted, was perfectly legal is certainly not the best way to enforce legislation – the more so when the Law introduced is far from clear for the vast majority of people whose conduct is to be regulated by it.

Until 26 April 1982, one of the drawbacks of the Law was that it did not make provision for any sort of practical co-operation between the now abolished CPC and the Minister of Commerce during the decision-making process. It appears that it had been completely forgotten that the Minister of Commerce should have been the person to direct and shape the Government's policies on anti-trust matters, and certainly he was not able to exercise any influence on competition policy at all if like any other individual he could only appeal against the formal resolutions of the CPC after the process was completed.

The abolition of the CPC – whose powers to resolve had been taken over by the Minister on 26 April 1982 – and the formation of a mere advisory body, the CC, has introduced a status diametrically opposed to the one previously prevailing, thus allowing the present Socialist Government to carry out its anti-trust policies through the competent Minister without interference from other administrative bodies. Of course, the formal decisions of the Minister are subject to judicial review, but no doubt until the judgment on appeal is issued, the impact of the Minister's decision – at least psychologically if not pecuniarily – would be present.

There are also technical and methodical defects in the Law; the notification system introduced clearly seems to have failed, considering the extremely low number of voluntary notifications made within the six years of the Law's application (less than 25 so far),[20] although as it stands today, the Law obliges all undertakings, regardless of size and turnover, to notify their agreements, decisions and concerted practices to the CPS. There is nevertheless a very good explanation for the small number of notifications made if one considers:

(a) that before 26 April 1982 the CPC, and the Minister now, is empowered to impose fines on undertakings for duly notified agreements if the agreements notified are found to violate the Law – this was enough to destroy the whole notification system;

(b) the short notification period introduced (one month for new

---

20   This number does not include notifications made after a formal complaint was lodged with the CPS by third parties affected.

agreements and four for old), combined with the heavy fines for failure to notify in time; and

(c) the very poor promotion of the 'notification' idea by the Ministry – how can one expect to receive vast numbers of notifications with only three information pamphlets issued and one seminar organised by the Ministry on anti-trust matters so far.

Another major drawback of the Law is that, being so wide in scope and allowing any physical or legal person to lodge formal complaints before the Competition Protection Service, this time-consuming procedure (investigations, reports, decisions, appeals by the complainant) is usually made to no avail. This has distracted the anti-trust authorities from what should be their main target, namely practices of undertakings operating in sectors of the Greek economy characterised by monopolistic or oligopolistic structures.

If one attempts to apportion responsibility among the administrative organs entrusted with the application and enforcement of the Law, certainly the one least to blame is the Competition Protection Service (CPS). It is true that the CPS has failed to expand its own initiative and to concentrate its activities on sensitive areas. Scrutiny of trade associations by laws and attention focused on agreements and decisions taken in their framework by their members could, for example, serve as a means of obtaining valuable information on the structure and competitiveness of the relevant product markets, and could offer the opportunity of investigating practices whose impact on free competition is as a rule more profound. No doubt five years of investigation in the right place would have produced far more than the 26 formal resolutions of the Competition Protection Committee so far issued, out of which only one[21] has benefited consumers. One should, however, take into account that the CPS remains extremely understaffed (although it was as a result of Greece's liaison with the EEC on anti-trust matters that three directors consecutively have changed posts), and that it was always lacking concrete support (administrative, moral and financial) from the Ministers, who seemed to be rather indifferent to its function.

The CPC, which was abolished in 1982, was mainly responsible for some unfortunate resolutions – particularly those issued up to September 1981 – but it was improving progressively, especially after a professor of law and a judge of the Athens Court of Appeal became members of the Committee. The CPC was also responsible for the failure to initiate group exemptions under Article 1(3) of the Law, and for a lack of courage to grant a single individual Article 1(3) exemption although there were many opportunities to do so.

The present advisory CC has not yet demonstrated its abilities, since no advisory opinion has been passed to the Minister to date. It is true that the composition of the CC now allows certain representative bodies, which participate in shaping competitive pressures in the Greek market, to be heard

---

21   *The Newspaper Cartel*, CPC Resolution No. 9/9.4.81, [1981] ECLR 285.

through delegates, but one wonders if such delegates will cast their votes impartially, whether they will have the necessary knowledge to interpret the current anti-trust legislation correctly, and if they will have time to become fully conversant with the subject in view of the fact that their work on the CC is a part-time, secondary occupation. It was a relief that the new Chairman of the CC is a professor of law, but it must be pointed out that the advisory opinions are issued by majority vote, therefore his opinion might be overruled where four members of the CC vote against it.

It seems that an intermediate system would be more preferable, with a panel of experts sitting in committee, whose decisions would be subjected to the approval (veto) of the Minister. Such a committee would be made up of full-time judges, lawyers, economists and high ranking public servants, the latter at least being always aware of Government policies on the subject (probably through consultations with the director of the CPS and with the Minister's personal advisers). The CPS role should of course also be strengthened, since no committee (advisory or decisive) works efficiently lacking the necessary support from the CPS, which should be fully responsible for the investigation preparation and introduction of the cases to be discussed.

Whilst the drafters of the Law and the other organs entrusted with its application each bear part of the blame for the poor performance of the Law to date, it seems that the underlying reason for the Law's failure to justify its presence in the Greek legal system is hesitation at each point by the competent Ministers (regardless of their political beliefs) to entrust the new anti-trust legislation with what Governments have tried to achieve for decades by immediate and direct intervention in the market through the Market Police Control legislation. It is evident that in Greece, anti-trust legislation is still deemed a second class measure, when compared with those traditionally used, for defeating inflation and promoting efficiency, productivity and competi-tiveness. It seems that it is not yet widely acknowledged in Greece that eventually an effective competition law produces more than the immediately impressive – but usually illusive – results of price controls imposed by the Market Police Control legislation.

Although a dramatic change in attitude towards anti-trust law in Greece is not contemplated in the near future, it is expected that the forthcoming Ministerial resolutions on anti-trust cases already pending before the Com-petition Committee shall provide the incentive for a review of the anti-trust legislation and of its potential effects in Greece.

Appendix A

Law 703/77 Article 1 'Prohibited Collaboration'

(1) All agreements between undertakings, all decisions by associations of undertakings and concerted practices in whatever form, which have as their

object or effect the prevention, restriction or distortion of competition, shall be prohibited, and in particular those which consist of:

(a) directly or indirectly fixing purchase or selling prices or any other trading conditions;

(b) limiting or controlling production, supply, technical development or investment;

(c) sharing markets or sources of supply;

(d) applying dissimilar trading conditions to equivalent transactions in a manner raising difficulties over the operation of competition, and in particular by unjustifiably refusing to sell, purchase or engage in other transactions;

(e) making conclusion of contracts subject to acceptance by the other parties of supplementary obligations which by their nature or according to commercial usage have no connection with the subject of such contracts.

(2) Agreements and decisions prohibited pursuant to the preceding paragraph are absolutely void, unless this Law provides otherwise.

(3) Agreements, decisions and concerted practices or categories thereof, falling within paragraph 1 of this article may by resolution of the Minister of Commerce[1] be declared completely or partially valid, provided they meet the following cumulative requirements:

(a) they contribute to improving the production or distribution of goods or to promoting technical or economic progress, while allowing the consumers a reasonable share of the resulting benefit;

(b) they do not impose on the undertakings concerned more restrictions than those which are absolutely necessary for the realisation of the above objectives;

(c) they do not afford such undertakings the possibility of eliminating competition in respect of a substantial part of the market in question.

Appendix B

Law 703/77 Article 2 'Abusive Exploitation of Dominant Position'

Any abusive exploitation by one or more undertakings of their dominant position within the whole or part of the home market is prohibited. Such abusive exploitation may in particular consist of:

(a) directly or indirectly imposing either purchase or selling price fixing or imposing fixing of other unreasonable trading conditions;

(b) limiting production, consumption or technological development to the prejudice of consumers;

(c) applying dissimilar conditions to equivalent transactions, in particular by unjustifiably refusing to sell, purchase or engage in other transactions, thereby placing certain undertakings at a competitive disadvantage;

---

1 As amended in effect by Joint Ministerial Decision No. B3/395 of 26 April 1982.

(d) making the conclusion of contracts subject to acceptance by the other parties of supplementary obligations or subject to conclusion of additional contracts, which by their nature or according to commercial usage have no connection with the subject of such contracts.

ITALY
Italian Competition Law
GUGLIELMO MAISTO

Introduction

During the last 25 years the Italian legislative assembly has made substantial changes to the normative discipline of business activities. More recently, these changes were reflected by the Tax Reform of 1973, by a clear and more defined discipline of the Stock Exchange, and by a major change to the company law concerning joint stock companies.

This approach constituted the legislative reaction to a change in the economic climate, which was distinguished by more aggressive competition between enterprises, and by a certain tendency towards concentrations and to special forms of economic co-operation.[1] The above legal and economic environment would thus justify the existence (or the introduction) of rules disciplining undertakings' competitive behaviour also in the light of the view of many experts who in the past have always held that, in order to be effective, a set of competition law provisions should be placed within the framework of a wider reform involving taxation, company law and other business areas.

On the contrary, the Italian legal order does not have a co-ordinated and autonomous set of rules on competition.[2]

Despite the absence of a rational and organic body of provisions disciplining anti-competitive arrangements, the Italian Constitution and the Civil Code contain some rules which have the primary function of restricting the entrepreneurs' freedom of economic initiative.

It should, however, be emphasised that these rules cannot be compared to

---

1 A. Frignani 'Concorrenza e consorzi in Italia: dieci anni di dibattiti e di disegni di leggè', (1976) Giur. Comm. I at 529.
2 The term 'competition law' is here used to define those provisions in the field of restrictions imposed by one or more enterprises on competition between themselves, between themselves and third parties, or between third parties. The term is sometimes replaced by the more restrictive 'anti-trust law'. The two terms correspond to the French *droit de la concurrence* and *droit des ententes*. The definition is used by W. Van Gerven. *Principes du droit des ententes de la Communauté Economique Européenne*, Bruxelles, Bruylant, 1966, at 3. The term does not cover those provisions to prevent or sanction unfair business practices, which go under the term *concurrence deloyale* or *concorrenza sleale*.

the restrictive business practices' legislation in force in other countries or applied at EEC level, inasmuch as:

(1) the rules concerned are part of Italian civil law (as opposed to criminal law),

(2) they have the mere function of limiting the contractual freedom to exercise an economic activity;

(3) the governmental authorities do not exercise a control over the arrangements stipulated by the entrepreneurs and no discretion is exercised by the authorities as to whether an agreement is harmful or not to the competitiveness of the market.

The Constitutional Principle of Freedom of Economic Activity

Article 41 of the Constitution

As a general constitutional principle 'private economic initiative is free'. This statement is made by Article 41 of the Constitutional Chart which, further, stipulates that the private economic initiative 'cannot be conducted in contrast with social interests' and that the law determines the programmes and the controls which may be deemed opportune in order to co-ordinate and address the private and public economic activities to social ends.[3]

Being a 'programmatic provision' Article 41 of the Constitution,[4] cannot be held directly applicable, but it stresses the need to take into account the interests of consumers together with those of society in general in evaluating the correctness of special business behaviour influencing competition.

Constitutional Legal Protection

Thus, the Constitution presents double legal protection (market freedom and consumer protection) and shows that the introduction of a competition law would be well supported by constitutional principles; however, the legislative authority has up to now concentrated its work almost exclusively within the framework of the limitation of the contractual power of initiative.

Non-Competition Clauses

Article 2595 of the Civil Code

The only provision of the Civil Code which seems to be oriented towards the

---

3 For a detailed analysis see V. Panuccio in Riccardo Petron (ed.), *Studi sull'art. 41 della Costituzione*, Bologna, 1969.

4 See Minervini, *Concorrenza e consorzi*, Cedam, Padova, 1961, at 6; Spagnuolo-Vigorita, *Iniziativa economica privata nel diritto pubblico*, 850 ss.; for the case law, see Constitutional Court, 14 February 1962 in (1962) Giur. Cost. 31.

anti-trust law principles is Article 2595 of the Italian Civil Code under which 'competition shall be conducted in such a way as not to harm the interest of the national economy, and shall remain within the limits provided by law and by corporate norms'.[5] Despite the efforts of the doctrine,[6] the provision can, however, hardly be applied in practice, being too general and having a programmatic nature.

Article 2596 of the Civil Code

Thus, in order to find a provision with a more substantive and practical value reference must be made to Article 2596 of the Italian Civil Code which states that

> . . . an agreement that limits competition shall be evidenced in writing. It is valid if confined to a specified territory or a specified activity, and cannot exceed five years in duration.
>
> If the duration of the agreement is not specified or is established for a period greater than five years, the agreement is valid for a period of five years.

This provision shows the civil nature of the Italian legislation relating to competition. Indeed, the legislative power has pursued the goal of protecting the freedom of economic activity of one of the contracting parties (the weaker): the power by one entrepreneur to limit another's freedom of activity should not go beyond certain limits.

The interest of the legislative authority is, thus, not directed to the market condition of competition, so that if the requisites set forth by Article 2596 are satisfied, the consequence and the effect of the agreement on the competitiveness of the market is immaterial.

Scope of Application of Article 2596

With regard to its scope of application, the provision covers all contractual clauses which have as their scope the discipline of the conduct of competing commercial activities.

In particular the rule applies to 'cartels', that is, according to a leading Supreme Court judgment,[7] to the bilateral discipline having as its object 'the

---

5 'Corporative norms' is a relic of the corporative State that was for a time the official programme of Italian fascism. Corporative norms were generally applicable rules affecting the organisation and operation of the Italian economy, and derived from a variety of sources. These included the so called 'corporations', which were public bodies composed of representatives of capital, management and labour. The corporative system was abolished in 1944.

6 In a recent study, G. Schiano di Pepe made some efforts to build a theory on the abuse of dominant position, to be applied at national level on the basis of Article 2595. See 'Note sulla disciplina dell'impresa in posizione dominante nel vigente diritto italiano della concorrenza. Intorno ad una ipotesi di concorrenza illecita' in (1975) *Annali della Facolta di Giurisprudenza dell'Università di Genova* at 684.

7 Court of Cassation, 28 October 1965, No. 2287 in (1966) For. It. I, 1629.

quantity or quality of the production, the areas reserved to the commercial penetration of the parties, prices and other conditions of sale', and other aspects of the economic activity of the entrepreneurs having the scope of restricting competing activities.

Despite the Supreme Court ruling cited above, it is still disputed in the literature whether a reciprocal non-competition clause, under which two enterprises undertake a reciprocal obligation not to compete with each other in their field of activity, falls within the scope of application of the provision.

Indeed, according to the opinion expressed by some authors,[8] this latter class of arrangements would be governed by the special set of rules regarding consortia that is 'contracts between enterprises engaged in the same economic activity, or in related economic activities, which have the object of regulating such activities *through a joint organisation*'. The dilemma should be solved by making a 'distinction' based upon the joint organisation Article 2602 refers to, so that cartels in the classic sense would certainly fall within the sphere of application of Article 2596.[9]

Violation and Remedies

Violation of the provision may occur where:

(1) the non-competition arrangement exceeds five years: in this case the duration is automatically limited to five years.

(2) the non-competition arrangement is undetermined as to the activities and the areas to be covered.

Non-compliance with the above requirements would give rise to the nullity of the agreement if it appears that the contracting parties would not have entered into it without that part of its content which is affected by nullity.[10] Alternatively, the creditor of a non-competition obligation might decide to renounce the obligation as set forth in the agreement, and to limit it as to activity and area so as to comply with Article 2596.[11]

Non-Competition Clause and Exclusive Distributing Agreements

When the non-competition clause constitutes an ancillary part of an exclusive dealing contract at undetermined time, (or of another contract having auto-

---

8 For a survey of the various opinions of the literature, see G.G. Auletta - V. Mangini, *Invenzioi industriali - Modelli di utilità e disegni ornamentali - Concorrenza*, Zanichelli, Bologna, 1973, at 127.
See also Guglielmetti, *Limiti negoziali della concorrenza*, Cedam, Padova, 1961 at 172; Ascarelli, *Teoria della concorrenza e dei beni immateriali*,Giuffrè, Milano, 1960 at 86; Franceschelli, *Consorzi per il coordinamento della produzione e degli scambi*, Zanichelli, Bologna.
9 In this respect see Guglielmetti, quoted above, at 172.
10 The nullity would, indeed, originate from a general principle applied to contracts, and based upon Article 1419 of the Civil Code.
11 On this latter possibility see G. Auletta, *Invenzioni industriali, modelli di utilità e disegni ornamentali, concorrenza*, quoted above, at 128.

nomous discipline) Article 2596 is held not to apply to it, inasmuch as the nature of the limitation of competition contained in an exclusive arrangement is the result of particularly intensive economic co-operation, and is not determined by the necessity to impede an anomalous compression of freedom of economic initiative:[12] the non-competition clause cannot be evaluated individually but together with the other stipulations effected by the entrepreneurs.

Refusal to Sell

Article 2597 of the Civil Code

The third important provision which might partly characterise a competition legislation is Article 2597 of the Civil Code which stipulates that 'one who operates an enterprise in a condition of legal monopoly has the obligation to contract on equal terms with anyone who requests the performance that is the object of the enterprise'.

Considering that the monopoly enterprise has an interest in selling at excessive prices and none is refusing to sell, the obligation to contract would be useless if not accompanied by rules or conditions according to which the contract must be concluded by the monopoly enterprise. These conditions are clearly set forth in the law and regulations disciplining monopolies.

Indeed, Article 2597 applies only to 'legal monopolies,' that is where the monopolistic position of the entrepreneur depends on a legislative provision prohibiting other undertakings from conducting the same business and stating the conditions under which the monopoly undertaking must contract.

Violation and Remedies

In case of refusal to contract, the customer is entitled to claim a judgment which grants him an equivalent effect to that of the contract which was not concluded.

Applicability to Private Monopolies

The provision illustrated constitutes the only legislative norm which could play a function in the field of competition law, especially in favour of consumers; the non-applicability of Article 2597 to private monopolies weakens, however, the scope of application of the provision.[13]

---

12   See G. Ferri, 'Exclusiva (Patto di)', in (1960) Nss D.J. VI at 691.
13   The case law clearly clarified the non-applicability of Article 2597 to non-legal monopolies (Supreme Court judgment of 6 August 1962, No. 2387).
   The approach is also shared by the prevailing literature: see Ascarelli *op.cit.* at 55; Guglielmetti, *op.cit.* at 433; Asquini, 'L'impresa dominante', (1963) Riv. Dir. Common. I at 3.

Domestic Competition Law and the EEC Treaty

The disorganised and insufficient character of domestic rules of competition strengthens the importance of EEC provisions on competition which, although applicable to arrangements and/or situations which are harmful to the trade between Member States, may partly be used to cope with the lack of a satisfactory domestic discipline.

A supreme example is given by the *Salonia* case,[14] which was recently decided by the European Court of Justice.

The plaintiff, who carried on a newsagent's business in Ragusa, requested a local distributor to supply her on a regular basis. The distributor refused to supply the retailer on the ground that the agreement stipulated by the *Federazione Italiana Editori Giornali* (Italian Federation of Press Publishers) and the *Federazione Unitaria Giornalai* (Federation of Newsagents) allowed distributors to sell periodicals only and exclusively to retailers provided with a special licence granted by a regional Commission formed by representatives appointed by the two organisations, this latter requirement not being fulfilled by Mrs Salonia.

The case could hardly be solved in favour of the plaintiff according to domestic legislation. The tribunal of Ragusa asked the European Court of Justice to establish whether or not a similar arrangement could be contrary to Article 85 of the EEC Treaty. The European Court held that in principle the agreement could be contrary to Article 85. In particular it held that

> . . . even though the agreement in object has the sole scope of distributing national press and does not apply to similar products from other Member States, a distribution system as closed circle, applied to the majority of press retail outlets within the territory of the State, can affect the distribution of these latter products if the retail outlets are the same ones in which the products from other Member States are ordinarily sold.

Due to the case-law[15] developed by the Court, the prerequisite of aptness adversely to affect trade between Member States is so easy to satisfy that the EEC law of competition can partly fill the gap which is due to the non-existence of a domestic anti-trust legislation.

---

14   M. *Salonia v G. Poidomani and F. Giglio*, Case 126/80, 16 June 1981 in (1981) ECR 1563.
15   *Cadillon v Höss* Case 1/71, 6 May 1971 in (1971) ECR 351; *Brasserie de Haecht v Wilkin-Janssen* Case 23/67, 12 December 1967 in (1967) ECR 407; *Volk-Vervaecke* Case 5/69, 9 July 1969 in (1969) ECR 295; *Vereeniging van Cement-Handelaren v EEC Commission* Case 8/72, 17 October 1972 (1972) ECR 977.

JAPAN

The Prohibition of Cartels and Industrial Defences Against It

HISAO HIROSE

Introduction

It is often said that the Japanese market is closed to European and American companies. This is due to the so-called 'non-tariff barrier' which causes trade imbalance between Japan and Western countries, and it is widely believed that as one of the aspects of the closed market, many cartels must be approved by law in Japan because of pressure from Japanese industry, or else they will be illegal. Whether this is true or simply prejudice, it might be interesting and important for those who deal with competition law in each country to consider what exceptions to the general prohibition of cartels are available to industry in Japanese law and practice.

Outline of Japanese Cartel Law

The title of the main statute in the field of competition law is the 'Law concerning Prohibition of Private Monopoly and Maintenance of Fair Trade'. It is usually referred to as the Anti-Monopoly Law, although the maintenance of fair trade is an equally important object of this law. Both cartels and other anti-competitive practices are covered by the Anti-Monopoly Law but this article will be considering cartels only.

Cartels are, in principle, prohibited by section 3 of the Law. It does not speak about cartels directly, but it can be understood from section 2, item 6, which is the definition of unreasonable restraint of trade, that this restraint mainly refers to cartels. An international agreement which contains such matters as unreasonable restraint of trade is also prohibited by section 6 of the Law. Section 8 of the Anti-Monopoly Law provides similar regulation for trade associations.

Apart from criminal punishment and compensation for damages, there are two measures in the Anti-Monopoly Law intended to effect the prohibition of cartels. One consists of measures to eliminate the violation of the Law. The other is a system of surcharge on profit.

Measures to Eliminate Cartels

Under section 7 of the Anti-Monopoly Law, the Fair Trade Commission may take any measures necessary to eliminate illegal cartels, for example the Fair Trade Commission (FTC) may order the undertaking concerned to file reports, or to cease such illegal cartels or to transfer a part of its business. Measures to be taken even when illegal cartels have already ceased to exist have been provided in section 7, paragraph 2. This paragraph was added in a significant amendment in 1977.

Surcharge System

The system of surcharge was introduced by the amendment of the Anti-Monopoly Law in 1977. Under section 7B, the FTC is empowered to order the participants in illegal cartels to pay a surcharge upon profits made by a price fixing agreement. The amount of the surcharge is equivalent to 1.5 per cent of the value of the goods sold or the services supplied during the period in which an illegal cartel was operated. The ratio of 1.5 per cent varies for certain types of business, namely two per cent in the case of manufacturing industry, one per cent in the case of retail business and 0.5 per cent in the case of wholesale business.

During 1981, the FTC ordered surcharges to be paid by 82 undertakings in seven cartel cases. The total amount of these surcharges was 3,212,310,000 Yen (about US $14 million). In these 1981 surcharges, we find the highest amount for any one case since the surcharge system was introduced in 1977, was 1,170,070,000 Yen (approximately US $5 million) and the highest amount for any single undertaking was 351,160,000 Yen (US $1.5 million). (See Table A)

Exempted Cartels (See Table B)

Exemptions by the Anti-Monopoly Law

(i) Depression cartels (crisis cartels), section 24(C)
In a free market economy, supply and demand should be adjusted through the mechanism of free market and inefficient enterprises may be destroyed. However when depression is so serious that a certain industry may be almost completely destroyed and may not recover for a long time, it is considered that there might be an exceptional case for the permission of a depression cartel.

A depression cartel is approved by the FTC when the following four conditions are recognised as existing:

(1) the supply of a particular commodity far exceeds the demand for it;
(2) the price of the commodity falls below the average cost of production;

(3) a considerable number of producers of the commodity are likely to be forced to discontinue their businesses and
(4) it is impossible to use rationalisation of enterprises to overcome the circumstances mentioned in (2) and (3) above.

However the operation of this depression cartel, for example the type and period of restraint, must not exceed a necessary degree. It is also necessary that there should be no risk of unreasonable injury to the interests of customers and ultimate consumers. There must be no unjust discrimination among the participants of the cartel and their customers. Undertakings may not be unreasonably restricted in taking part in the cartel and withdrawing from it.

Depression cartels, by their nature, may be formed by manufacturers of commodities or associations of producers, but not by undertakings whose businesses are wholesale, retail, banking and so on.

As depression cartels are approved in order to improve an imbalance between supply and demand, the restriction of the volume of production and of sales or the restriction of facilities for production are usually approved as part of a depression cartel. The producers are allowed to fix prices in very exceptional cases where restriction of production is impracticable for technical reasons or is entirely inadequate to overcome the circumstances of depression.

As is clear from the strict conditions for approval, depression cartels are not easily permitted. At the end of last year, there were seven depression cartels. As you will find in Table C at the end of this paper, of these seven cartels the volume of production was restricted in three, three were concerned with facilities for production, and one consisted of both restraint of the volume of production and restraint of the use of facilities. No price fixing depression cartel was in existence at the end of 1981. As at 10 September 1982 there were no depression cartels.

(ii) Rationalisation cartels, section 24(D)

Enterprises should be rationalised through free competition in a free market economy. However, in some exceptional cases, rationalisation is much more effective through co-operation among undertakings than within one company.

Rationalisation cartels may be permitted where they are found particularly necessary for such rationalisation as improvement in technology and quality of products, and reduction of cost. The types of concerted activities approved in such cartels are limited to restraint of the type of technology used and kind of products manufactured, common use of facilities for transport or storage of raw materials or goods, or common utilisation or purchase of scrap or waste materials.

At 31 December 1981 only one rationalisation cartel had been approved, namely one organised by five companies to restrict the kind of goods to be produced. The products involved were dyestuffs for synthetic fibre. This rationalisation cartel ended in January 1982 and since then no rationalisation cartel has been approved.

Exemptions by Separate Statutes

(i) The Small and Medium-sized Enterprise Organisation Law

This Law allows an association of such enterprises to form stabilisation and rationalisation cartels under certain conditions, subject to the approval of the supervising minister of the Government. The FTC is consulted by such a minister before the approval. The purposes of this law are to preserve opportunities of fair business activities for small or medium-sized enterprises and to promote the stabilisation and rationalisation of their business operations.

(ii) The Law Governing Improvement of Operation of Sanitary Business

This statute permits the formation of price fixing cartels in order to prevent excessive competition in businesses which are related to local health conditions such as hair salons, laundries and so on. The approval of cartels is made by the Minister of Health and Welfare after consultation with the FTC.

(iii) The Export Import Trade Law

The Export Import Trade Law enables the Minister of International Trade and Industry to approve export cartels and import cartels after consultation with the FTC in order to prevent unfair export trade and to establish order in the export and import trade.

(iv) The Marine Transportation Law

This Law provides that terms of transportation such as freight charges can be fixed by ship operators but they are subject to regulations issued by the FTC.

Proportion of Exempted Cartels that Involve Small Enterprises

Sanitary businesses are almost always carried on by small enterprises. Twenty-one cartels mentioned as 'Others' in Table B were mostly related to small enterprises. Taking these facts into account, it can be seen from the table that apart from 65 export and import cartels, at least 90 per cent of exempted cartels were approved in relation to comparatively small enterprises, which needed protection against large companies.

Administrative Guidance and Illegal Cartels

Administrative guidance, which is called *gyosei shido* in the Japanese language, is often discussed from various points of view. Someone once said that administrative guidance is one of the key words to an understanding of the power of Japanese economy. This paper will consider this term in connection with the prohibition of cartels.

Administrative guidance is defined in Japan as the duty of the administrative Government agency to achieve a policy by means of guidance advice or recommendation to the business world or to a subordinate office. It is not necessarily made or based on laws or ordinances. Typical examples of administrative guidance can be seen in the businesses of steel, oil, spinning, cars and finance. Supported by the expansion of the administrative function, the administrative agency is now trying to intervene by way of guidance in other industries.

The point which is the subject of discussion is that administrative guidance may sometimes induce illegal cartels. As an administrative guidance may be based on no specific law and moreover as a result of such an administrative guidance, free trade may be restrained, this guidance must be considered in connection with the cartel law.

In ECLR volume 2 number 2, it was reported by Mr N. Nakagawa of Nakagawa Law Office, Tokyo that:

> In September, 1980, in the case of a production cartel and a price cartel of oil companies, the Tokyo High Court held that actions taken by companies in response to an administrative guidance from Government ministries could be in violation of the law, and that the fact that a company had acted pursuant to administrative guidance could not constitute an absolute defence against prosecutions of the Anti-Monopoly Law violations.
>
> In this judgment, the court condemned the administrative guidance of the Ministry of International Trade and Industry (MITI), and said that although MITI had the power to make production plans for industry as a whole, this power should not contravene the Anti-Monopoly Law in affecting market conditions by reducing or limiting the production of individual members of the oil companies' association.
>
> Six months later, the FTC published its opinion on this matter.
>
> In this opinion, the FTC distinguished different types of administrative guidance, on the basis that some types of administrative guidance usually produce cartels whereas other types rarely do so, and the FTC warned Government ministries not to induce illegal cartels by their administrative guidance.
>
> The Ministry of International Trade and Industry (MITI) reacted to this opinion and the proposal of the FTC from the point of view of industrial policy. The conflict between the FTC and MITI can be seen as a conflict between competition policy and industrial policy.[1]

It is difficult to make any judgments about this dispute, because in order to present an opinion on this issue, historical aspects of the Japanese economy, industrial conditions today, and Japanese ways of thinking must be taken into account. However, so long as Japan remains a free market economy, it can be said that it should be governed by competition policy in principle, and that industrial policy should be carried out in accordance with and subject to competition policy.

---

1   This was reported at [1981] ECLR 392 under 'Continuing Disagreement between the FTC and MITI on "Administrative Guidance"'.

In connection with this matter, two newspaper articles, both of which were published on 24 August, should be noted. According to a Japanese daily newspaper which is equivalent to the *Financial Times*, MITI had drawn up its opinion entitled *Industrial policy and Administrative Guidance in Japan* and presented it at the meeting with the Antitrust Division of Department of Justice of the United States on 25 August. MITI justified industrial policy and administrative guidance. The other article was about the FTC's formal opinion on Government restrictions imposed on enterprises. A weekly newspaper written in English published in Japan, the *Japan Economic Journal*, reported that the FTC disclosed its feeling that Government restrictions imposed upon enterprises constitute obstructions to free competition and from this stand-point proposed that the restrictions should be modified or greatly reduced in many cases. These opinions of MITI and the FTC are reported again in detail in the *European Competition Law Review*.[2]

---

2   See [1982] ECLR 233.

Table A
Number of cases investigated by the FTC in 1981

carried over from 1980: 105			new investigation in 1981: 195	
total number of cases investigated in 1981: 300				
price cartels: 77	other cartels: 23		unfair business practices: 166	others: 34
Cartels: 100				
dealt with in 1981: 39	carried forward to 1982: 61			
recommendation: *(i) 9	warning: *(ii) 21	discontinuation: *(iii) 9		

*(i) Recommendation. The FTC recommended the undertakings concerned to take the necessary measures to cease cartels. The recommendation does not have any legal compelling force but if the company accepts it, the FTC may make a decision without a hearing and if the company does not accept it, the FTC may hold a hearing and issue a decision. The FTC's decisions have the same force as judgments of the courts.
*(ii) Warning. The undertakings concerned accepted the warnings of the FTC to cease cartels and the FTC considered that there no longer existed a violation of law, so the FTC did not take any further measures, such as making a recommendation.
*(iii) Discontinuation. The FTC stopped investigating for lack of sufficient evidence.

Table B
Exempted Cartels as at 31 December 1981

Types of exempted cartels	*Number of cartels*
Anti-Monopoly Law (Depression Cartel)	7
Anti-Monopoly Law (Rationalisation Cartel)	1
Small and Medium sized Enterprise Organisation Law	292
Law Concerning Improvement of Operations of Sanitary Businesses	123
Export and Import Trading Law	65
Marine Transportation Law	6
Others (various laws concerning rationalisation measures etc.)	21
TOTAL	515

Table C
Depression cartels as at 31 December 1981

Commodity concerned	Number of participants	Types of restraint
steel vessel	34	volume of production
chloride vinyl resin	20	volume of production and use of facilities
high quality paper	13	use of facilities
coated paper	11	use of facilities
kraft paper	9	use of facilities
low-and-medium density polyethylene	13	volume of production
glass long fibre	9	volume of production

Appendix

Partial Translation of the Law Concerning Prohibition of Private Monopoly and Maintenance of Fair Trade (Law Number 54 of 14 April 1947 as amended)

Chapter I General Provisions

(i) Section 1 (purpose)
This Law by prohibiting private monopolisation, unreasonable restraint of trade and unfair business practices, by preventing the excessive concentration of economic power and by eliminating unreasonable restraint of production, sale, price, technology, and the like, and all other undue restriction of business activities through combinations, agreements and otherwise, aims to promote free and fair competition, to stimulate the initiative of undertakings, to encourage business activities of undertakings, to heighten the level of employment and people's real income, and thereby to promote the democratic and wholesome development of the national economy as well as to assure the interests of consumers in general.

(ii) Section 2 (definition)
(6) The term 'unreasonable restraint of trade' as used in this Act means such business activities, by which undertakings by contract, agreement, or any other concerted activities mutually restrict or conduct their business activities in such a manner as to fix, maintain, or enhance prices, or to limit production, technology, products, facilities, or customers or suppliers, thereby causing, contrary to the public interest, a substantial restraint of competition in any particular field of trade.

Chapter II Private Monopolisation and Unreasonable Restraint of Trade

(i) Section 3 (prohibition of private monopolisation and unreasonable restraint of trade)
No undertaking shall effect private monopolisation or any unreasonable restraint of trade.

(ii) Section 6 (prohibited international agreements)
(1) No undertaking shall enter into an international agreement or an international contract which contains such matters as constitute unreasonable restraint of trade or unfair business practices.

(iii) Section 7 (measures against private monopolisation, restraint of trade and international agreements)
(1) Where there exists any act in violation of the provisions of section 3, or paragraph (1) or (2) of the preceding section, the Fair Trade Commission may, in accordance with the procedure as provided for in division II, chapter VIII, order the undertaking concerned to file reports, or to cease and desist from such acts, to transfer a part of his business, or to take any other measures necessary to eliminate such acts in violation of the said provisions.

(2) The Fair Trade Commission may, when it deems particularly necessary, even when an act in violation of the provisions of section 3 hereof has already ceased to exist, order the undertaking concerned, in accordance with the procedure as provided for in division II, chapter VIII, to take measures to publicise that the said act has been discontinued and order any other measures necessary to ensure elimination of the said act: provided that the foregoing shall not apply to cases where one year has elapsed since the date of discontinuation of the said act without recommendation being given to the entrepreneur concerned or a proceeding being initiated with respect to the said act.

(iv) Section 7B (surcharge on profits made by unreasonable restraint of trade)
(1) Where any undertaking effects an unreasonable restraint of trade or enters into an international agreement or an international contract containing such matters as constitute an unreasonable restraint of trade, which pertains to the price of goods or services or, as a result of curtailing substantially the volume of supply thereof, affects the price of such goods or services, the Fair Trade Commission shall order the entrepreneur concerned, in accordance with the procedures as provided for in division II, chapter VIII, to pay to the Treasury a surcharge of an amount equivalent to one half of an amount arrived at by multiplying the turnover of such goods or services, computed in accordance with the method prescribed by a cabinet order, for the period from the date on which the undertaking was engaged in the business practices to the date on which the undertaking discontinued such practice (hereinafter referred to as 'period of such practice') by three per cent (or by four per cent for manufacturing industry, by two per cent for retail business or by one per cent for wholesale

business): provided, that in case the amount thus computed falls below Yen 200,000, the Commission may not order the payment of such a surcharge.

Chapter III Trade Association

(i) Section 8 (prohibited activities and filing requirement)
(1) No trade association shall engage in any one of the following acts:

(i) substantially restricting competition in any particular field of trade;
(ii) entering into an international agreement or an international contract as provided for in section 6(1).

(ii) Section 8B (Measures against trade associations)
(1) When there exists any act in violation of the provisions of the preceding section, the Fair Trade Commission may, in accordance with the procedure as provided for in division II, chapter VIII, order the trade association concerned to file a report, or to cease and desist from such act, to dissolve the said association, or to take any other measures necessary to eliminate the said act.

(2) The provision of section 7(2) shall apply *mutatis mutandis* to any act in violation of the provisions of paragraph (1)(i), (iv) or (v) of the preceding section.

(3) The Fair Trade Commission may, in accordance with the procedure as provided for in division II, chapter VIII, in ordering a trade association to take any of the measures set forth in paragraph (1) above or section 7(2) applied *mutatis mutandis* under the provision of the preceding paragraph, when it deems particularly necessary, at the same time, order an officer, manager or constituent undertaking of the said association (including another undertaking when a constituent undertaking is acting for the benefit of the said undertaking) to take measures necessary to ensure the measures provided for in paragraph (1) above or section 7(2) which is applied *mutatis mutandis* under the provisions of the preceding paragraphs.

(iii) Section 8C (surcharge on profits made by trade association)
The provisions of section 7B shall apply *mutatis mutandis* to cases where an act is committed in violation of the provisions of section 8(1)(i) or (ii) (applying only to such an undertaking which is a party to an international agreement or an international contract which contains such matters which would constitute an unreasonable restraint of trade). In this case, the term 'undertaking' appearing in paragraph (1) of section 7B shall read 'trade association' and the phrase 'the undertaking' appearing therein shall read 'the constituent undertaking (including another undertaking when a constituent undertaking is acting for the benefit of the said undertaking) of the trade association'.

Chapter VI Exemptions

(i) Section 24C (depression cartels)
(1) Where there exists an extreme imbalance of supply and demand for a par-

ticular commodity, resulting in circumstances falling under each of the following paragraphs, the provisions of this Law shall not apply to concerted activities of undertakings (including an act of a trade association which causes its constituent undertakings to be involved in concerted activities) who produce the said commodity or a trade association consisting of such undertakings (hereinafter referred to as 'manufacturers') approved in accordance with either of the following two subsections: Provided that the foregoing shall not apply when undertakings employ unfair business practices or when any undertaking is caused to employ such practices:

(i) the price of the said commodity is below the average cost of production, and a considerable proportion of the undertakings in the trade concerned may eventually be forced to discontinue production;

(ii) it is difficult to overcome such circumstances as mentioned in the foregoing paragraph by the rationalisation of individual enterprises.

(2) When circumstances provided for in the preceding subsection exist, those producers who desire to effect concerted activities relating to restrictions on output or sales, or on facilities (excluding such as will impede the renovation or improvement of facilities) may, in order to overcome such circumstances, obtain from the Fair Trade Commission prior approval of the said activities.

(3) When circumstances provided for in subsection (1) above exist and if restriction on output of the commodity in a particular trade is found extremely difficult for technical reasons, those producers who desire to effect concerted activities involving price-fixing may, in accordance with the rules of the Fair Trade Commission, obtain from the Fair Trade Commission, prior approval of the said activities. The same shall apply to a price fixing agreement entered into concurrently with an agreement provided for in the preceding subsection, when the concerted activities have been effected upon approval under the preceding sub-section, and such concerted activities alone proved to be entirely inadequate to overcome the circumstances provided for in subsection (1) above.

(4) The Fair Trade Commission shall not grant approval as provided for in the preceding two subsections unless the concerted activities for which approval is requested fall under the conditions provided for in the preceding two subsections and conform with each of the following requirements:

(i) that they do not exceed the action necessary to overcome the circumstances provided for in subsection (1) above;

(ii) that there is no risk of unduly injuring the interests of the consumers in general, and of related undertakings;

(iii) that they are not unjustly discriminatory;

(iv) that they do not restrict unreasonably participation in or withdrawal from such activities.

(5) When the Fair Trade Commission has approved or dismissed an application for approval under subsection (2) or (3) above, or has taken action pursuant to the provisions of section 66(1) with regard to approval under sub-

section (2) or (3) above, it shall without delay make public its decision giving reasons.

(6) The producers engaged in concerted activities after approval under subsection (2) or (3) above shall, without delay, file a report thereof with the Fair Trade Commission, when they have discontinued the said activities.

(7) The Fair Trade Commission shall, where an objection to approval under subsection (2) or (3) above has been made, conduct a public hearing in accordance with the rules of the Fair Trade Commission.

(8) The Fair Trade Commission shall, prior to granting such approval under subsection (2) or (3) above, or to rejecting an application therefor, consult with the competent minister in charge of the business concerned. The same shall apply when the Fair Trade Commission takes action provided for in section 66(1) with respect to such approval under subsection (2) or (3) above.

(ii) Section 24D (rationalisation cartels)
(1) The provisions of this Act shall not apply to concerted activities of producers approved in accordance with the following subsection, where they are found particularly necessary for effecting an advancement of technology, an improvement in the quality of goods, a reduction in costs, an increase in efficiency and any other rationalisation of enterprises.

(2) Manufacturers desirous of undertaking concerted activities regarding restrictions on technology or kinds of products, utilisation of facilities for storage of raw materials or products or for transport thereof, or utilisation or purchase of by-products, waste, or scrap in the case provided for by the preceding subsection may, in accordance with the rules of the Fair Trade Commission, obtain prior approval from the Fair Trade Commission.

(3) The Fair Trade Commission shall not grant approval under the preceding subsections unless the concerted activities applied for fall under the conditions provided for in the preceding subsection, and conform with each of the following requirements:

(i) that there is no risk of injuring the interests of customers;
(ii) that there is no risk of unduly injuring the interests of consumers in general and of related undertakings (excluding customers);
(iii) that they are not unjustly discriminatory;
(iv) that they do not restrict unreasonably the participation in or withdrawal from such activities;
(v) that where restrictions on kinds of product are imposed differently on participants in the concerted activities, such differentiation is not designed unduly to concentrate production of a particular kind of product in the hands of any one undertaking.

(4) The provisions of the proviso to subsection (1) and of subsections (5) to (8) of the preceding section shall apply *mutatis mutandis* to the concerted activities as provided for in subsection (2).

NETHERLANDS

Dutch Cartel Law - The Impact on Dominance

R. HEIN HOOGHOUDT

In this article some general remarks will first be made on Dutch cartel legislation, and in particular on the law on dominant positions.[1] Subsequently some case law on dominant positions will be discussed, with special emphasis on the *Hoffman-La Roche* case.

Dutch Cartel Legislation

Its Nature

The Dutch Economic Competition Act,[2] which forms the basis of the present Dutch cartel legislation, is based on a system of combating abuses on the one hand and imposing necessary restraints on unlimited competition on the other, rather than on a system of mere direct prohibition.[3] The Act establishes the means for governmental intervention if a situation capable of affecting workable competition arises and such situation is deemed by the Government to be contrary to the public interest.

The public interest is the sole criterion for deciding whether the measures provided for under the Act should be applied. As appears from the Explanatory Memorandum to the Act, it is the intention that the measures should be applied in such a way as to ensure that the aims or effects of different forms of economic power will not conflict with the aims of social and economic policy of the Government, such as, for example, those of its policy on wages and prices.

The Minister defending the Bill in Parliament admitted that under the Act the Government would have large powers, and that the subjective insight of the

---

1 An elaborate treatise in English on the Dutch cartel legislation has been written by A.D. Ham in *World Competition Law*, Volume 3, Part 7 - The Netherlands, (looseleaf edition of Matthew Bender).
2 *Wet Economische Mededinging*, Act of 28 June 1956, as amended several times, for the last time by the Act of 29 June 1977.
3 An exception to this rule is Article 9b in combination with Article 15 of the Act, which concern agreements restricting competition and providing for sanctions to be imposed under binding arbitration by arbiters who are not independent or do not have to comply with certain basic rules of procedure and rights of defence.

Minister concerned[4] in respect of what the public interest requires with regard to a system of workable competition would often be decisive. In order to give the Government total flexibility the original Bill did not even provide for a possibility of appeal against the decisions of the Minister to an independent judicial body. In the final Bill, however, as it was adopted by Parliament, Article 33 provides for appeal to the independent Court of Appeal for Trade and Industry (CBB) and as will subsequently be observed from the *Hoffman-La Roche* case,[5] this may have considerably narrowed the scope of the Government's discretion in applying the Act in practice.

Measures Under the Act

The basic assumption of the Act that workable competition is not necessarily identical with unlimited competition on the one hand, and should not allow for the suppression of all and any competition on the other, is reflected in the measures which the minister can apply in respect of the two categories of restrictions on competition defined under the Act - that is, the dominant position and the restrictive agreement.[6]

If the economic situation in a certain sector of industry is such that some restraint of competition, for example, in respect of prices, is desirable, the Minister may, at the request of a majority (either in number or in sales) of the sector concerned, declare a restrictive agreement generally binding on all enterprises in that particular sector if the interests of that sector in agreement with the public interest so require.[7]

In the same spirit, although not at the request of the enterprises involved, the Minister has used his powers under Article 27 of the Act (provisional measures against dominant positions) in the *Haarlem Bakeries* case in order to end a local price war and to impose minimum prices for bread. This peculiar case will be discussed in greater detail below.

The Government can not only take measures to restrain competition, but

---

4 This is the Minister of Economic Affairs either alone or in collaboration with one or more other ministers responsible for particular sectors of the economy, for example, agriculture or transport. Hereinafter the Minister(s) concerned will be referred to as 'the Minister'.

5 The first case on a dominant position ever to reach the CBB, decision CBB of 24 July 1979 NJ/AB 1980, 457.

6 For the purposes of the Act 'restrictive agreement' means any binding agreement or group decision which regulates competition between the owners of enterprises (Article 1(1) of the Act). The meaning of 'dominant position' will be discussed later.

7 Article 6 of the Act. So far this Article has been applied only once. On this occasion minimum prices were imposed in respect of sugar. Measures under Article 6 could of course raise questions as to compatibility with the EEC Treaty, in particular Article 5 in conjunction with Articles 85 and 86 and Articles 30 to 36. It is not possible within the scope of this paper to comment on these interesting questions.

also measures[8] to promote it; and in fact it has more often taken the latter course.

Under Article 10 of the Act the Government may declare all agreements of a certain type invalid by Order in Council, if it is of the opinion that the public interest so requires. Under this authority the Government has declared invalid all provisions purporting to impose a system of collective resale price maintenance, and furthermore, the individual resale price maintenance provisions of vertical distribution agreements for certain durable consumer goods, including radios, television sets, household appliances and motor cars.[9]

Furthermore, the Minister may by Ministerial Decree declare individual restrictive agreements invalid,[10] either on his own initiative or after notification of the agreements, if he deems them to be contrary to the public interest. Under Article 2 of the Act, each restrictive agreement has to be notified to the Minister of Economic Affairs within one month of it taking effect.[11]

Conduct tending to comply or to cause compliance with an agreement provisionally suspended or declared to be invalid by either Royal or Ministerial Decree is prohibited.[12]

Finally, the Minister can take certain measures against enterprises holding dominant positions within particular markets which will be discussed later.

Enforcement

Enforcement of the Act is secured by penal as well as civil sanctions. Violations committed unintentionally or of a less serious nature are punishable as summary offences (*overtredingen*). The latter include the failure to notify restrictive agreements and the submission of false information to the Minister. Serious violations which are committed intentionally are indictable offences (*misdrijven*). They include intentional conduct contrary to instructions given to undertakings in a dominant position or contrary to the prohibitions against compliance with agreements which have been suspended or declared invalid.[13]

---

8   The measures can be either provisional or of a more permanent nature. In cases of urgency provisional measures like the suspension of a certain agreement may be taken after the advice of an advisory body called the Economic Competition Commission has been sought but before it has been obtained. Such measures cannot last longer than one year after they have come into effect.

9   Royal Decrees, 1 April 1964, OJ 110 and 31 August 1964, OJ 353, as prolonged by Acts of Parliament.

10   Article 19 of the Act.

11   This obligation rests *inter alia* on the owners of the enterprises established in the Netherlands to which the agreement relates and on the parties to the agreement. Some categories of restrictive agreements have been exempted from the obligation to notify. These include agreements not regulating competition in the Netherlands, exclusive agency and distribution agreements between only two parties and joint purchase agreements.

12   Articles 12(8), 15, 22 and 23(5) of the Act.

13   Penalties have been provided for in the Act on Economic Crimes (*Wet Economische Delicten*). They include fines, imprisonment, forfeiture of goods and cessation of the activities of the enterprise for up to one year. According to A.D. Ham at Net 5 to 9 of the work cited in Note 1, no judicial decisions imposing penalties have so far been rendered. Ham can state this with particular authority, since he is the Deputy Director of the Competition and Mergers Directorate of the Ministry of Economic Affairs.

Apart from penal sanctions which may be imposed by the ordinary courts at the request of the Public Prosecutor, any person or legal entity having a 'reasonable interest' may start a civil action in court in order to compel an enterprise to which an agreement declared generally binding applies, or on which in connection with its dominant position certain rules or obligations have been imposed, to comply with that agreement or those rules and obligations. [14] Furthermore, acts contrary to the prohibitions referred to above could constitute a tort under the Dutch Civil Code if damage is caused.

Dominant Position

Before the second world war Dutch cartel legislation did not have special provisions in respect of dominant positions. In the present Act, Articles 24 to 27 have been introduced in order to enable the Government to give certain instructions to enterprises in a dominant position, even if this dominant position is not the result of a restrictive agreement. As has previously been noted, the only criterion for taking any measures against a dominant position is whether it produces effects contrary to the public interest. The Act does not prohibit any specific conduct of a dominant enterprise unless special instructions pursuant to Articles 24 and 27 of the Act have been issued to it, or unless the conduct tends to comply with an agreement declared to be invalid.

Under Article 1 of the Act, a dominant position is defined as 'a factual or legal relationship in trade or industry involving a predominant influence by one or more owners of enterprises on a market for goods or services in the Netherlands'. As the *ABG* case reveals later in this article, this definition is wide enough to cover not only monopolistic and oligopolistic positions, but also non-binding gentlemen's agreements and conscious parallel behaviour which result to some extent in market domination. This domination does not necessarily have to cover the entire Dutch market. Domination of a local market, for example Haarlem or Rotterdam, can be sufficient.

If a dominant position produces effects detrimental to the public interest, the Minister may take three types of measure:

(1) publication of data on the dominant position (Article 24 paragraph 1(a)); [15]

(2) the issuance of certain instructions to the persons involved with the dominant position (Article 24 paragraph 1(b));

(3) in cases of urgency, the same instructions as provided for under Article 24 paragraph 1(b) in the form of a provisional measure (Article 27).

Furthermore, if the dominant position is embodied in a restrictive agreement, the Minister can also act against it by declaring the agreement invalid.

---

14   Articles 9 and 26 of the Act.
15   Under Article 9 the Minister has a similar power in respect of restrictive agreements in so far as they are contrary to the public interest.

Under Articles 24 and 27, the Minister can give the following instructions:
(1) to refrain from inducing, *de facto* or *de jure*, owners of enterprises designated by the Minister to pursue certain market practices to be specified in the decree;
(2) to supply certain goods or services to designated persons for cash at customary prices and terms;
(3) to charge certain prices for certain goods or services;
(4) to apply certain terms of delivery, service and payment, including the instruction not to impose tie-ins.

The maximum period of validity for the foregoing measures is five years if taken pursuant to Article 24 and one year in the case of Article 27.

The Act contains no provisions as to merger control or the dissolution of monopolies. The intervention by the Minister can only be directed against actual market conduct, and therefore there is no room for a 'Continental Can doctrine' under the present Dutch cartel law. In 1977 the Social Economic Council (SER) advised the Government that preventive control on mergers should be introduced, but so far no Bill has been submitted.[16]

Application of the Economic Competition Act in Respect of Dominant Positions

Some Statistics

So far the Act has been formally applied to dominant positions only eight times:[16a] six times in connection with refusals to deal, once with regard to prices which were considered too high and once to end a local price war.[17]

Twice a measure under Article 24 has been applied. Three times formal proceedings under Article 24 were started but were eventually called off because the enterprises concerned decided to give in.[18] In three instances provisional measures under Article 27 were applied.

In connection with the foregoing statistics it should be noted that most cases

---

16   The only existing general rules on mergers are laid down in the non-binding SER Merger Code. This Code contains certain procedural rules to protect shareholders of quoted companies and employees. Furthermore, the Act on the Supervision of the Credit System contains certain rules as to mergers of banks for which the approval of the Dutch Central Bank is required.

16a   Since this paper was presented at the 1982 Oxford International Anti-trust Conference, Article 27 has been applied once more in connection with a refusal to deal in the *Vihamij* case (decision of 1 March 1983, Official Gazette 2 March 1983).

17   This classification is somewhat arbitrary since at least two of the refusals to deal were not downright refusals but refusals after the purchaser had refused to accept certain terms and conditions of delivery, which included too high a purchase price in one case and a resale price maintenance obligation in the other.

18   If formal proceedings have been entered into by referral of the case by the Minister to the Economic Competition Commission for advice, the Minister is required under Article 25(5) to make an announcement in the Official Gazette in case he eventually decides not to apply Article 24.

are dealt with informally, and they may include practices by dominant positions other than boycotts and pricing, although the Annual Ministerial Reports on the application of the Act[19] do not mention any such cases.

Refusals to Deal

The foregoing statistics demonstrate that the application of the Act has been mainly concerned with refusals to deal.

It is stressed once more that a refusal by a dominant enterprise to deal is in no way in itself prohibited. This will only be the case if a measure under Article 24 or Article 27 has been taken. Moreover, it has been stated that a refusal to deal (like any other practice) is not *per se* detrimental to the public interest and that in each individual case the possible benefits to society should be weighed against the disadvantages. The 1966 Annual Ministerial Report stressed that intervening with the suppliers by imposing an obligation to supply is justified only if there is a real need for such a decision where, for example, the boycott represents a severe impediment to developing an efficient distribution system. If there are available to dealers sufficient supplies of comparable quality from competitors of the supplier(s) concerned, the Minister will in general refuse to take action.[20]

In the following cases, however, the Minister found both a dominant position and effects contrary to the public interest to be present.

In the *Lymar* case[21] independent wholesalers of tobacco products put pressure on cigar manufacturers not to supply wholesale grocers. This attempt by the independents to keep the chain-affiliated enterprises from the market was apparently successful because almost all manufacturers refused to supply Lymar, a wholesale grocery chain.

After having deduced from the refusal to supply and its effectiveness the existence of a dominant position of the manufacturers on the local market, the Minister went on to say that as a result of the refusal Lymar was severely restricted in the way it could organise its business, that is, as a chain-affiliated enterprise instead of an independent one. On the one hand the system of free enterprise gave each entrepreneur the right within the limits of the law to organise his own business as he chose, while on the other, each supplier had the right to choose his own distribution channels. If, however, the supplier is in a dominant position, a refusal to supply - which purports to restrict the freedom of the dealer to organise his own business - would only then meet no objection 'if - from the viewpoint of society - the benefits largely outweigh the disadvantages of this restriction of freedom'. In the present case the Minister could not find such benefits, and under Article 24 he ordered the manufacturers

---

19 Such Annual Reports are required under Article 43 of the Act.
20 This can be inferred (*inter alia*) from the respective Annual Ministerial Reports, which under the sub-heading 'Complaints' report on the informal policy in respect of refusals to deal.
21 Decision of 4 August 1961, Official Gazette 7 August 1961, No 151.

to supply Lymar at the usual prices to be paid in cash and on the usual terms and conditions.

As can be concluded from the above Ministerial decision, the Minister can also move against a dominant position if its detrimental conduct is not the result of its own independent decision, but is in fact brought about by others. In the Lymar case it was the independent wholesalers rather than the cigar manufacturers who had an interest in cutting supplies to Lymar because they feared the competition of a more efficient organisation. It would therefore perhaps have been more appropriate to impose an obligation on the independents to refrain from inducing the manufacturers to refuse to supply Lymar or other chain-affiliated wholesalers. The reason for not taking this course was probably that compliance with such obligation would have been more difficult to check than the obligation to supply.

In a similar case, the *Sipkes* case,[22] the Minister announced pursuant to Article 25(5) that he would take no further action against the manufacturers, since under the threat of a formal decision pursuant to Article 24, they had resumed the supply of cigarettes to Sipkes. In the same way the Minister eventually announced in the *Rotterdam Commission for the Protection of Trade Interests of the Home Furnishing Industry* case that he would take no action.[23] In this case an organisation of retailers - the Commission - put pressure on manufacturers and wholesalers of furniture not to supply certain discount shops. After having taken the unusual step of announcing that he would take action against the Commission[24] if these practices continued, the Minister eventually announced that the Commission's practices of excluding discount shops had been discontinued, and that possible pressure, from others than the Commission, not to supply to discount stores was unlikely to be effective enough to justify formal measures. In the earlier announcement the Minister made clear that in reaching the decision to make the threat to take formal measures against the Commission it was considered important that the discounts of the excluded discount shops were realistic.

Finally an announcement pursuant to Article 25(5) was made in the *VNU* case.[25] Following a complaint from some distributors of magazine portfolios that VNU was not willing to supply them at the usual wholesale prices and conditions, the Minister asked advice from the Economic Competition Commission on the application of Article 24. The Minister did not have to pursue the matter, however, since the parties involved reached agreement on the outstanding issues - the prices, the timing and supply and the level of the wholesale margins.

Apart from the four above cases which concerned measures under Article 24 or the formal beginning of procedures that purported to lead to such measures,

---

22   Announcement of 20 June 1961, Official Gazette 21 June 1961, No. 118.
23   Announcement of 11 November 1970, Official Gazette 12 November 1970, No. 219.
24   Announcement, Official Gazette 7 March 1968, No. 48.
25   Announcement of 10 April 1972, Official Gazette 13 April 1972, No. 72.

there have been two cases concerning refusals by dominant positions to supply where provisional measures under Article 27 have been applied.

In the first one, the *Sitos* case,[26] Sitos refused to supply bread to a chain of supermarkets, de Gruyter, after de Gruyter had turned down Sitos's request to raise the resale price. The bread in question was sold under the de Gruyter brand name. Sitos continued to supply other bread which was sold under Sitos's trade marks and which was more expensive. The Minister found that de Gruyter could not obtain the same regular supplies of similar non branded bread from other suppliers for all its outlets in the provinces of North and South Holland. He further said that in view of the nature of the business of de Gruyter it would be difficult for it to confine itself to the sale of the more expensive bread which was still being supplied. After stressing that suppliers have the freedom to choose their distribution channels and to establish their own terms of delivery including resale price maintenance,[27] the Minister continued that where a supplier enjoyed a dominant position, he had to refrain from imposing resale prices on a level not justified by his own commercial interests, if that level harmed the retailer concerned disproportionately in the conduct of his business. Since in the present case Sitos did not have a sufficient interest in a higher resale price, and since de Gruyter, because of the nature of its business, had to be able to supply low priced bread to its customers, Sitos was ordered to resume delivering at the former terms including a resale price maintenance obligation at the level before the suppliers were cut off.

The Sitos case is interesting for the way in which the Minister narrowed the scope of the relevant product market on the supply side by considering only suppliers who could supply non-branded bread in sufficient quantities to all the outlets of de Gruyter.

Another case which is particularly interesting for the way in which a dominant position has been construed is the *ABG* case,[28] which also led to proceedings before the European Commission and the European Court of Justice.[29] During the fuel shortage of 1973 to 1974 nine major oil companies refused to supply ABG, a central buying organisation of independent oil wholesalers in the Netherlands. The oil companies argued that in view of the general shortage - supplies had been reduced to 85 per cent of the previous level - they had to give priority to their longstanding customers with whom they had long term supply contracts.

The Minister rejected this argument. He pointed out that ABG was unable to function as a result of the refusal to supply, and concluded therefore that the nine oil companies were in a dominant position. Although he acknowledged that the general oil supply in the Netherlands had been severely hampered since

---

26 Decision of 6 March 1968, Official Gazette 6 March 1968, No. 47.
27 In general individual resale price maintenance is not prohibited, except in respect of certain consumer durables.
28 Decision of 4 April 1924, Official Gazette 4 April, No. 67
29 Commission 19 April 1977, OJ L 117 of 9 May 1977; Court of Justice 19 June 1978, (1978) ECR 1513.

November 1973, he thought that this was not sufficient justification for the oil companies to eliminate an independent enterprise from an already oligopolistic market. The argument of shortage had furthermore only a limited validity, since some oil companies were apparently willing to supply the wholesalers organised within ABG if they were to conclude long term purchasing agreements with the oil companies concerned. The Minister held that this would even further reinforce the present tendency to eliminate independent market participants. On the basis of these considerations the Minister reached the conclusion that the oil companies' behaviour and the resulting elimination of the independent ABG conflicted with the public interest. The nine companies were ordered to supply ABG with certain quantities of oil at a price fixed by the Minister.[30]

In their appeal lodged against this decision with the Crown,[31] the oil companies argued *inter alia* that they did not have a dominant position in the sense of the Act since in the case of a dominant position of more than one enterprise, there should be a certain consensus among them which was absent in the present case. On the other hand the Minister argued that in order to exist a dominant position in no way required the enterprises involved to have a certain legal or factual relationship. No concerted practice was needed; mere factual parallel behaviour was sufficient. The Crown[32] shared the view of the Minister and held that the history of the Act showed that the decisive element is the existence of a predominant influence on the market. This includes not only domination by one enterprise, but also non-binding gentlemen's agreements and other parallel conduct, not resulting from any arrangements, by enterprises that together have a predominant influence.

In view of the approach taken by the Dutch authorities it is interesting to note that the European Commission in its decision in the *ABG* case did not rely on the concept of a collective dominant position, but rather rested its decision on the ground that because of the general shortage, the customers of the oil companies were unable to turn to sources of supply other than their traditional suppliers, and that therefore each of the major oil companies was in a dominant position with regard to its customers. Unfortunately this approach was not put to the test before the Court of Justice since the Court, without passing judgment on the issue of BP's dominant position, reversed the Commission's decision on the ground that BP's conduct had not been abusive.

---

30   The quantity to be supplied by each individual company was determined in a separate decision of 11 April 1974, Official Gazette 11 April 1974, No. 51.
31   At the time no appeal against provisional measures was provided for under the Economic Competition Act. An appeal was therefore lodged with the Crown under the general Act of Appeal against Administrative Decisions. At present under the Economic Competition Act such appeals should be lodged with the CBB.
32   Royal Decree of 5 June 1974, No. 76.

Application of Article 27 in Order to End a Price War

In the unusual *Haarlem Bakeries* case[33] the Minister had to apply an exceptionally wide interpretation of the notion of 'dominant position' in order to end a local price war. In an effort to outbid each other, sixteen bakeries in Haarlem and the vicinity had reduced bread prices to an extremely low level. As a result other bakeries were forced to bring their prices down to a level which was so low that even an efficient enterprise would operate at a loss. This was held to be contrary to the public interest since it endangered the future survival of the firms involved. The Minister therefore imposed minimum prices on the sixteen bakeries engaged in the price war.

The decision does not clearly explain why a dominant position was deemed present. It must be assumed that the Minister inferred the dominant influence from the fact that other bakeries were forced to lower their prices as well. Nevertheless, it seems quite unusual to infer a collective dominant position from the activities of a number of enterprises which fight each other rather than co-operate. From a formal legal standpoint it would probably have been more appropriate for the Minister to wait until the other Haarlem bakeries had organised themselves and put forward a request pursuant to Article 6 of the Act to the effect that a minimum price cartel be imposed on all the bakeries in Haarlem and the vicinity. This, however, would have taken much more time than a provisional measure under Article 27 and it could have been done only if the bakeries putting forward the request formed a majority either in number or in sales. At present a Bill is pending which will amend the Economic Competition Act and provide the Government with a more appropriate tool to deal with situations as in the *Haarlem Bakeries* case. It will give the Government the power to impose minimum prices without having received a prior request to that effect. [34,34a]

Application of Article 24 to Excessive Prices

The *Hoffman-La Roche* case[35] has been the first and so far the only case in which measures under the Act have been applied because of excessive pricing. The Dutch authorities' attention was drawn to the prices charged by Hoffman-

---

33   Decision of 18 January 1960, Official Gazette 19 January 1960, No. 12.

34   The Dutch legislation on prices is rather complicated. Apart from the Economic Competition Act, the Act on Prices (*Prijzenwet*) provides for the possibility of imposing maximum prices, while the Act on the Organisation of Trade and Industry (*Wet Publiekrechtelijke Bedrijfsorganisatie*) also creates certain regulatory powers in respect of prices.

34a   Since this paper was presented at the 1982 Oxford International Anti-trust Conference the Government announced that it will withdraw the Bill in question.

35   In this case, three Ministerial decisions were taken. The one discussed is the main decision of 14 July 1977, Official Gazette 18 July 1977, No. 137. In the two other decisions (Official Gazettes 22 September 1978, No. 185 and 29 December 1978, No. 253) permission for some limited price increases was given.

La Roche BV (HLR) following the price reductions of approximately 60 per cent imposed by the British Government on Roche Products Ltd in respect of its sales of Valium and Librium in the UK. The Dutch authorities found that the prices for Valium and Librium in the Netherlands were much higher than those charged in the UK before the UK reductions were imposed. Eventually the Minister ordered HLR to reduce its prices for the different Valium and Librium tablets by 13 to 30 per cent for Valium and 31 to 38 per cent for Librium.

After having determined the relevant market as the Dutch market for tranquillisers, the Minister noted that HLR possessed a market share of 60 per cent in 1973, which fell to 34 per cent in 1976. He then went on to analyse this market, which has a number of particular structural characteristics as a result of which there is almost no price competition. Since tranquillisers are available on prescription from a doctor only, the influence of price on demand is negligible. In addition, producers, importers and wholesalers are bound by systems of vertical resale price maintenance, while the chemists have concluded horizontal price arrangements. Besides the absence of price competition the Minister found that the market structure was an oligopolistic one on the supply side of producers and importers whose positions were further strengthened by patents and trade marks. Although as a result of a number of decisions of the European Court of Justice some obstacles to parallel imports had been removed, the Minister did not notice any appreciable influence as to price conduct on the relevant market. In view of these circumstances he concluded that HLR was not forced into competitive conduct as to prices. This conclusion, according to the Minister, is confirmed by the fact that the prices of HLR are considerably higher than the ones of Roche Products Ltd. Finally, taking into account the absence of price competition and the market share of HLR which, although it had been reduced, was still deemed 'considerable', the Minister held that HLR had a dominant position.

Subsequently it was held that in view of the different prices on the UK and Dutch markets HLR was apparently using its dominant position to the disadvantage of customers by charging higher prices than it would have done in a situation of active competition. In the absence of proof that the higher prices were necessary to avoid an economically prejudicial situation for HLR, the Minister concluded that such conduct was against the public interest. The investigation conducted by the Minister found that in fact the low UK prices were sufficiently profitable, and as a result the Minister ordered the reduction of the Dutch prices to the UK level, to which was added a margin to cover the difference between promotional costs in the UK and those in the Netherlands, which were higher.

HLR lodged an appeal against the Ministerial decision with the CBB and simultaneously started summary proceedings before the President of the District Court of The Hague in which it claimed damages and requested the President to order the Government not to execute the Ministerial decision. The summary proceedings were started since an appeal to the CBB does not suspend measures under Article 24. The President, however, dismissed the action. The decision of the President of 2 September 1977 was upheld by the Court of Appeal of The Hague in its decision of 29 December 1977.

Hoffman-La Roche was more successful in its appeal to the CBB. Although HLR's objections as to the definition of the relevant market were rejected, the CBB nevertheless held that the Minister could not reasonably have come to the conclusion that HLR was involved in a dominant position on the Dutch market of tranquillisers. The market share of HLR had dropped from 73.4 per cent in 1972 to 35 per cent in 1977 and further down to 30.7 per cent in 1978. It was not contested by the Government that this reduction was caused by the fact that a competitor of HLR had already long before the Ministerial decisions introduced tranquillisers of a better quality than Valium and Librium. Despite the considerably higher sales prices of these tranquillisers the competitor had acquired a large part of the relevant market at HLR's expense. HLR could not therefore have had a dominant position on its own.

The CBB went on to hold that HLR was also not involved in a collective dominant position. Although it acknowledged that none of the suppliers on the relevant market was forced into competitive pricing and that each supplier had a large discretion in determining its own prices, it did not find that this particular market structure resulted in or was the result of any parallel behaviour - whether interrelated or not - of several of such suppliers including HLR.

On the basis of these arguments the CBB annulled the decisions of the Minister, without having to pass judgment on the issue whether the prices charged by HLR were against the public interest.

The judgment of the CBB has met with some severe criticism. [36] First it was felt that, *inter alia* in view of the EEC developments in the field, the CBB had applied too narrow a concept of a dominant position. In respect of Article 86 of the EEC Treaty, it had already several times been held by the European Commission and the Court of Justice that in principle no absolute domination of the market was needed, but that the ability for independent market conduct without the need to take account of competitors, customers or suppliers would suffice. It was submitted that the CBB, by just focusing on the market shares of HLR, had omitted to take other relevant factors into account.

Although the CBB could have given more consideration to the arguments of the Minister, it seems unjustified to say that the CBB conclusion was based only on the finding that the market share was insufficient for a dominant position. The CBB did consider whether a collective dominant position existed, and took the lack of price competition into account, but concluded that the lack of evidence of any sort of parallel behaviour gave no grounds for finding that such a collective dominant position existed. This does not seem a totally unreasonable conclusion. More important though, and this relates to the individual dominant position, the CBB found that the position of HLR had been

---

36   See M.R. Mok, February 1980 SEW at 135 *et seq.* and J.G. van der Wielen NJ/AB 1980, 457 at page 1105 *et seq.*

severely weakened in the course of the previous six years as a result of effective competition. It was not so much the mere market share of HLR at a given moment, but the fast and rather persistent process of the decrease of its market share as a result of competition from a better quality product, which seemed to matter.

In this respect it is interesting to note that the Minister made the following statement when defending the Bill in Parliament:[37]

> In connection with a general investigation into dominant positions, one should realise that these dominant positions are not static but extremely flexible phenomena. It is definitely not the case that each big concern, because it is big, has a dominant position. This depends entirely on its market strength. Whether a big concern has a predominant influence on the market on one day and not on the next cannot be measured or investigated. Only after some time can one determine whether such concern in a given period of time has had a predominant influence on the market.

In view of this statement one would have expected the Minister to pay more attention in his decision to the decline of the market shares of HLR and the reasons for it, rather than simply stating that this was due to an earlier voluntary price reduction of 25 per cent and a less intensive promotion of sales.

Another criticism of the decision of the CBB which should be mentioned is that the CBB exceeded its jurisdictional powers by examining the issue of the dominant position in full. Article 24 provides the Minister with the power to take certain measures 'if in (his) opinion . . . a dominant position exists the consequences of which conflict with the public interest'. The way Article 24 is worded indicates that it is the opinion of the Minister that counts and that the Court should not simply replace the judgment of the Minister by its own, unless it feels that the Minister could not reasonably have come to the conclusion that a dominant position is involved. It is not sufficient merely for the Court to disagree. The way the Minister has come to his opinion must be clearly unreasonable if the Court is to act. It was felt that in the present case the CBB had gone beyond the marginal test of whether the Minister could reasonably have found a dominant position and that it had actually put the question whether such position existed to a full test.

The only comment the writer would make in respect of the above criticism, which seems to be to some extent justified, is that according to the wording of Article 24 two requirements must be satisfied in the opinion of the Minister before he is allowed to apply the measure referred to in this Article, namely:

(1) there should be a dominant position as defined under Article 1 and

(2) this position should have consequences contrary to the public interest.

It would seem that any decision in respect of the public interest is more a matter of policy in principle reserved for the executive branch than the finding of a dominant position, which is largely a matter of fact and interpretation of the

---

37   MvAII (Memorandum of Reply) quoted in S&J 12 at XXXV.

law. In this respect it is not surprising that the Act contains a definition of 'dominant position' while a definition of 'the public interest' is not provided for. One would therefore assume that the CBB would show more caution in its attack on the Minister's opinion with regard to the public interest than in attacking his findings as to the existence of a dominant position. In this respect it is interesting to note that in Article 19, which concerns measures in respect of individual restrictive agreements, the words 'in their opinion' (this is, the opinion of the Minister) only relate to the public interest and not to the existence of a restrictive agreement as defined under Article 1. In the writer's opinion, it would have been desirable had the drafters of the Act taken the same approach with regard to Article 24.

The HLR case was the first case in which the CBB was called upon to review a Ministerial decision and a dominant position, and it is therefore as yet uncertain in which direction its case law will develop. It is to be hoped that its approach will not be so cautious as to put Ministerial decisions almost beyond its scrutiny, and indeed the HLR case does suggest that the CBB is willing to play an active role in the future.

The HLR case did not end with the judgment of the CBB. Apparently encouraged by the outcome, HLR subsequently sued the Dutch state for damages, including lost profits as a result of the price reductions imposed. The action was based on tort and it was brought before the District Court of The Hague since the CBB - being an administrative court - is not competent with regard to tort actions. HLR argued that the Minister and therefore the State committed a tort by wrong-fully applying Article 24 and therewith causing damage for HLR. In its judgment of 24 March 1982[38] the District Court sided with HLR and held that the state was liable for the damages suffered by HLR as a result of the Ministerial decisions annulled by the CBB.

The interesting question in the proceedings before the District Court was whether the decision of the CBB in itself was already sufficient ground for an award for damages against the State or whether additional facts and circumstances should be established before the State could be held liable. The District Court clearly stated that it was its own responsibility to establish whether the Ministerial decisions were tortious and whether any guilt could be imputed to the Minister. It, however, agreed with the CBB that the Minister could not reasonably have come to the conclusion that HLR was involved in a dominant position on the Dutch market for tranquillisers and concluded - without mentioning any additional circumstances - that the fact of the unreasonableness of the conclusion of the Minister as to dominance was in itself sufficient to establish guilt.

If it is to be upheld, the result of this judgment is that in practice a company which succeeded with the CBB in getting a Ministerial decision *ex* Article 24 annulled stands a very good chance of subsequently obtaining an award for damages. Although there are other grounds for the annulment of Ministerial

---

38 Not yet published

decisions under the Economic Competition Act, it is generally difficult to defend any ground for annulment other than that 'the Minister could not reasonably have reached the conclusion that, etc.' When the CBB annuls the Ministerial decision on that ground the ordinary judiciary[39] (like the District Court in The Hague in the above mentioned decision) will probably be inclined to recognise the CBB as an expert court and, despite its independent responsibility, in most cases adopt the conclusion of the CBB and the arguments on which this conclusion is based without too much investigation of its own. Once the Court itself decides that the conclusion of the Minister was unreasonable if follows from the above mentioned decision of the District Court of The Hague that guilt can be imputed to the State and that, provided there was any damage, the State is liable for such damage.

The State has lodged an appeal against the decision of 24 March 1982 of the District Court of The Hague.

---

39   In actions against the state the District Court in The Hague and in appeal and cassation the Court of Appeal and the Supreme Court, both in The Hague, have jurisdiction.

SWEDEN

Swedish Competition Law
A General Survey

JOHAN COYET

Introduction

It was not until after the second world war that Sweden took its first important step towards a system to control restrictive business practices. In 1946 an Act on Supervision of Restrictive Business Practices was passed and a Registration and Investigation Officer (the Office) was set up as a division of the Board of Trade. The Office was charged with the tasks of keeping a public cartel register to record restrictive agreements and of carrying out special investigations, the results of which were to be published by the Office. Through the activities of the Office numerous examples of restrictive practices were brought to light. As a consequence, the legislation of 1946 was supplemented in 1953 by an Act to Counteract Restrictions on Competition in Business in Certain Instances (the RBP Act). Some important changes in this Act were undertaken in 1956 and in 1966. In connection with the changes made in 1956, the 1946 Act was repealed and a new act entitled the Act Concerning the Obligation to Submit Information as to Conditions of Price and Competition (the Information Act) came into force.

The RBP Act together with the Information Act constituted the present Swedish legislation on restrictive business practices until 31 December 1982.

In 1974 a Government commission was mandated to undertake a thorough overhaul of the Swedish legislation dealing with restrictive business practices. One of the main reasons for appointing the Commission was that development in trade and industry was moving towards the formation of larger corporate entities and the trend towards corporate concentrations was deemed to require a new system of legislation dealing more effectively with such practices. In 1978 the Commission presented a proposal for a new act against restrictive business practices which substantially differed from the RBP Act, the most important change perhaps being the proposal included a set of rules for merger control. The proposal became the subject of some severe criticism especially as regards the proposal for merger control, and for some time it seemed that the Ministry of Trade, under which the Commission worked, had put a stop to work on a new Act. However, in all probability largely because a number of mergers and acquisitions took place during 1981 leading to or strengthening dominant positions of certain companies and unsuccessfully attacked by the Anti-trust authorities under the RBP Act, work on a Bill for a new Act was again given priority in the autumn of 1981, and in April 1982 the Government presented a Bill (1981/82:165) for a new Competition Act (the Competition Act). The Bill was passed by the Riksdag at the beginning of June and the Competition Act came into force on 1 January 1983.

As the Competition Act has come into force fairly recently this survey will concentrate on giving a presentation of the new Act. In order to understand the new Act it is, however, important to have some basic knowledge of the former legislation.

The authorities discharging the duties of both the old and the new legislation are the Market Court, functioning as a specialised court for this field (as well as in the field of consumer protection), the Anti-Trust Ombudsman, being the cartel authority who may also be regarded as a public prosecutor in this field and the National Price and Cartel Office, which acts as an investigative body.

The RBP Act

Prohibited Practices

Under the RBP Act only types of restrictive business practices, resale price maintenance and collusive tendering are prohibited *per se*. The prohibitions are found in sections 2 and 3 of the Act and read as follows:

> *Section 2.* Unless otherwise required by law an entrepreneur may not without the permission of the Market Court require a reseller to maintain a specified minimum price in the resale of goods in Sweden or otherwise specify a price as a guidance to the establishment of resale prices in Sweden unless it is clearly stated that a price lower than that price may be charged.
> *Section 3.* An entrepreneur may not without the permission of the Market Court enter into or carry out an agreement stipulating that consultation or other forms of co-operation shall take place between a number of entrepreneurs before any of them submits a tender for a contract to supply goods or to render a service in Sweden. [1]

Intentional breaches of the prohibitions are criminal offences and may be subject to fines or, if the breach is serious, to imprisonment for up to one year. It should be noted that the prohibition against resale price maintenance applies to goods only while the prohibition against collusive tendering applies to both goods and services.

The ban on resale price maintenance is not applicable to agreements between an entrepreneur and his trade agents (as distinct from distributors) as no proper

---

1   The word 'entrepreneur' as used throughout the Act in the official English translation merely means anyone engaged in business.

sale takes place between them prior to the agent's order solicitation or conclusion of agreements with the final customers. In this connection it should also
be mentioned that, broadly speaking, Swedish competition law accepts the concept of parent and subsidiary companies being single economic entities, which
means that agreements between a parent company and its subsidiary do not fall
under the Act provided that the subsidiary does not enjoy any real autonomy in
the determination of its course of action on the market.

As to the ban on collusive tendering it is to be noted that for the ban to apply, an agreement stipulating some sort of future co-operation must have been
reached between the parties concerned. Consequently neither mere negotiating
to enter into such an agreement nor collusive tendering on a case by case basis,
without this being based on an agreement previously reached, is hit by the ban.
Such practices are instead handled in accordance with the negotiating system of
the Act applicable to non-prohibited practices.

As indicated in sections 2 and 3, exemptions from the bans may be granted
by the Market Court. Such exemptions may, however, be granted only if the restraint of competition can be expected to result in lower costs, be substantially
beneficial to consumers or otherwise contribute to the public interest, or if there
are other particular reasons for granting such exemptions. Exemptions from
the bans have in fact been granted in only a very few special cases.

As breaches of the bans are criminal offences, they are judged by the ordinary
courts, but proceedings may be instituted by the public prosecutor only at the
request, or with the consent, of the Anti-Trust Ombudsman.

Other Types of Restrictive Business Practices

For preventing and eliminating all other types of restrictive business practices
other than resale price maintenance and collusive tendering, the RBP Act relies
on a fairly unusual method of negotiation between the Market Court and the
parties concerned. The legal basis for this system of negotiation is found in section 1 of the Act where it is stated that it is the duty of the Market Court to en-
deavour to eliminate through negotiations the harmful effects of restraints of
competition submitted for its consideration. It is further found in section 5,
where it is stated that a restraint of competition shall be deemed to have a harmful effect if, contrary to the public interest, it unduly affects the formation of
prices, restrains productivity in business or impedes or prevents the trade of
others.

The Act does not define the term 'restraint of competition'. The preparatory
works to the Act indicate that a restraint of competition may be defined as any
practice or circumstance which in one way or another restrains completely free
competition. In practice this means that almost all restrictive business practices
may be the subject of negotiations by the Market Court provided that the requirements set out in section 5 are fulfilled. One important limitation to the applicability of the Act should be pointed out. The preparatory works clearly state
that negotiations may not be aimed at eliminating restraints of competition

which are due to the structure of the industry. That statement has generally been interpreted – and this has been confirmed by the Market Court – to mean that the Court is unable to conduct negotiations concerning possible harmful effects of an acquisition, a merger or any similar concentration leading to a change in the structure of an industry.

In order for a restrictive business practice to have 'harmful effects' two criteria must be fulfilled, namely

(i) it must unduly affect the formation of prices, restrain productivity in business or impede or prevent the trade of others; and

(ii) that it does so must be contrary to the public interest.

The preparatory works to the Act devote some space to examining what kind of circumstances or practices would normally fall under the first criterion mentioned above. But for the present purposes, suffice it to say that it is difficult to envisage any restraint of competition which could not be construed as falling under at least one of the requirements set out. Instead the crucial issue in competition cases in Sweden is whether a restrictive business practice is also contrary to the public interest. This issue is, of course, not simplified by the fact that public interest varies, not only from one type of restraint to another or from sector to sector, but also from time to time depending on aspects such as the economic situation in a particular line of business, the situation in Sweden and so on. Consequently a practice which at one time when the overall situation in a certain line of business was sound may well have been contrary to the public interest might well at another time be in the public interest, if the same industry at that time suffered from great problems. This also means that previous case law may often be of only limited interest, when trying to decide whether a certain type of restrictive practice will at any given time have a harmful effect. At any rate it is clear that when deciding whether or not a restrictive practice is contrary to the public interest, any and all circumstances which could serve as a motivation or excuse for the restraint in question should be taken into consideration and be balanced against the negative effects the restraint may cause.

Procedure

The principle of eliminating restraints of competition through negotiations has quite naturally led to the vast majority of cases being settled out of the Market Court in direct negotiations between the Anti-Trust Ombudsman and the parties concerned. Only where these negotiations do not lead to a result – very often a compromise – acceptable to the Ombudsman will he submit the case to the Market Court.

The proceedings before the Court are divided into two stages. The first stage of the procedure resembles an ordinary court procedure. On the basis of the evidence submitted, the Court establishes whether or not the effects of the restraint in question are harmful. If they are, negotiations will be arranged between the

Market Court and the defendant with a view to eliminating those harmful effects.

The sanctions available, should negotiations lead nowhere, are virtually non-existent. Should the matter concern a refusal to sell to an entrepreneur at a later stage of distribution on conditions which correspond to those offered to other comparable customers, the Market Court may order the party concerned to effect such a sale on pain of a fine. In all other cases the only consequence of a failure to eliminate the harmful effects by negotiation is that where the matter is found to be of major importance, the Court must report the matter to the Government. If the harmful effect is manifested by a particular price being obviously too high having regard to costs and other circumstances the Government may, at the request of the Market Court, specify a certain maximum price which may not during a fixed period be exceeded by the entrepreneur in question without permission of the Court. In other cases the Government would have to take some legislative action in order to stop the restraint.

It may surprise some that a system with such limited sanctions functions at all. However, it is a fact that the Market Court and the Anti-Trust Ombudsman have succeeded in developing a competition law fairly similar to the competition law of countries where the legal framework provides for much heavier sanctions.

The Information Act

Government action against restrictive business practices presupposes fact-finding activities which to a considerable extent must be based on documentation available in company files as well as on information provided by executives or others concerned. In Sweden the legal framework for this fact-finding is the Information Act. According to this Act, on request of the National Price and Cartel Office, an entrepreneur is bound to submit information on such restraints of competition as are specified in the request and which concern his operations and relate to conditions of prices, production, trade or transport as well as information on prices, revenues, costs, profits and other conditions affecting the general price structure. Both failure to comply with such a request and the intentional supply of incorrect information are criminal offences punishable by a fine or imprisonment.

It is to be noted that the obligation to submit information under the Act is subject to the Price and Cartel Office making a specific request therefore, specifying to which particular restraint of competition the information should relate. However, the Office may also impose an obligation to keep the Office continuously informed for a fixed period of any and all restraints of competition in specified trades to which the entrepreneur in question is a party.

The obligation to submit information includes an obligation to submit copies of any restrictive agreement, letter, correspondence and other documentation except trade secrets of a technical nature. The Office is under an obligation to classify such information or part thereof as may be deemed to be trade secrets.

The Information Act also requires the National Price and Cartel Office to keep a public cartel register in which all restrictive agreements coming to the attention of the Office shall be recorded. What is in fact published is a summary of the agreements. The Office is obliged to inform the parties concerned of its decision to publish a summary of their agreement only after the decision has been taken. In the practice established by the Office, however, the Office always informs the parties concerned prior to taking a final decision to publish a summary. The parties also have the opportunity to comment upon the summary to be published. The cartel register is continually updated and is generally thought to have at least some preventive effect.

The New Competition Act

The proposal for a new Act against restrictive business practices made in 1978 by the Government Commission appointed to undertake an overhaul of the RBP Act quite naturally aimed at making the legislation more rigorous. To that end the Commission proposed two new punishable bans, one against price cartels and the other against market division. Further, in order to render the negotiating system covering other restrictive practices than those prohibited *per se* more effective, the Commission proposed that the Market Court should be given the right to impose sanctions such as prohibiting a certain contract or terms of contract or other restrictive practices in case the negotiations failed. Moreover, and perhaps most important, the Commission proposed rules for merger control according to which any merger where the acquired company was of a certain minimum size should be examined. According to the proposal the government was to be given the right to intervene against a merger by imposing a ban or injunction should this be necessary in order to prevent any inconvenience of major importance to the public interest. The rules for merger control were deemed by the Commission to be of particular importance as the RBP Act is in principle not applicable to acquisitions, mergers or similar forms of concentration.

Although the Competition Bill presented by the Government and passed by the Riksdag in June 1982 followed the general intentions of the Government Commission in making the legislation more rigorous than the RBP Act it differed in many respects from the Commission's proposals. In particular the Competition Act does not include any new punishable bans, and although some rules for merger control have been introduced these are limited to such acquisitions or mergers which lead to one of the parties reaching a dominant position or strengthening an already existing dominant position on a certain market.

Prohibitions Per Se

As mentioned above no new punishable bans have been incorporated into the

Competition Act. The two previous bans against resale price maintenance and collusive tendering are, however, retained and in the latter case substantially enlarged and its enforcement made more effective. Also the penalties have been made heavier. Intentional breaches are subject to fines or imprisonment for up to one year and serious breaches are subject to imprisonment for up to two years.

The only major material change in the ban against resale price maintenance is that the ban in the new Act also covers leasing. The enlarged ban against collusive tendering provides that an entrepreneur may not enter into or carry out an agreement, or otherwise collaborate or consult with another entrepreneur, or try to induce another entrepreneur so to collaborate or consult if the object or effect of the agreement or the collaboration is to require that in a contest for a tender

(1) someone shall abstain from submitting a bid or tender;
(2) a certain bidder shall submit a higher tender than another or
(3) any other collaboration is to occur in the course of tendering with respect to fixing the total amount of the tender or the terms of payment.

Excluded from the ban are agreements or conducts which

(1) are due to several entrepreneurs acting through a joint sales organisation in the form of a separate legal entity, or
(2) intend to bring several entrepreneurs together for collective performance on the basis of a common tender or in a form such that any of them participates as sub-contractor to the bidder.

A bidder being privy to conduct that would have been forbidden unless it was permitted in accordance with one of the two exemptions is obliged to notify the client of the existence of the agreement or conduct in writing when the tender is submitted at the latest.

Unlike the previous ban the enlarged ban on collusive tendering covers not only agreements but any kind of concerted practice with the objects set out in the ban. Moreover, collusive tendering on a case by case basis is hit by the new ban. Although the ban is still geared to prohibiting agreements and practices the objects of which are collusive tendering, its wording is much more far-reaching. Obviously, a market sharing agreement, whether on a quota, geographical or customer basis, could well fall under the ban, since such an agreement would normally mean that one of the parties would have to abstain from submitting a bid or tender to a customer belonging to the other party's market. This is a fairly strange consequence since the Government decided against proposing a separate market sharing ban although such a ban had been suggested by the Government Commission. Furthermore, exclusive distribution agreements could well fall under the ban although this was clearly not the intention of the legislative authority as such an agreement also normally means that the principal has to abstain from submitting a bid or tender on the market covered by the exclusive agreement. It is therefore to be expected that the enlarged ban on collusive tendering will create major problems and concern until the limits of its application have been fixed by future adjudication. Exemptions from the bans on resale price maintenance and collusive tendering may be granted by the Market Court on the same conditions as under the RBP Act.

Other Types of Restrictive Practices

The legal construction of the RBP Act – containing a general clause which covers restrictive practices that have harmful effects other than those practices prohibited *per se*, as well as the system of negotiations between the Market Court and parties concerned for the removal of such harmful effects – is largely retained in the Competition Act. However, according to the new legislation, where negotiations fail the Court is entitled to issue penalty-sanctioned bans and injunctions.

According to the general clause the Market Court may take action in accordance with the Act in order to prevent any restrictive business practice having a harmful effect within Sweden. Such action may be taken against the entrepreneur which induces the harmful effect. There are three bans or injunctions at the Market Court's disposal. It can

(1) prohibit the entrepreneur from applying a certain agreement, term of agreement or other restrictive practice or from applying any practice similar to that which has been so prohibited;

(2) order the entrepreneur to supply to another entrepreneur certain goods, services or other commodity on conditions which correspond to those offered to other comparable customers;

(3) order the entrepreneur to change a restrictive practice applied by him or to fulfil a certain condition or give specified information in connection with such restrictive practice or take other action counteracting the restrictive practice.

Moreover, if the harmful effect is manifested by a particular price being obviously too high having regard to costs and other circumstances and the matter is of major importance, then the Market Court may order the entrepreneur not to exceed a certain maximum price specified by the Court during a fixed period not exceeding one year.

All the aforementioned bans and injunctions may be sanctioned by a penalty fixed by the Court.

Prior to the Court issuing a ban or injunction the Court shall try to prevent the harmful effect in question by negotiation unless the circumstances require otherwise. This means that in fact the question of whether a negotiation shall take place or not is to a large extent within the discretion of the Market Court. It is, however, likely that the Court in most cases will try to negotiate prior to issuing any ban or injunction.

The Competition Act also introduces a simplified procedure for matters of minor importance. In such matters the Anti-Trust Ombudsman may himself impose the same penalty sanctioned bans and injunctions as those available to the Market Court except that relating to the fixing of a maximum price. The ban or injunction imposed must, however, be approved by the entrepreneur concerned. If it is approved it has the same legal effect as a ban or injunction issued by the Market Court. If not approved it has no effect whatsoever and the Anti-Trust Ombudsman is left with the option of taking the matter before the Market Court. This simplified procedure has its roots in the Swedish consumer protection legislation where such a procedure has been used for some years with some success. Its primary object within the field of competition law is to allow the Anti-Trust Ombudsman to take swift action with sufficient authority in comparatively clear-cut matters.

The Act does not contain any definition of 'matters of minor importance' nor do the preparatory works to the Act give any clear indication of when the simplified procedure can or cannot be used. It is therefore to be expected that the Anti-Trust Ombudsman will try to use the simplified procedure fairly often. This should, however, not pose any major problems for industry as it is entirely up to the party concerned to accept or refuse any ban or injunction imposed by the Ombudsman.

The two criteria which have to be fulfilled in order for a restrictive business practice to be deemed to have harmful effects remain unchanged in the new Act. This means that under the Competition Act also the crucial issue is whether or not a restrictive business practice is contrary to the public interest. It also means that all previous case law relating to the interpretation of the concept of harmful effects also remains valid when interpreting the new Act.

Concentrations

As mentioned above the new Competition Act contains a set of rules concerning company acquisitions and mergers. Section 5 of the Competition Act lays down that if the harmful effect consists of an entrepreneur reaching a dominant position on the market for certain goods, services or other commodity by making a company acquisition or if such an acquisition leads to the strengthening of an already dominating position then the Market Court shall try to prevent the harmful effect by negotiation. If the matter is of particular importance to the public interest the negotiations may aim at making the entrepreneur abstain from the acquisition.

Section 5 defines a company acquisition as the acquisition of a company performing business within Sweden as well as purchase of stock, shares in a partnership or the purchase of a business or a part thereof. Moreover, for the purposes of section 5, mergers are regarded as company acquisitions. The section is also applicable if the entrepreneur is one of several entrepreneurs jointly owned or controlled if the jointly owned group of companies reaches or strengthens a dominant position on the market through the acquisition.

It is quite clear that the applicability of the Competition Act to concentrations is limited to such concentrations as are covered by section 5, in other words, those leading to a dominant position or the strengthening of such a position. All other concentrations by way of mergers or acquisitions fall outside the Act and cannot be attacked.

The Act does not define the concept of dominant position. The preparatory works to the Act indicate, however, that the definition of a dominant position is similar to the definition adopted by the European Court in Luxemburg, namely a position giving a company the capability of acting without having to take the reactions of actual or potential competitors into any real regard. In addition, when establishing the relevant market tests similar to those applied by the European Court will be used.

Section 5 gives the Market Court two options when dealing with an acquisition leading to or strengthening a dominant position. The Court can either try to prevent the harmful effects through negotiations which would obviously aim at making the entrepreneur in question accept certain limitations on his future actions in order to limit or eliminate, the risk of the entrepreneur abusing his dominant position or if the matter is of particular importance to the public interest it can negotiate in order to make the entrepreneur abstain from the acquisition. In both cases the Court can also apply the bans and injunctions mentioned above to other types of restrictive business practices covered by the general clause. If, however, firstly the negotiation is aimed at making the entrepreneur abstain from the acquisition, secondly the negotiation is ended without the harmful effect having been prevented and thirdly provided that the Market Court is of the opinion that a ban or injunction either should not be issued or is insufficient, then the Market Court may prohibit the acquisition. Such a prohibition may not, however, be issued in case of purchase of shares at the Stockholm Stock Exchange or at executive auctions. In such cases the Market Court may instead order the entrepreneur to divest himself of the shares or property in question.

A decision by the Market Court to prohibit the acquisition or an order of divestiture is not automatically binding upon the entrepreneur in question. For it to become binding upon him the Government must confirm the decision. If the decision is confirmed by the Government it shall be executed within six months from the date when the Government issued its decision or within such longer period as the Government may decide. Should the Government confirm the decision to prohibit an acquisition, the acquisition is null and void.

The Competition Act also contains certain procedural rules specifically relating to the implementation of the provisions concerning concentrations.

As soon as the Anti-Trust Ombudsman finds any reason to study a certain acquisition he shall make a specific decision to that effect. Any party to an agreement concerning a company acquisition may also notify the acquisition to the Anti-Trust Ombudsman. If so notified the Ombudsman must as soon as possible decide whether to study the acquisition or abstain from further action. If the Anti-Trust Ombudsman has decided to abstain from action he may not thereafter request the Market Court to prohibit the acquisition or order a divestiture unless the company notifying the acquisition has given incorrect information of particular importance to the decision not to act on the acquisition. In a case where the Anti-Trust Ombudsman has decided to study the acquisition and wishes the Market Court to prohibit the acquisition or issue an order of divestiture the Ombudsman must make an application therefore with the Court within three months from his decision, unless the parties agree to a prolongation of this period. In extraordinary circumstances the Market Court may also prolong the time limit for a specified period of not longer than one month at a time at the request of the Anti-Trust Ombudsman. In extraordinary circumstances the Market Court and when relevant the Government may also prohibit the entrepreneur from making the acquisition until a final decision in the matter has been reached.

The Market Court may not issue a prohibition or an order of divestiture later than six months after an application therefore has been made. This period may however be prolonged by the Court if the parties so agree or in extraordinary circumstances. In no circumstances, however, may a prohibition or an order of divestiture be issued later than two years after the date when the agreement concerning the acquisition was made. Correspondingly, if the Market Court has decided to prohibit the acquisition or order a divestiture, the Government must make its decision in the matter not later than three months thereafter. Again the Government is entitled to prolong this period under the same conditions as those applicable to the Market Court.

A matter concerning a company acquisition may not be retried unless the entrepreneur in question has given incorrect information of particular importance to the decision not to act against the acquisition.

The various time limits laid down in the procedural rules are of course aimed at forcing the authorities to act swiftly in such matters. It is however open to debate if any period exceeding a few days is not too long when it comes to deciding actions relative to acquisitions or mergers. Many practitioners at least agree that the periods laid down are far too long and will jeopardise future acquisitions 'good or bad' which could fall under the Act. Further the value of the various time limits, except the maximum final two year time limit and of the possibility of notifying an acquisition or a merger to the Anti-Trust Ombudsman, may well be questioned. The Anti-Trust Ombudsman is not the only party allowed to take action before the Market Court. Such action may also be taken by any organisation of consumers, employees or employers as well as by any entrepreneur affected by the restrictive business practice in question. This means that even if the Anti-Trust Ombudsman decides not to act upon a certain acquisition or merger, action may well be taken by any other such party. The threat of taking such action and thereby at least suspending an acquisition or merger can of course become an important weapon in the hands of competitors, consumer groups, or for that matter trade unions.

Jurisdictional Aspects

The primary objective of the Competition Act is of course to protect the

Swedish market against harmful restrictive business practices. The Act therefore does not normally apply to agreements or practices entered into or decided in Sweden having their effect only outside Sweden. Of course to the extent that a restrictive practice will have an effect also in Sweden that part of the practice would fall under the Act. However, contrary to what is the case in several countries, the Act itself contains a provision which makes it possible for the Market Court – upon the approval of the Government – to take action in order to eliminate harmful effects outside Sweden of a restrictive business practice, provided that this is considered necessary because of international treaties to which Sweden is a party. In such cases a restrictive practice shall always be deemed to have harmful effect if it is contrary to the international treaty in question. A corresponding provision is found in the previous RBP Act. Both provisions have their background in the efforts made in the post-war years under the auspices of the United Nations Economic and Social Council to create an international order to counteract the harmful effects of restrictive practices. Sweden therefore has the legal framework to implement provisions relating to restrictive business practices in its international trade agreements, such as for instance Article 23 of the Free-Trade Agreement between Sweden and the EEC.

As to the extra-territorial application of the Act the preparatory works to the Act indicate a change as compared to the previous position as established by the Market Court in the so called *Bayer-Kerr* case of 1977.[2] The *Bayer-Kerr* case concerned a refusal by Bayer AG of West Germany and the Kerr division of Sypron (Europe) AG of Switzerland to sell certain dental products to a Swedish company. In that case it was established that for the RBP Act to be applicable to restrictive practices implemented by non-Swedish entities but with their effects on the Swedish market, three conditions must be fulfilled. First the practice in question must be directly aimed at the Swedish market. Secondly it must have perceptible effects on the Swedish market. Thirdly the foreign entity in question must have some permanent or at least notable connection with Sweden. According to the Market Court the weaker this connection the more unlikely it would be that the RBP Act would have been applicable. The Court was not unanimous in its opinion as to the relevance of the third condition. Three of the members of the Court felt that it was quite sufficient that the effects of a practice were direct and perceptible in order for the RBP Act to be applicable and that the question of whether or not the parties concerned had any notable connection with Sweden was irrelevant. This opinion also tallies with the consensus of opinion as expressed in legal writing as well as with the view expressed by the Government Commission appointed in 1974. According to the preparatory works to the Competition Act the legislative authority has chosen to follow the view established by the minority in the *Bayer-Kerr* case. Thus the Competition Act applies if the practice in question is directly aimed at the Swedish market and has perceptible effects on that market regardless of whether the foreign party concerned has any notable connection with Sweden.

---

2   Judgment of the Market Court 1977: 16, of 17 July 1977.

Legal Validity of Restrictive Agreements

Generally speaking under Swedish law nullity does not automatically follow from breaches of every form of legal prohibition. It is therefore by no means certain that an action which from a certain point of view is unlawful or even criminal is automatically null and void. When examining this aspect one must in each case look at the purpose of the prohibition, the consequences of the nullity and the need for such a consequence. The same considerations apply in relation to restrictive business practices falling under the previous RBP Act or the new Competition Act. This means that it is not certain that for example a restrictive agreement deemed by the Market Court to have harmful effects and hit by one of the bans or injunctions in the Competition Act is enforceable between the parties. The question whether such unenforceability will occur will depend on the circumstances of each case. On the other hand it seems quite clear that no Swedish court would enforce an agreement or practice falling under one of the two criminal offences in the Competition Act, namely the bans against resale price maintenance and collusive tendering.

Third Party Rights to Damages

A very important aspect of competition law is of course the possible liability towards third parties for damages sustained by them as a consequence of a certain restrictive practice.

Neither the RBP Act nor the Competition Act contains any provision concerning liability to pay damages to third parties suffering from a restrictive practice. Instead for guidance one must look to the Swedish Tort Liability Act. According to that Act financial loss only is in principle recoverable – unless otherwise expressly provided in other statutes – when it has been caused by a criminal offence. This being the case liability to pay damages for restrictive practices would normally only arise in consequence of a judgment for breach of either of the bans against resale price maintenance and collusive tendering. Such a liability could possibly also arise in a case where a company, in spite of having been ordered on pain of a fine to start selling a product to a customer, refuses to do so and in other cases of breaches of a penalty-sanctioned ban or injunction issued by the Market Court. In all other cases the risk of having to pay damages to third parties is very limited indeed. A certain reservation should however be made as it is stated in the preparatory works to the Swedish Tort Liability Act that the question of an enlarged liability for financial loss is left to future case law. So far, however, no case concerning claims for damages sustained due to a restrictive business practice has been decided by a Swedish court.

Conclusion

A comparison betwen the RBP Act and the new Competition Act makes it quite clear that the Competition Act indeed makes Swedish competition law more rigorous. Leaving aside the enlarged ban on collusive tendering and the new system for merger control, it seems unlikely, however, that the Competition Act will lead to a general enlargement of Swedish competition law to apply to practices which have hitherto not been considered restrictive or as having harmful effects. The fact that the criteria which have to be fulfilled in order for a restrictive practice to be deemed to have harmful effects have been kept unchanged indicates that future development of Swedish competition law will in most material respects be the same under the new Act as it would have been if the RBP Act had been retained. The main difference is found in the sanctions, the importance of which should not of course be underestimated. There is a vast difference in the Court's negotiating position between the former situation where the Court knew that if negotiations for the removal of harmful effects failed, no sanctions could be imposed, and the position under the new Competition Act where the Market Court can immediately impose both bans and injunctions.

The most interesting part of the new Competition Act is of course the merger control established by the Act. Only the future will tell whether the system chosen is workable or if the worries expressed by industry and legal practitioners that the system will at best lead to severe problems and at worst prevent acquisitions and mergers wholly in the public interest from taking place will be sustained.

UNITED KINGDOM
United Kingdom Law
VALENTINE KORAH

Historical Introduction

By the end of the second world war, the UK economy was far from competitive. Some wartime rationing, price and other controls continued until the 1950's. Imports were subject to high tariffs and to quotas. Several important industries were nationalised shortly after the war, and it looked as if the UK might be moving towards a planned economy. Towards the end of the war, however, a group of temporary civil servants responsible for planning post-war reconstruction became concerned that production should be transferred to lower cost producers through the stimulus of competition. They did not convince the permanent officials in the Board of Trade, who had attempted to organise crisis cartels in the 1930's. The Labour and Conservative political parties were also divided.

In the famous *White Paper on Employment Policy*[1] it was argued however that measures to maintain effective demand might lead, in the presence of widespread monopoly and restrictive practices to higher prices and profits rather than to increased output and higher employment. Control over the restrictive practices both of business and unions was suggested.

Creation of the Monopolies and Restrictive Practices Commission

Although there was no clear decision to rely on market pressures for efficiency rather than on intervention, the Commission (now called the Monopolies and Mergers Commission) was established to see how widespread restrictive practices were in industry, and to consider whether in particular industries they operated or might be expected to operate against the public interest.

The definition of the public interest is open ended. The Commission is required to take into account anything it considers necessary, and in particular a list of matters. The list was revised by the Fair Trading Act in 1973, but it has

---

1   May 1944, Cmnd 6527.

never been very important. Unless the Commission considers a particular item on the list important, it is not relevant, and if it is important, it may be considered anyway. The criteria used by the Commission may have altered since it was set up, but this has been due to changes in industrial structure, conduct and performance and changing economic views, not to changes in the list.

Originally, the Board of Trade (now the Secretary of State) was enabled to refer to the Commission the supply and export of any goods (now also services) it might specify, if one third (now one quarter) was supplied by or to a single firm, group of companies, or persons who

> . . . whether voluntarily or not, and whether by agreement or not, so conduct their respective affairs as in any way to prevent, restrict or distort competition in connection with the supply of goods of that description, whether or not they themselves are affected by the competition and whether the competition is between persons interested as producers or suppliers or between persons interested as customers or producers or suppliers.

The final situation is now called a 'complex monopoly'. It is sometimes thought that the Commission is not concerned with the relevant market, but this is not so. The Commission must consider only the products specified in the reference when deciding whether the reference was properly made, but having made a very limited enquiry, it is then required to consider whether the existence of the dominant position or any steps or conduct taken as a result of it or to maintain or exploit it is contrary to the public interest. This is the important part of the Commission's reports, and it has a good record for analysing the market and for taking into account competition from other products. In *Frozen Foodstuffs*[2] for instance, it recognised that frozen hamburgers might be no substitute for frozen peas or fruit, but observed that these were substitutes on the supply side: supplies of each had to compete for the space of retailers' freezer cabinets. Habitually, the Commission has considered competitive pressures not only from identical products to those referred, but also from substitutes. In *Cat and Dog Foods*[3], it considered the competition offered to tinned foods by scraps, and in *Frozen Foodstuffs*, it pointed out that most frozen foods were easier to prepare than their fresh equivalents. The Commission rarely defines the relevant market, but does analyse the competitive pressures on the firm(s) found dominant on the statutory definition. Of course, this does not enable it to establish presumptions that large market shares are bad, but it analyses each group of products referred to it.

For a monopoly to exist in respect of exports, the one third (now one quarter) test must be satisfied by production in the United Kingdom − at least a quarter of the goods specified in the reference that are produced in the UK are produced by a single firm or group of companies, or there exist agreements affecting at least a quarter of the goods so produced which restrict competition in relation

---

2 *Frozen Foodstuffs* [1976] HCP 674.
3 *Cat and Dog Foods* [1977] HCP 447.

to exports of such goods generally, or to particular markets. It was not desired to subject the entrepôt trade of the UK to control, even to discretionary control, under the monopolies legislation.

It is not illegal to enjoy a dominant position as defined in the legislation; indeed, until the reference products have been specified, it is not possible to say whether a firm is dominant. Nor does condemnation by the Commission have any immediate effects. However much the Commission may disapprove of the conduct and power of the dominant firm, no immediate sanctions apply. The Secretary of State (in practice the Minister of Trade and Industry) is authorised to make such order as he thinks fit to remedy the adverse effect on the public interest found by the Commission. In practice, since 1973 he has delegated to the Director General of Fair Trading the task of persuading the principal firms involved to give voluntary undertakings. If they do not, the Director will advise the Minister on the conduct to be controlled by order. Few orders have been made since they tend to be too inflexible. Both firms and the government usually prefer to give and receive undertakings, which can be renegotiated when circumstances change, without the need to return to Parliament to revise an order. If undertakings are infringed the only sanction is that the Minister might well make an order on the basis of the original report, and then any future infringement could be restrained by an injunction requested by the law officers of the Crown. It is not clear whether the victim of the breach of an order can sue for breach of statutory duty. It is clear that victims cannot obtain compensation for breach of an undertaking.

Between 1949, when it started to function, and 1956 the Commission considered some twenty products. These were often quite narrowly defined, for example cast iron rainwater goods. Frequently it found price fixing, usually supported by market sharing with quotas. Often the members of a manufacturers' trade association agreed to supply on trade terms only members of the equivalent traders' association and in return the traders' association recommended that its members should give preference to those manufacturers when ordering supplies. It is hardly surprising that the Commission condemned such practices almost universally. In 1955 its report on *Collective Discrimination*[4] was published in which it condemned the various practices referred to it, but suggested that there might possibly be circumstances in which they might not operate against the public interest. The majority recommended, therefore that the practices should be condemned generally, but should be capable of exemption after being considered by some tribunal created for the purpose.

Creation of the Restrictive Practices Court

The Restrictive Trade Practices Act of 1956 and various amending Acts have been consolidated by the Restrictive Trade Practices Act 1976. It was less rad-

---

4 *Collective Discrimination* [1955] Cmnd 9504

ical than the recommendations of the majority of the Commission. What is now section 6 of the 1976 Act defines the kinds of agreements relating to the supply or acquisition of goods that are subject to control. The citizen is required to furnish particulars of these to the Director General of Fair Trading. If the Director considers that the agreement is indeed caught by the legislation, he places it on a public register (there is a special section containing trade secrets etc. that is not subject to public scrutiny), and is required to refer each of the agreements on his register to the Restrictive Practices Court for a declaration where the restrictions are contrary to the public interest.

Originally control was limited to goods, but in 1976 it was extended to services. The Act is drafted in formalistic terms, since it was thought wrong to require citizens to initiate proceedings on a test as vague as agreements with the object or effect of restricting competition. Lawyers in the United Kingdom are unlikely to have studied economics, and it would be difficult to get reliable advice as to what prospective agreements were likely to restrict competition. To be caught by part II of the Act the agreement must be made between at least two parties who carry on a business in the production, supply or processing of goods. If a monopolist is exploiting foreigners, the matter can be referred to the Monopolies Commission, but any agreement only one party to which carries on business here should not be open to public inspection. Particulars of export agreements are required to be notified to the Director General, but these do not appear on the public register – they are not subject to registration or reference to the Court.

Not only must two persons party to the agreement carry on business in the UK, two persons must accept restrictions of certain kinds in relation to goods.

> 6(1) This Act applies to agreements (whenever made) between two or more persons carrying on business within the United Kingdom in the production or supply of goods, or in the application to goods of any process of manufacture, whether with or without other parties, being agreements under which restrictions are accepted by two or more parties in respect of any of the following matters:
>
> (a) the prices to be charged, quoted or paid for goods supplied, offered or acquired, or for the application of any process of manufacture to goods;
>
> (b) the prices to be recommended or suggested as the prices to be charged or quoted in respect of the resale of goods supplied;
>
> (c) the terms or conditions on or subject to which goods are to be supplied or acquired or any such process is to be applied to goods;
>
> (d) the quantities or description of goods to be produced, supplied or acquired;
>
> (e) the processes of manufacture to be applied to any goods, or the quantities or descriptions of goods to which any such process is to be applied; or
>
> (f) the persons or classes of persons to, for or from whom, or the areas

or places in or from which, goods are to be supplied or acquired, or
any such process applied.

There are very similar provisions relating to services, and set out in the
Services Order, made under what has since become part III of the Act of 1976.
There is, however, no intermingling of parts II and III. If I carry on a service
business in the UK, but no goods business, and you carry on a goods business,
with ancillary services, such as a motor dealer who also services or repairs vehicles, an agreement between us would be caught if it relates to service restrictions of the kind listed in the order, but not if it refers only to goods. No valid
reasons have been given for this segregation. The formalistic legislation has
become so complex, especially in relation to services, that many practitioners
wonder whether we should continue to use a formalistic definition.

Section 9 (section 18 for services) provides that in deciding whether two or
more persons have accepted restrictions, certain restrictions shall not count at
all. These can be ignored. The third schedule provides another list of exceptions, but these cannot be ignored. If after deleting the restrictions let out by
section 9 (or 18), the only restrictions of the kind listed in section 6(1) (or the
Order) come within one of the paragraphs, the agreement is not subject to the
legislation. Many vertical agreements such as exclusive supply and purchase,
can be drafted to take advantage of these excepting provisions. Care should be
taken in trying to decide whether the Act does apply to a particular agreement.
'Agreements' are defined to include arrangements, and the mutual arousing of
expectations in circumstances where it would be ungentlemanly not to make
them come true has been held to constitute an arrangement. This does not include conscious parallelism, unless there is something more: unless it would be
ungentlemanly not to follow or maintain the price rise announced by one seller.

The legislation is so complex that there is little point in going into one layer
of detail after another. Suffice it to say that it is very seldom that one can draft
a horizontal price fixing agreement so as to avoid the legislation, but many vertical arrangements can be drafted so as to avoid control. In the case of horizontal collaboration which may increase competition, such as joint ventures, there
is a possible escape under section 21(2). If the restrictions are not of such importance as to warrant investigation by the Court, the Director may ask the
Minister for directions discharging him from the duty to refer the agreement to
the Restrictive Practices Court. Often the restrictions in an important joint venture are insignificant, because the ownership of a joint subsidiary is not a restriction. Parents are unlikely to compete with their joint baby, so any restriction is unimportant. Section 2 is the only provision giving a measure of administrative power to exempt. Such agreements remain on the register, but it is legal
to give effect to them.

The registration provisions are supported by sanctions. An agreement that
was not notified when it should have been is incurably void in respect of the restrictions. Moreover, the Director may seek an order from the Restrictive Practices Court forbidding the parties to give effect to the agreement, or seek to en-

force it, or make any other agreement to which the Act applies without duly furnishing particulars. This final sanction applies only the second time a party is caught, but is then very powerful, since directors may be sent to prison for contempt of court. So may the other parties to the second contract, since they may have aided and abetted someone bound by a court order or an undertaking given to it. Unfortunately the Director's powers to obtain information have been construed narrowly, so the sanctions apply in rather a haphazard way: some firms have had to pay quite large fines, while others may never be caught. It is clear that the victims of an agreement that should have been notified, but was not, can sue for breach of statutory duty. I know of no reported case, but the Post Office did obtain £9 million when the cartel over telephone cables was discovered. Damages are single.

Agreements that have been duly notified may be operated and are treated as entirely valid (subject to two incomprehensible cases.) Proceedings on the public interest tend to be lengthy and expensive. Restrictive provisions are deemed to be contrary to the public interest unless the Court is satisfied on one of eight circumstances, and also that it is not unreasonable having regard to the balance between those circumstances and any detriment to the public (section 10). The gateway most often pleaded is:

> (b) that the removal of the restriction would deny to the public as purchasers, consumers or users of any goods other specific and substantial benefits or advantages enjoyed or likely to be enjoyed by them as such, whether by virtue of the restriction of information provision itself, or of any arrangements or operations resulting therefrom;

The first two gateways are based on benefits to the public, the next two on the need to counteract the market power of others, the fifth to increasing exports (but not minimising imports), the sixth to counteracting persistent regional unemployment, the seventh covers necessary ancillary restrictions, and the last cases where competition is not restricted or discouraged to any material extent in any relevant trade or industry and is not likely to be. Very similar provisions are contained in section 19 for service agreements.

Few goods agreements have survived a reference to the Court, and most effort is devoted to drafting agreements which escape the legislation. Few are defended before the Court. Hearings in the more recent ones have lasted 40 days or more, although most of the facts are exchanged in written form before the hearing starts. The procedure is adversary, and far more legalistic than the inquisitional procedure of the Monopolies and Mergers Commission. Recently the hearing of the first agreement under the Services Order – ABTA – has taken place.

This area of law is incredibly complex and formalistic. When a lawyer tidies up an agreement to avoid the need to furnish particulars, he may well not make the market more competitive. (The author has just wasted time persuading clients to grant exclusive copyright licences – copyright is treated as being neither goods nor services – instead of exclusive rights to distribute discs and cassettes.) At least when one advises on transactions under US or EEC law, one removes some anti-competitive aspects. It is high time the Restrictive Trade Practices legislation was amended and based on competitive effects. Note how delayed the sanctions are in the case of an agreement duly notified. It is legal to implement such an agreement until the Director has time to refer it to the Court. Only after it has lost on the public interest will the Court make an order restricting the parties from implementing it or from making any other agreement to the like effect. That order is enforceable for contempt of court. No one has yet been imprisoned, but in a recent case on *Concrete Pipes*,[5] the Court did issue stern warning that those who commit or aid and abet a contempt of court may be punished.

The Functions of the Monopolies Commission after 1957

When restrictive agreements about goods became subject to control through the Restrictive Practices legislation, they ceased to be capable of reference to the Commission, and even if the goods affected were referred to it on other grounds, the Commission was not allowed to consider the effects on the public interest of agreements that might be referred to the Court. So from 1957 until 1965 the Commission had the difficult task of considering only monopolisation problems. It introduced few reports and each took several years.

In 1965 the competence of the Monopolies Commission was extended to include services and the minister was empowered to refer to it the question of whether mergers or probable mergers might be expected to operate against the public interest. At first only about two per cent of the mergers qualifying for reference were referred, although nearly a decade ago the proportion rose to three per cent. The qualifications for reference were that as a result of the merger a single firm or corporate group would supply or acquire more than a third (now a quarter) of the reference products, or that the assets taken over exceed £5 million (now £15 million) according to the company's books of account. The definition of merger is also very wide, drafted in terms of a single person being able to control or materially to influence policy. Mergers cannot be referred more than six months after they take place, but of course the products giving rise to concern may be the subject of a Monopolies reference.

The Commission rapidly established precedents unfavourable to collective agreements about services. Although service agreements might differ from those affecting goods, it said in *Fire Insurance*[6] that

> a collective agreement such as that adopted by the [Fire Offices Committee] which significantly limits the freedom of the parties in the conduct of their

---

5 *British Concrete Pipe Association's Agreement* [1982] ICR 182: noted, Korah, (1980) Law Soc. Gaz. 961.
6 *Fire Insurance* [1972] HCP 396.

business, will tend to have some or all of the following effects – higher prices, less efficient use of resources, discouragement of new developments and rigidity in the structure and trading methods of businesses.

It failed to find special circumstances to convince them that there were counter-vailing benefits sufficient to balance these detriments to the public. On the basis of its experience it has accepted economic postulates about the likely effect of cartels both for goods and services.

Resale Price Maintenance

The collective enforcement of resale price maintenance through blacklists was made illegal in 1956, but individual resale price maintenance was made easier, through a non-signer clause. A supplier could enforce conditions as to the price at which goods might be resold against sub-purchasers who bought with notice of the condition. By the Resale Prices Act 1964 (now of 1976), this was made illegal, subject to the possibility of exemption. Two classes of goods survived a reference to the Restrictive Practices Courts, books and medicaments. For all other products not only are such conditions void, it is illegal to refuse to supply a firm on the ground that it is a price cutter. There are a few branded products for which it is difficult to prove the grounds for refusing supplies to multiple retailers, but in general the practice seems to have been stamped out.

Creation of Office of Fair Trading

A major innovation made by the Fair Trading Act of 1973 was the creation of the Office of the Director General of Fair Trading. He is independent of Government, although he must work closely with the Minister of Trade and Industry. He has been given power to make references to the Monopolies Commission, and it was hoped that he would be subject to less political pressure to refrain from making such references since the Minister can veto a reference only after it has been published, but the number does not seem to have increased much since 1973. The Director also assumed the responsibilities under the restrictive practices legislation of maintaining the register, referring cases to the Restrictive Practices Court, and is a competent authority liaising with the Commission of the European Communities in competition matters. He cannot refer mergers himself, but his Office prepares the cases for references to be made by the Minister.

The Competition Act 1980

Yet another layer of control was added two years ago. The Director General may now not merely instigate investigations by the Commission or the Court; he may himself investigate anti-competitive practices. If he finds that the practice is anti-competitive and the firm does not undertake in terms satisfactory to the Director to abrogate it, he can refer the practice of that person to the Commission. That body is asked not only whether the practice is anti-competitive, but also, whether it may be expected to operate against the public interest. The Competition Act was not intended to cover a gap in the United Kingdom law – such practices, if carried on by a firm supplying or acquiring a quarter of the products specified in the reference, can be referred to the Monopolies and Mergers Commission by the Director or Minister. Indeed, even if several firms together supplying a quarter of the products so act as to restrict competition, whether by agreement or not, a monopoly situation exists which may be referred. Such a reference could even be limited to the specific practices causing concern. In many ways, such a reference would be more sensible than the investigation under the Competition Act of the specific practice of named persons, in that the Commission would consider the supply of the product generally, and not merely the conduct of the firm specified by the Director. It is hard if a complaint is made against one firm for refusing supplies, and it is investigated and restrained, and its competitors are not. It was hoped that the Director might be able to make quicker, simpler investigations than the Commission. In the event, firms have been unhappy to be found to be acting anti-competitively through a rough and ready, speedy procedure, and several of those found to be carrying on an anti-competitive practice have refused to give undertakings to abrogate it, and have had to submit to a second enquiry to bring out public interest justifications. In the first such case, on *Raleigh Bicycles*,[7] the Commission's condemnation was narrower than the Director's.

> A person is engaged in an anti-competitive practice if, in the course of business, that person pursues a course of conduct which, of itself or when taken together with a course of conduct pursued by persons associated with him, has or is intended to have or is likely to have the effect of restricting, distorting or preventing competition in connection with the production, supply or acquisition of goods in the United Kingdom or any part of it or the supply or securing of services in the United Kingdom or any part of it. (section 2(1).)

The Director has powers to obtain information only when he has started his statutory investigations and cannot write round to large firms requiring them to tell him in respect of which products they adopt requirements contracts. Consequently, he relies on complaints. He has treated as anti-competitive conduct which makes it difficult for firms to enter into or stay in business. This has been criticised as including conduct which merely prevents potential competitors from taking a free ride on the back of an existing firm, such as forbidding service dealers to service competing brands of refrigerated vehicles. The Director is per-

---

7 *Raleigh Bicycles* [1981] HCP 67.

mitted only to decide whether the agreement restrains competition, not whether it is contrary to the public interest. If he finds a practice anti-competitive, he may make reference of the practice of the specified person to the Monopolies Commission which is required to say whether it considers the practice anti-competitive, and if it does, to decide whether it operates against the public interest. Consequently, to defend a practice a firm picked upon may have first to suffer an investigation by the Director, and then either give undertakings, or submit to one by the Commission, at which stage additional justifications are relevant. This double test may cause great hardship to small firms, or to big ones in relation to a small business. Complainants have considerable power to increase the costs of leading firms.

Conclusion

The United Kingdom law is now so complex, with so many layers of control, that competition law is understood in detail by only a small number of specialists. The Restrictive Trade Practices legislation is particularly complex and litigation very expensive so few agreements are being made with a view to justifying them before the Restrictive Practices Court. Ways round the legislation can often be found without making agreements less restrictive, although this is rare for naked cartels. Practices not caught by that legislation may be referred to the Monopolies and Mergers Commission or become the subject of an investigation under the Competition Act or under Community law. The Monopolies Commission did produce fairly consistent adverse views on cartels in both the goods and services industries, but its views are far harder to predict in relation to other matters. They are particularly difficult to predict in relation to mergers. The public interest test includes everything. It looks not merely at effects on competition, but also directly at efficiency, though the Commission is rarely satisfied that a merger will lead to economies of scale or other efficiencies. It often considers whether the managers of the acquiring firm will be able to manage the resources of the target firm as ably as would its existing management.

There are so many layers of control, that one cannot give a short and satisfactory description of the law to a client. It seems to the writer that it is high time that the Restrictive Trade Practices legislation was either abandoned and its task left to the Commission, or remodelled in terms of effects on competition within the UK. The difficulty of such radical alterations is that the Court has been successful in driving naked cartels underground, at least. Any amendment would either have to forbid them *per se*, apart from the very few agreements which have survived a reference to the Court, or provide for the continuation of the orders and undertakings of or given to the Court.

No one would recommend such a complex system as we have – like Topsy, it 'just growed', as Governments wished to seem to be doing something about competition. It has one major advantage: firms cannot be fined for past conduct unless they were subject to an order at the time.

Bibliography

Bibliography taken from Valentine Korah, *Competition Law of Britain and the Common Market*, Nijhoff, (3rd ed.), 1982.

Part I: Monopolies and Mergers, Competition and Protection of Trading Interests Act

J. P. Cunningham, *The Fair Trading Act 1973: Consumer Protection and Competition Law*, London, Sweet & Maxwell, 1974. (Lucid analysis of the legislation, with illustrations from the reports of the Monopolies Commission, by a lawyer accustomed to advise a large industrial group of companies, written in terms easy for a layman to understand.)

Valentine Korah, in Ed. D. J. Gijlstra, *Competition Law in Western Europe and the USA*, Deventer, Kluwer, looseleaf, Volume A, UK Commentary. (This includes the two statutes of 1980, as well as analysis of the monopolies and mergers legislation, and of the public interest criteria applied by the Commission.)

Barounos and Allan, in Ed. von Kalinowski, *World Law of Competition*, Unit B, Western Europe, Volume 4.

A. Sutherland, *The Monopolies Commission in Action*. Cambridge, CUP, 1969. (Critical analysis of the then recent reports of the Commission on Monopolies and Mergers.)

W. R. Cornish, *Intellectual Property: Patents, Copyrights, Trade Marks and Allied Rights*, London, Sweet & Maxwell, 1981. (The first elementary analysis of the legislation covering all sorts of intellectual property by the leading academic lawyer in the field. Perceptive, basic, highly compressed, very readable, but also critical.)

J. F. Pickering, 'The Implementation of British Competition Policy on Mergers,' [1980] 1 ECLR at 177.

J. F. Pickering, *Industrial Structure and Market Conduct*, London, Martin Robertson, 1974 (2nd ed. in preparation). (Not merely economic theory, but also description and appraisal of governmental policy towards mergers and competition by a professor who has done considerable empirical work in the field. Lucid and illuminating for both beginninner and expert.)

J. P. Cunningham and J. Tinnion, *The Competition Act 1980*, London, Sweet & Maxwell, 1980. (A copy of the Act, with a section by section commentary by Tinnion, and a preliminary analysis with a wider focus by Cunningham. Lucid and perspective.)

Valentine Korah, 'The Competition Act 1980: Narrow interpretation by the

Office of Fair Trading of its Functions' [1981] 78 *The Law Society's Gazette* 745. (Criticism of the first two reports into anti-competitive practices by the Director.)

Annual reports of the Board of Trade and Secretary of State under the Monopolies and Mergers Act until 1973. Thereafter chapters in the Annual Report of the Director General of Fair Trading.

Mergers: A guide to the procedures under the Fair Trading Act 1973. Office of Fair Trading, 1978.

Part II: Restrictive Practices

Books for Lawyers

J. F. Lever and C. Bellamy, *Chitty on Contracts*, Sweet & Maxwell, 1977 (24th ed.), and 1979 1st Supp. Volume II at Chapter 10. This is a revised version of his book, *The Law of Restrictive Practices and Resale Price Maintenance*, London, Sweet & Maxwell, 1964. (A carefully prepared book for lawyers, succinct, clear, accurate and brought up to date as needed by supplements. The book is too expensive for many individuals to buy, but is to be found in most law libraries. There is little reference to works by economists. Difficult to understand without introduction.)

J. P. Cunningham, *The Fair Trading Act 1973*. See under Part I.

Valentine Korah, in Ed. Gijlstra. See under Part I. Introduction only.

Books and Articles of More General Interest, Largely on Economics

R. B. Stevens and B. S. Yamey, *The Restrictive Practices Court: A Study of the Judicial Process and Economic Policy*, London, Weidenfeld & Nicolson, 1965. (A classic analysis of the work of the Restrictive Practices Court in its early and active years, and of the problems with which it is confronted, both legal and economic. Now out of print. The authors consider how far the court has access to the relevant evidence and whether the orders it is permitted to make are appropriate for furthering the public interest.)

D. Swan, D. P. O'Brien, W. P. J. Maunder, W. S. Howe, *Competition in British Industry*, London, Unwin University Books, 1974. (Survey of effects of restrictive practices legislation on British industry.)

G. C. Allen, *Monopoly and Restrictive Practices*, London, Unwin University Books, 1968.

B. S. Yamey (ed.), *Economics of Industrial Structure*, Harmondsworth, Penguin, 1973.

B. S. Yamey (ed.), *Resale Price Maintenance: Studies*, London, Weidenfeld & Nicolson, 1966. (Studies of the effect of resale price maintenance in seven countries, and of its abolition where this has occurred. The editor describes the main economic issues in an introduction.)

B. S. Yamey, *Resale Price Maintenance and Shoppers' Choice*, Hobart Paper No. 1, London, Institute of Economic Affairs, 1964 (4th ed.). (An influential attack on the practice, in more polemical terms than the more academic book by the same author, which has long been out of print and for that reason is not listed here.)

J. F. Pickering, 'The Abolition of Resale Price Maintenance in Great Britain', [1974] 26 *Oxford Economic Papers* 120. (An empirical study of the consequences of abolishing the practice as it became illegal for one class of goods after another under the Resale Prices Act 1964.)

W. R. Cornish, *Intellectual Property: Patents, Copyrights, Trade Marks and Allied Rights*. See under Part I.

Law Reports

The official reports of the judgements of the Restrictive Practices Court, including summarised versions of counsel's submissions, were published by the Incorporated Council of Law Reporting in seven volumes of Restrictive Practices Cases, cited as for example [1960] ☆ LR 2RP 00. These were amalgamated with labour law cases in 1972 in the *Industrial Court Reports*, but only a few cases have been reported there. The Council decided to continue that series under the name *Industrial Cases Reports*, and it continues to include any restrictive practices cases.

Before being so published, the cases are reported without counsel's arguments in the *Weekly Law Reports*, cited as for example [1962] 1 WLR 00. Butterworths also publish the *All England Reports*, cited as for example [1960] 2 All ER 00. All these reports are reliable, and references to each are given in the table of cases.

Reports of the Registrar have described the Registrar's work over the years, the state of register, and sometimes his views about amendments he would like to make in the law. These are obtainable from Her Majesty's Stationery Office, Cmnd Nos 1273, 1603, 2246, 3188, 4303, 5195. Since 1973 they have been replaced by a chapter in the annual report of the Director.

UNITED STATES OF AMERICA

Anti-trust Enforcement in the US

DAVID H. MARKS

It is a privilege to be asked to speak on American anti-trust law in the country whose own laws in this area, as in so many other areas, have served as a fountainhead for the American law. American anti-trust law can be traced to the English common law prohibition against restraints of trade,[1] and the 1624 Statute of Monopolies, which limited the Crown's prerogative to establish exclusive rights.

Courses on anti-trust law in the American law schools only begin to plumb the depths of the subject after 60 or more hours of classes; so this short paper will focus on three major topics which should give a foundation on which to build an understanding of American anti-trust laws. First, the major anti-trust legislation and the various governmental and private enforcement mechanisms will be introduced. Second, an attempt will be made to explain two of the most important concepts in proving an anti-trust violation – the *per se* rule and the rule of reason. And finally the concept of anti-trust damages in private treble damage actions will be discussed.

The Major Anti-Trust Laws And Their Enforcement

The most important substantive anti-trust laws are stated in a few short provisions of a handful of statutes – the Sherman Act[2] the Clayton Act[3] the Federal Trade Commission Act[4] and the Robinson-Patman Act.[5] The oldest and most important is the Sherman Act, enacted in 1890. It outlawed monopolisation and contracts, combinations and conspiracies in restraint of trade.[6] The Clayton Act, passed in 1914, specified a number of specific trade practices that

---

Mr Marks appreciates the assistance of Carolyn T. Ellis and Douglas Broder in preparing this paper.

1   See *Mitchel v Reynolds*, 1 PWms 181, 24 Eng Rep 347 (Ch. 1711); *Darcy v Allen*, 77 Eng Rep 1260(K.B. 1602); *Dyer's Case*, Y.B. 2 Hen. v, fs, pl 26 (1415). See generally *National Society of Professional Engineers v United States*, 435 US 679 (1978).
2   Act of 2 July 1890, Ch. 647, 26 Stat. 209, *as amended*, 15 USC §§1 to 7.
3   Act of 15 October 1914, Ch. 323, 38 Stat. 730, *as amended*, 15 USC §§ 12 to 27.
4   Act of 26 September 1914, Ch. 11, 38 Stat. 717, *as amended*, 15 USC §§ 51 to 58.
5   Act of 19 June 1936, Ch. 592, 49 Stat. 1526; 15 USC §§ 13, 13a, 13b, 21a.
6   15 USC §§ 1, 2.

are illegal when they tend substantially to lessen competition or create a monopoly: price discrimination,[7] exclusive dealing and tying practices,[8] mergers and acquisitions of other companies,[9] and interlocking directorates.[10] The Federal Trade Commission Act, also passed in 1914, created the Federal Trade Commission as an independent agency to enforce the anti-trust laws. The Robinson-Patman Act of 1936 expanded the price discrimination provisions of the Clayton Act.[11]

The most significant anti-trust law is the Sherman Act, section 1 of which declares that 'every contract, combination . . . or conspiracy in restraint of trade' is illegal; persons engaging in such conduct are guilty of a felony punishable by a fine of up to $1 million for a corporation and one $100,000 for an individual, or by imprisonment of up to three years, or both.[12] Section 2 of the Sherman Act makes it illegal to monopolise, to attempt to monopolise or to conspire to monopolise any part of trade or commerce. A section 2 violation carries the same criminal penalties as a violation of section 1.[13]

The Clayton Act was designed to deal with specific restraints of trade which Congress felt had not been adequately prohibited by the courts under the broad mandate of section 1 of the Sherman Act.[14] Unlike violations of the Sherman Act, Clayton Act violations carry no criminal penalties.

Section 3 of the Clayton Act prohibits certain transactions linking the sale or lease of two products and certain exclusive dealing arrangements where the ef-

---

7   15 USC § 13.
8   15 USC § 14.
9   15 USC § 18.
10   15 USC § 19.
11   Scores of other federal laws deal with trade regulation. Many statutes which set up regulatory agencies specify that those agencies must consider the competitive impact of their decisions. See for example Bank Holding Company Act of 1956, Ch. 240, 70 Stat. 133, *as amended*, 12 USC § 1842(c).
12   Section 1 states:

Every contract, combination in the form of trust or otherwise, or conspiracy, in restraint of trade or commerce among the several States, or with foreign nations, is declared to be illegal. Every person who shall make any contract or engage in any combination or conspiracy hereby declared to be illegal shall be deemed guilty of a felony, and, on conviction thereof, shall be punished by fine not exceeding one million dollars if a corporation, or, if any other person, one hundred thousand dollars or by imprisonment not exceeding three years, or by both said punishments, in the discretion of the court.

13   Section 2 states:

Every person who shall monopolize, or attempt to monopolize, or combine or conspire with any other person or persons, to monopolize any part of the trade or commerce among the several States, or with foreign nations, shall be deemed guilty of a felony, and, on conviction thereof, shall be punished by fine not exceeding one million dollars if a corporation, or, if any other person, one hundred thousand dollars or by imprisonment not exceeding three years, or by both said punishments, in the discretion of the court.

14   See for example *United States v United Shoe Machinery Co.* 258 US 451 (1921).

fect of such transactions or arrangements may be substantially to lessen competition or to tend to create a monopoly in any line of commerce. [15]

Section 7 of the Clayton Act concerns mergers. As at present written, section 7 prohibits any acquisition of stock or assets the effect of which may be substantially to lessen competition or to tend to create a monopoly in any line of commerce in any section of the country. [16]

As originally enacted, the Clayton Act included provisions dealing with price discrimination. These provisions were amended and expanded in 1936 by the Robinson-Patman Act. There Congress declared that section 2 of the Clayton Act would prohibit discrimination in price between different purchasers of commodities of like grade and quantity, where the effect of such discrimination may be substantially to lessen competition or to tend to create a monopoly, or to injure, destroy or prevent competition with any person who either grants or knowingly receives the benefit of such discrimination, or with customers of either of them. Statutory defences were provided for discrimination intended only to meet competition, and for discrimination based on cost justifications. [17]

The other major anti-trust statute is the Federal Trade Commission Act of 1914, which established the Federal Trade Commission (the FTC) as an independent anti-trust enforcement agency. The FTC is authorised, after appropriate administrative hearings, to issue cease and desist orders prohibiting '[u]nfair methods of competition in or affecting commerce'. [18] 'Unfair methods of competition' include, but are not limited to, violations of the other anti-trust laws. [19]

Each of these statutes contains provisions establishing mechanisms for its enforcement, and as a result, it is safe to say that in the United States anti-trust is everybody's business. Two federal Government agencies, a myriad state government agencies and private parties injured in their business or property have explicit authority to bring cases to enforce the various anti-trust laws. Turning first to the federal anti-trust enforcement agencies, there are two federal agencies with explicit powers to enforce the anti-trust laws: the United States Department of Justice and the Federal Trade Commission.

---

15   Section 3 states:

> That it shall be unlawful for any person engaged in commerce, in the course of such commerce, to lease or make a sale or contract for sale of goods, wares, merchandise, machinery, supplies or other commodities, whether patented or unpatented, for use, consumption or resale within the United States or any Territory thereof or the District of Columbia or any insular possession or other place under the jurisdiction of the United States, or fix a price charged therefor, or discount from, or rebate upon, such price, on the condition, agreement or understanding that the lessee or purchaser thereof shall not use or deal in the goods, wares, merchandise, machinery, supplies or other commodities of a competitor or competitors of the lessor or seller, where the effect of such lease, sale or contract for sale or such condition, agreement or understanding may be to substantially lessen competition or tend to create a monopoly in any line of commerce.

16　Section 7 states, in pertinent parts:

That no person engaged in commerce or in any activity affecting commerce shall acquire, directly or indirectly, the whole or any part of the stock or other share capital and no person subject to the jurisdiction of the Federal Trade Commission shall acquire the whole or any part of the assets of another person engaged also in commerce or in any activity affecting commerce, where in any line of commerce or in any activity affecting commerce in any section of the country, the effect of such acquisition may be substantially to lessen competition, or to tend to create a monopoly.

. . . .

This section shall not apply to persons purchasing such stock solely for investment and not using the same by voting or otherwise to bring about, or in attempting to bring about, the substantial lessening of competition.

17　Section 2 states:

(a) That it shall be unlawful for any person engaged in commerce, in the course of such commerce, either directly or indirectly, to discriminate in price between different purchasers of commodities of like grade and quality, where either or any of the purchases involved in such discrimination are in commerce, where such commodities are sold for use, consumption, or resale within the United States or any Territory thereof or the District of Columbia or any similar possession or other place under the jurisdiction of the United States, and where the effect of such discrimination may be substantially to lessen competition or tend to create a monopoly in any line of commerce, or to injure, destroy, or prevent competition with any person who either grants or knowingly receives the benefit of such discrimination, or with customers of either of them: Provided, That nothing herein contained shall prevent differentials which make only due allowance for differences in the cost of manufacture, sale, or delivery resulting from the differing methods or quantities in which such commodities are to such purchasers sold or delivered . . . And provided further, That nothing herein contained shall prevent persons engaged in selling goods, wares, or merchandise in commerce from selecting their own customers in bona fide transactions and not in restraint of trade. . . .

(b) Upon proof being made, at any hearing on a complaint under this section, that there has been discrimination in price or services or facilities furnished, the burden of rebutting the prima-facie case thus made by showing justification shall be upon the person charged with a violation of this section, and unless justification shall be affirmatively shown, the Commission is authorized to issue an order terminating the discrimination: Provided, however, That nothing herein contained shall prevent a seller rebutting the prima-facie case thus made by showing that his lower price or the furnishing of services or facilities to any purchaser or purchasers was made in good faith to meet an equally low price of a competitor, or the services or facilities furnished by a competitor.

. . . .

(d) That it shall be unlawful for any person engaged in commerce to pay or contract for the payment of anything of value to or for the benefit of a customer of such person in the course of such commerce as compensation or in consideration for any services or facilities furnished by or through such customer in connection with the processing, handling, sale, or offering for sale of any products or commodities manufactured, sold, or offered for sale by such person, unless such payment or consideration is available on proportionally equal terms to all other customers competing in the distribution of such products or commodities.

(e) That it shall be unlawful for any person to discriminate in favor of one purchaser against another purchaser or purchasers of a commodity bought for resale, with or without processing, by contracting to furnish or furnishing, or by contributing to the furnishing of, any services or facilities connected with the processing, handling, sale, or offering for sale of such commodity so purchased upon terms not accorded to all purchasers on proportionally equal terms.

(f) That it shall be unlawful for any person engaged in commerce, in the course of such commerce, knowingly to induce or receive a discrimination in price which is prohibited by this section.

The Antitrust Division of the Justice Department

The Sherman Act is a criminal statute and its enforcement is the principal work of the Antitrust Division of the United States Justice Department. The Antitrust Division has authority to seek either criminal indictments or, pursuant to section 4 of the Sherman Act, a civil injunction for violations of the Act. [20] In addition, it enforces the Clayton Act and, when it chooses in the exercise of its discretion as to prosecution, the Robinson-Patman Act, by means of an injunctive action. [21]

The Antitrust Division is headed by an assistant attorney-general of the Department of Justice. With a small staff, the Assistant Attorney-General supervises the enforcement activities of the several hundred career anti-trust attorneys in the Antitrust Division. The Division's enforcement activity is carried out by 'Sections' responsible for various functions or subject areas. [22] In addition, the Division has eight field offices located in major US cities, each of which is responsible for enforcement in its geographical area.

The Antitrust Division may initiate both criminal and civil actions and uses two investigatory devices: the federal grand jury for criminal investigations and the civil investigative demand (CID) for civil investigations. [23] Because of constitutional issues involving the rights of potential defendants, the Antitrust Division considers carefully what type of proceeding will be initiated.

In a criminal investigation, the Antitrust Division follows the federal rules of criminal procedure. It may call upon a grand jury to investigate violations of the

---

18   Sections 5(a) and (b) state:

(a) (1) Unfair methods of competition in or affecting commerce, and unfair or deceptive acts or practices in or affecting commerce, are hereby declared unlawful.

(2) The Commission is hereby empowered and directed to prevent persons, partnerships, or corporations, except [certain regulated industries] from using unfair methods of competition in or affecting commerce and unfair or deceptive acts or practices in or affecting commerce.

(b) Whenever the Commission shall have reason to believe that any such person, partnership, or corporation has been or is using any unfair method of competition or unfair or deceptive act or practice in or affecting commerce, and if it shall appear to the Commission that a proceeding by it in respect thereof would be to the interest of the public, it shall issue and serve upon such person, partnership, or corporation a complaint stating its charges in that respect and containing a notice of a hearing upon a day and at a place therein fixed at least thirty days after the service of said complaint. The person, partnership, or corporation so complained of shall have the right to appear at the place and time so fixed and show cause why an order should not be entered by the Commission requiring such person, partnership, or corporation to cease and desist from the violation of the law so charged in said complaint. . . . The testimony in any such proceeding shall be reduced to writing and filed in the office of the Commission. If upon such hearing the Commission shall be of the opinion that the method of competition or the act or practice in question is prohibited by this Act, it shall make a report in writing to which it shall state its findings as to the facts and shall issue and cause to be served on such person, partnership, or corporation an order requiring such person, partnership, or corporation to cease and desist from using such method of competition or such act or practice. . . .

19   *FTC v Sperry & Hutchinson Co.* 405 US 233 (1972). But see *Official Airline Guides v FTC* 630 F.2d 920 (2d Cir. 1980), cert. denied, 450 US 917 (1981); *FTC v Boise Cascade Corp.* 637 F.2d 573 (9th Cir. 1980).

criminal anti-trust statutes, principally sections 1 and 2 of the Sherman Act. The grand jury's broad investigatory powers under these sections include, as with investigations of violations of other federal criminal statutes, the power to compel witnesses to testify and to produce documents, records, books, and other information. A witness before a grand jury has no right to have counsel present. If the grand jury determines that a criminal violation of the anti-trust laws has probably occurred, it will return an indictment against the suspected participants.

Since 1962 the Antitrust Division has had a civil alternative to grand jury investigation. Before instituting a proceeding, whenever the Attorney-General or the Assistant Attorney-General in charge of the Antitrust Division has reason to believe that a person, including a corporation, may be in possession of information relevant to the investigation, it may serve a CID on him.[24] Using these

---

20 Section 4 states:

> The several [district] courts of the United States are hereby invested with jurisdiction to prevent and restrain violations of this act; and it shall be the duty of the several district attorneys of the United States, in their respective districts, under the direction of the Attorney-General, to institute proceedings in equity to prevent and restrain such violations. Such proceedings may be by way of petition setting forth the case and praying that such violation shall be enjoined or otherwise prohibited. When the parties complained of shall have been duly notified of such petition the court shall proceed, as soon as may be, to the hearing and determination of the case; and pending such petition and before final decree, the court may at any time make such temporary restraining order or prohibition as shall be deemed just in the premises.

21 While section 3 of the Robinson-Patman Act provides that a knowing violation for the purpose of destroying competition or eliminating a competitor is a criminal violation punishable by a fine of 'not more than $5,000' or imprisonment of 'not more than 1 year, or both', there has been no criminal prosecution under this section since *United States v H.P. Hood & Sons Inc*. Cr. 63-110-C D. Mass. (19 March 1965) (Case No. 1742).

22 These sections include the Intellectual Property Section, the Foreign Commerce Section, the Transportation Section, the Consumer Affairs Section, the Special Regulated Industries Section, the Energy Section, as well as sections for handling litigations, appeals, enforcement of judgments, legislation, policy planning and evaluation.

23 As originally enacted, the Antitrust Civil Process Act of 19 September 1962, Public Law 87-664, 76 Stat 548, was limited in scope. It was expanded in the Hart-Scott-Rodino Antitrust Improvements Act of 1976, Public Law 94-435 §§ 101 to 05, 90 Stat 1383. The current version is at: 15 USC §§ 1311 to 14 and 18 USC § 1505.

24 Section 3(a) of the Antitrust Civil Process Act states:

> Whenever the Attorney General, or the Assistant Attorney General in charge of the Antitrust Division of the Department of Justice, has reason to believe that any person may be in possession, custody, or control of any documentary material, or may have any information, relevant to a civil antitrust investigation, he may, prior to the institution of a civil or criminal proceeding thereon, issue in writing, and cause to be served upon such person, a civil investigative demand requiring such person to produce such documentary material for inspection and copying or reproduction, to answer in writing written interrogatories, to give oral testimony concerning documentary material or information, or to furnish any combination of such material, answers, or testimony. Whenever a civil investigative demand is an express demand for any product or discovery, the Attorney General or the Assistant Attorney General in charge of the Antitrust Division shall cause to be served, in any matter authorized by this section, a copy of such demand upon the person from whom the discovery was obtained and notify the person to whom such demand is issued of the date on which such copy was served.

civil investigative procedures, the Antitrust Division can insist on examining witnesses and obtaining documents before a complaint is issued. The Antitrust Division can use the CID to investigate possible violations of the Sherman and Clayton Acts, the Robinson-Patman Act and various other anti-trust statutes. After a complaint is issued, the Antitrust Division may also use ordinary civil discovery procedures to gather additional information before trial.

Criminal prosecutions are of substantial importance to United States anti-trust enforcement. The Sherman Act declares that certain conduct is criminal. Originally Senator Sherman's bill was introduced in Congress as a purely civil statute, but it was soon rewritten to include criminal penalties.[25] Indeed, the Sherman Act does not describe a civil offence at all. Sections 1 and 2 of the Act declare certain conduct to be 'illegal' and section 4 merely authorises a civil proceeding to prevent such illegal activity.

Throughout the years Congress has strengthened the criminal provisions of the anti-trust laws. In 1914 Congress enacted section 14 of the Clayton Act, which provides that a violation of the anti-trust laws by a corporation shall be deemed to be a violation by the individual directors, officers or agents of the corporation who authorised, ordered or committed any of the illegal acts.[26] In 1955 Congress increased the maximum fine under the Sherman Act from $5,000 to $50,000 per violation.[27] In 1974 a Sherman Act violation was made a felony and the maximum penalties were increased to their present levels.[28]

Perhaps the most important decision for any potential target of a Government investigation of Sherman Act violations is the decision that the Antitrust Division makes as to whether to proceed by a criminal indictment or a civil injunctive complaint. While, as noted above, all violations of sections 1 and 2 of the Sherman Act are criminal violations, the Antitrust Division has, as a matter of discretion over prosecution, limited criminal indictments to cases involving for the most part agreements among competitors to fix prices, to rig bids, or to allocate customers and territories.[29] During the previous administration a criminal indictment charging vertical price-fixing was brought.[30] However, given the often expressed beliefs of the present Assistant Attorney-General in charge of the Antitrust Division, it is unlikely that this administration will bring another criminal vertical price fixing case. Nevertheless, the current administration has reiterated the importance of criminal indictments, prosecutions and jail sentences for horizontal agreements among competitors, such as price fixing. The Government has demonstrated its faith in the deterrent effect of this

25   Senator Sherman's Bill, S. 3445, 50th Cong., 1st Sess. (1888), provided no criminal penalties when introduced on 14 August 1888; criminal penalties were added when it was reported by the Senate Committee on Finance on 11 September 1888.
26   Act of 15 October 1914, Ch. 323, § 14, 38 Stat 736 (current version at 15 USC § 24).
27   Act of 7 July 1955, Ch. 281, 69 Stat 282.
28   Act of 21 December 1974, Public Law 93-528, § 3, 88 Stat 1708 (current version at 15 USC § 1).
29   See US Department of Justice, *Antitrust Division Manual*, III-11 (1979); address by Richard J. Favretto, *A Prosecutor's Perspective on the Gypsum Opinion*, 5 Trade Reg. Rep. ¶ 50,412 (1980).
30   *United States v Cuisinarts Inc.* Cr. No. H-80-49 (D. Conn. filed 17 September 1980).

enforcement mechanism and has announced its intent to rely on it to an ever increasing extent, at least insofar as price fixing is concerned. It is important to
recognise, however, that not all conduct on which the Government bases a
charge of price fixing is obviously price fixing in the traditional sense, and in
these cases the Government may choose to bring a civil injunctive action rather
than a criminal action. Since proof of intent is a requirement in a criminal case,
criminal actions are reserved for that type of conduct which is clearly recognised
as being illegal.[31]

It is impossible to discuss the nature of representing individuals and corporations that are the targets of a federal criminal anti-trust investigation within
this paper. Suffice it to say that the Antitrust Division is ordinarily very cautious
in deciding whom to indict. On the other hand, there is an institutional preference to indict the most senior officers responsible for the violation even if they
were involved only in a supervisory capacity. Thus, those who are directly involved in the violation may be compelled to give testimony that implicates their
superiors who might not otherwise be implicated. In the author's experience
this is probably one of the most traumatic parts of the anti-trust practice, both
for the lawyer and for the client.

The Sherman and Clayton Acts authorise the federal courts 'to prevent and
restrain' violations of their provisions. Under this authority, the Supreme Court
has repeatedly held that the Government is entitled to whatever positive and
negative orders are necessary to prevent defendants from engaging in the same
or similar illegal practices, to deprive them of the fruits of their illegal activities,
and to restore competition in the affected area of the economy.[32] Thus, for
example, injunctive relief has been granted requiring a corporation to sell its
subsidiaries, to grant royalty-free licences on dominant patents and to adopt
and implement anti-trust compliance programmes.[33]

Many Government suits for injunctive relief are settled by the negotiation of
a consent decree. A consent decree is a final judgment in the form of an injunction entered on the consent of the parties and with the approval of the court.[34]
While it has the same force and effect as a final judgment entered in a litigated
case, it cannot be used by private litigants as *prima facie* evidence of a violation.[35]

The assistant attorneys general who have headed the Antitrust Division have
had divergent views concerning anti-trust enforcement policy. However, there
is one general principle that has consistently guided the Justice Department's
anti-trust enforcement policy, namely, that the objectives of anti-trust policy

31   See *United States v United States Gypsum Co.* 438 US 422 (1978).
32   See for example *Ford Motor Co. v United States* 405 US 562, 573-78 (1972); *United
States v United Shoe Machinery Corp.* 391 US 244, 252 (1968); *United States v Grinnell
Corp.* 384 US 563, 577 (1966); *United States v E.I. duPont de Nemours & Co.* 366 US 316,
326 (1961); *United States v United States Gypsum Co.* 340 US 76, 88-90 (1950); *Schine
Chain Theatres, Inc. v United States* 334 US 110, 127-29 (1948).
33   For example *Ford Motor Co. v United States* 405 US 562 (1972); *United States v General
Shoe Corp.* [1956] Trade Cas. ¶ 68,271 (M.D. Tenn. 1956).
34   15 USC § 16(b).
35   15 USC § 16(a). See below at 168 to 169.

must be accomplished by securing compliance with the law through all available techniques rather than through reliance on litigated victories alone. For this reason, everything Antitrust Division attorneys do – writing letters, making speeches, conducting investigations, conferring with businessmen and their counsel, as well as engaging in litigation – is aimed at educating businessmen as to the types of conduct the anti-trust laws prohibit and the types of conduct they encourage, and at creating a social environment in which businessmen are induced to conduct their business in accordance with not only the letter but also the spirit of the anti-trust laws.

In the last several years, the Antitrust Division has produced a number of 'guides' to provide businessmen with statements of the Division's thinking as to the applicability of the anti-trust laws to different fact patterns.[36] While these publications do not bind the Division as a matter of law, they reveal a great deal about the Division's enforcement policies. The Antitrust Division also has a statutory procedure whereby it will issue a 'business review letter' stating its present enforcement intentions with respect to specific proposed business conduct.[37] A party requesting such a letter must submit all the information it deems relevant to the proposed course of conduct as well as any additional information sought by the Antitrust Division. After reviewing the material, the Division may make whatever response seems appropriate, including declining to state its enforcement intentions. A favourable business review letter, however, does not immunise any conduct from future challenge by the Division. Moreover, neither a favourable business review letter nor compliance with the standards set out in one of the guides issued by the Antitrust Division will provide a conclusive defence to a private treble damage action.

The Federal Trade Commission

The second arm of the United States Government which is actively involved in anti-trust enforcement is the Federal Trade Commission. The FTC is specifically empowered to enforce the Clayton Act and the Federal Trade Commission Act's prohibition against unfair methods of competition. Its enforcement activity is of three types: investigation, adjudication and administrative rule-making.

The FTC has broad powers of investigation. Section 9 of the Federal Trade Commission Act authorises the FTC to issue compulsory process, in the form of a subpoena, to require the production of documentary evidence or testimony relating to a rule-making proceeding, an adjudication or to 'any matter under investigation'.[38] Section 20, which was added to the Act in 1980, provides the Commission with the power, similar in scope to that provided to the Antitrust

---

36   For example United States Department of Justice, *Merger Guidelines* (June 1982), 2 (CCH) Trade Reg. Rep. ¶ 4500; United States Department of Justice, *Antitrust Guide Concerning Research Joint Ventures* (November 1980), [466] (CCH) Trade Reg. Rep. (Pt. II).
37   The Antitrust Division's Business Review Procedure is set out at 28 CFR § 50.6 (1981).
38   15 USC § 49.

Division, to issue civil investigative demands to obtain documents or testimony.[39] The CID has the procedural advantage that it does not require the Commission to institute a formal proceeding before being able to obtain documents or testimony.

The FTC's investigatory powers extend to foreign corporations. In fact, section 6(h) of the Federal Trade Commission Act specifically grants the Commission authority to investigate trade practices in and with foreign countries whose practices may affect the foreign trade of the United States and to report to the Congress thereon with appropriate recommendations.[40]

Whenever the FTC has reason to believe that an unfair method of competition is being used, and that a proceeding against the practice would be in the public interest, it may issue a complaint stating its charges and, after holding a hearing and issuing written findings of fact, it may order the offending party to cease and desist from the violation of law so charged. The United States courts of appeals have authority to review and to affirm, enforce, modify or set aside such FTC orders.[41]

The FTC is a federal administrative agency and its practice is governed by the Federal Administrative Procedure Act[42] and the FTC Act. Thus, the Commission itself votes to institute a proceeding, which is then referred to a staff attorney called 'the complaint counsel' who prepares the case for presentation before an administrative law judge. While the hearings before the administrative law judge are not governed by the federal rules of civil procedure, much of the practice is similar. At the end of the hearings the administrative law judge issues findings of fact and, if he finds a violation, an order setting out the injunctive relief to be granted. Either side may then appeal the matter to the commission. The Commission as a whole then reviews the record and issues its own findings of fact and order if it finds a violation. The Commission, unlike a federal court of appeals reviewing the findings of fact of a district court judge, is not bound by the administrative law judge's findings. On the contrary, the Commission can review the entire record *de novo* and make its findings thereon even if it chooses to disregard evidence upon which the administrative law judge relied. Significantly, section 5(c) of the FTC Act provides that 'the findings of the Commission as to the facts . . . if supported by evidence, shall be conclusive'.[43]

In addition to the powers to conduct investigations and to adjudicate through the administrative procedures outlined in the Federal Trade Commission Act, the FTC has one significant enforcement power not found in the Antitrust Division. The FTC has power to promulgate rules concerning unfair methods of competition. Congress had passed an amendment to the FTC Act allowing the two Houses of Congress to veto a Commission rule. The courts,

39   15 USC § 57b-1.
40   15 USC § 46h.
41   15 USC § 45. Similar procedures apply to proceedings aimed at violations of the Clayton Act; see section 11(b) of the Clayton Act, 15 USC § 21(b).
42   5 USC § 500 *et seq.*
43   15 USC § 45(c).

however, held such a provision unconstitutional. Although at one time it was suggested that the Commission might be able to establish binding rules relating to the size of companies which would be allowed to merge, the Commission has never moved forward to attempt to apply its rule-making authority to any of the areas traditionally encompassed by the Sherman Act or the Clayton Act.

State Attorneys-General and State Laws

Each of the fifty states and the District of Columbia has some statutory provision dealing with anti-trust. The state attorneys-general are empowered to enforce these laws in their respective states. Indeed, certain state supreme courts have interpreted the private right of action provisions in their state laws more generously than has the US Supreme Court for the federal statutes. [45] While the Supreme Court has not had an opportunity to decide whether these laws are pre-empted by the Sherman and Clayton Acts, to the extent that they are more generous than the Clayton Act's provision, federal courts have upheld such statutes. [46] Nonetheless, the states are only empowered to regulate commerce within their respective territories and, therefore, the reach of a given state's anti-trust law is limited to acts occurring within or affecting the commerce of that state.

In 1976 Congress gave the state attorneys general additional means to enforce the Federal anti-trust laws. Section 4C of the Clayton Act gives the attorney-general of a state the right to bring a civil action in the name of the state as *parens patriae* 'on behalf of natural persons residing in such State . . . to secure monetary relief . . . for injury sustained by such natural persons to their property by reason of any violation of the Sherman Act'. [47] The purpose of this

---

44   15 USC § 57a-1. The Supreme Court in *Immigration & Naturalization Service v Chadha* 51 USLW 4907 (1983), held such a legislative veto unconstitutional. The result in *Chadha* was applied to the FTC specifically in *United States Senate v Federal Trade Commission* 51 USLW 3935 (US July, 1983).

45   See for example California's Cartwright Act, Calif. Bus. & Professions Code § 16750, discussed in *In re Sugar Antitrust* Litigation 588 F.2d 1270 (9th Cir. 1978); cert. denied 441 US 932 (1979).

46   See for example *Shell Oil Co. v Younger* 587 F.2d 34 (9th Cir. 1978); cert. denied 440 US 947 (1979) (§21,200 of Cal. Bus. & Prof. Code not in conflict with Robinson-Patman Act § 2(b) despite narrower defence under state law); compare *Alton Box Board Co. v Espirit De Corp.* 1982-1 Trade Cas. ¶ 64,711 (9th Cir. 1982) (whether *Illinois Brick Co. v Illinois*, 431 US 720 (1977) bars suits by indirect purchasers under California's Cartwright Act not reached because federal court is barred from enjoining state court action).

47   Section 4C states:

(a)(1) Any attorney general of a State may bring a civil action in the name of such State, as parens patriae on behalf of natural persons residing in such State, in any district court of the United States having jurisdiction of the defendant, to secure monetary relief as provided in this section for injury sustained by such natural persons to their property by reason by any violation of the Sherman Act. The court shall exclude from the amount of monetary relief awarded in such action any amount of monetary relief (A) which duplicates amounts which have been awarded for the same injury, or (B) which is properly allocable to (i) natural persons who have excluded their claims pursuant to subsection (b)(2) of this section, and (ii) any business entity.

provision was to allow a state attorney-general to bring a consumer class action to redress violations of the anti-trust laws. While relatively few actions have been brought under this statute, it remains a potentially significant weapon. In addition, of course, the attorney-general of a state has always had the right to represent the state as an actual purchaser of services or goods which have been the subject of an anti-trust violation. In that manner the state can obtain treble damages on its own behalf.

The Private Anti-trust Suit

The private anti-trust action, authorised by sections 4 and 16 of the Clayton Act, serves three functions. First, it provides recompense to persons who are injured in their business or property by reason of a violation of the anti-trust laws. Second, it allows individuals to protect themselves from injury by obtaining injunctive relief against would-be transgressors. Third, it has an important deterrent effect and supplements Government enforcement efforts. Private anti-trust suits may be based on violations of sections 1, 2 or 3 of the Sherman Act or sections 2(a) to (f), 3, 7 or 8 of the Clayton Act, when those violations inflict injury on the plaintiff. Private plaintiffs do not have standing to bring suits under the Federal Trade Commission Act.[48]

---

(2) The court shall award the State as monetary relief threefold the total damage sustained as described in paragraph (1) of this subsection, and the cost of suit, including a reasonable attorney's fee. The court may award under this paragraph, pursuant to a motion by such State promptly made, simple interest on the total damage for the period beginning on the date of service of such State's pleading setting forth a claim under the anti-trust laws.

. . .

(b)(1) In any action brought under subsection (a)(1) of this section, the State attorney general shall, at such times, in such manner, and with such content as the court may direct, cause notice thereof to be given by publication. If the court finds that notice given solely by publication would deny due process of law to any person or persons, the court may direct further notice to such person or persons according to the circumstances of the case.

(2) Any person on whose behalf an action is brought under subsection (a)(1) may elect to exclude from adjudication the portion of the State claim for monetary relief attributable to him by filing notice of such election with the court within such time as specified in the notice given pursuant to paragraph (1) of this subsection.

(3) The final judgment in an action under subsection (a)(1) shall be res judicata as to any claim under section 4 of this Act by any person on behalf of whom such action was brought and who fails to give such notice within the period specified in the notice given pursuant to paragraph (1) of this subsection.

(c) An action under subsection (a)(1) shall not be dismissed or compromised without the approval of the court, and notice of any proposed dismissal or compromise shall be given in such manner as the court directs.

(d) In any action under subsection (a)--

(1) the amount of the plaintiffs' attorney's fee, if any, shall be determined by the court; and

(2) the court may, in its discretion, award a reasonable attorney's fee to a prevailing defendant upon a finding that State attorney general has acted in bad faith, vexatiously, wantonly, or for oppressive reasons.

48 For example *Naylor v Case & McGrath, Inc.* 585 F.2d 557, 561 (2d Cir. 1978).

(i) The treble damage action

The deterrent effect of the private anti-trust action is amplified by the treble damage provision of section 4, which entitles the successful litigant to three times its proven damages plus the costs of suit, including reasonable attorneys' fees. While the Supreme Court has recently rendered a number of decisions limiting in some degree the availability of treble damages – decisions which I shall discuss in the last part of this presentation – the treble damage remedy has been a powerful vehicle for redressing injuries and deterring future violations, especially when it has been coupled with the procedural weapon provided by the class action rules. For example, class actions on behalf of purchasers of corrugated containers were settled by all but one of the defendants in a nationwide price fixing action, for more than $300 million dollars. The remaining defendant, Mead Corporation, went to trial and was found guilty. Because the treble damage provisions provide for joint and several liability, Mead may be liable for all the damages incurred by the class, trebled, and reduced only by the $300 million dollars in settlements. Mead subsequently settled the case by agreeing to pay $45 million.[49]

(ii) The effect of a Government action on private rights

Congress has eased the burden on private litigants who seek to bring suit against those who are defendants in Government suits arising from the same facts. Section 5(i) of the Clayton Act suspends the running of the normal four-year anti-trust statute of limitations during the pendency of Government suits and for one year thereafter. This provision is intended to give private litigants the benefit of any pleadings, testimony, exhibits or legal decisions that come out of the Government suit. This suspension provision also enables private litigants to take advantage of a second provision intended to ease their burden, section 5(a) of the Clayton Act,[50] which permits the private litigant to use a judgment or decree obtained by the Government (except consent decrees) as *prima facie* evi-

---

49   Counsel for the plaintiffs in the *Corrugated Container* litigation estimated Mead's potential damage liability at $700 million. *Hearings on S. 995 before the Senate Comm. on the Judiciary* 97th Cong. 2d Sess. 525 (1982). The damages in another class action – the *Plywood* case – were estimated to be as high as $1.5 billion to $2 billion. see *idem*. at 539 to 541. The defendants settled the *Plywood* case for $165 million, after the Supreme Court had agreed to review the lower courts' findings of liability, but before the case was argued.

50   Section 5(a) of the Clayton Act provides:

A final judgment or decree heretofore or hereafter rendered in any civil or criminal proceeding brought by or on behalf of the United States under the antitrust laws to the effect that a defendant has violated said laws shall be prima facie evidence against such defendant in any action or proceeding brought by any other party against such defendant under said laws as to all matters respecting which said judgment or decree would be an estoppel as between the parties thereto: Provided, That this section shall not apply to consent judgments or decrees entered before any testimony has been taken. Nothing contained in this section shall be construed to impose any limitation on the applications of collateral estoppel, except that, in any action or proceeding brought under the antitrust laws, collateral estoppel effect shall not be given to any finding made by the Federal Trade Commission under the antitrust laws or under section 5 of the Federal Trade Commission Act which could give rise to a claim for relief under the antitrust laws.

dence that the defendants have violated the anti-trust laws. Although a Government judgment or decree is not conclusive evidence of a violation, it is, unless successfully rebutted, sufficient evidence. A private litigant may also take advantage of any findings of fact made by the court in the prior action, under the principles of collateral estoppel.[51]

Per Se Rules Versus the Rule of Reason

Section 1 of the Sherman Act is the most extensively litigated and relied upon of the anti-trust laws. Much like the United States constitution, its generality makes it an instrument of great flexibility. Application of section 1 to a myriad different patterns of fact has generated two strikingly distinct approaches. Since they serve as the rules of decision in the majority of US anti-trust cases, this next section of the paper will discuss these two rules – the *per se* rule and the rule of reason.

Any analysis of section 1 must begin with the language of the statute. 'Every contract, combination . . . or conspiracy in restraint of trade . . . is declared to be illegal . . . .'[52] The difficulty with the language is that, as Justice Stevens recently said in the *Engineers* case, 'it cannot mean what it says'.[53] The purpose of every contract is to restrain. Thus, literally construed, this section of the Sherman Act 'would outlaw the entire body of private contract law'.[54]

Because of the breadth of the language in section 1, in its early years the courts struggled to develop a proper construction of its meaning. The Supreme Court initially rejected the contention that 'reasonable' contracts were permitted under section 1 as they were in restraint of trade cases decided under common law.[55] The Court held that all contracts that restrained competition 'directly' were illegal, but that the statute did not prohibit 'indirect' restraints.[56] These decisions were by sharply divided Courts, with four of the Court's nine justices agreeing with the defendants that the common law doctrine allowing reasonable restraints should be applicable. To these justices, even a price-fixing cartel could be found legal if the prices fixed were not unreasonably high.

The 'direct/indirect' restraint test proved difficult to apply[57] and was abandoned in 1911, twenty-one years after the Sherman Act was passed, when the Supreme Court adopted the 'rule of reason' test in the famous *Standard Oil*[58] and *American Tobacco*[59] cases. In announcing the rule of reason, the Supreme

---

51 15 USC § 16(a).
52 15 USC § 1.
53 *National Society of Professional Engineers v United States* 435 US 679, 689 (1978).
54 *Idem* at 689 to 90, citing *Chicago Board of Trade v United States* 246 US 231 (1918).
55 See for example *Mitchel v Reynolds* 1 P. Wms. 181 24 Eng. Rep. 347 (1711).
56 *United States v Trans-Missouri Freight Assn* 166 US 290 (1897); *United States v Joint Traffic Assn* 171 US 505 (1898).
57 See *Northern Securities Co. v United States* 193 US 197 (1904).
58 *Standard Oil Co. of New Jersey v United States* 221 US 1 (1911).
59 *United States v American Tobacco Co* 221 US 106 (1911)

Court's opinions avoided the central problem that had initially led to the Court's reluctance to impose a 'reasonableness' construction on the Sherman Act – the fear that even the most severe restriction on competition could be upheld on the basis of some 'reasonable' excuse for its use. In *Standard Oil* and *American Tobacco*, the Court refused to allow trade restraints to be justified on the basis of *ad hoc* notions of reasonableness. Instead, the rule of reason focused solely on the impact of the challenged restraint on competition. If the restraint unduly impaired competition, it was illegal, however 'reasonable' it might seem in some metaphysical sense.

Thus, in the 1927 *Trenton Potteries* case,[60] the Supreme Court made it clear that agreements among competitors to fix prices were always unreasonable, regardless of whether the prices fixed were unduly high, because the restraint on competition was inherently unreasonable. Although the term *per se* was not used in the opinion, *Trenton Potteries* is understood as having been the first case to hold that price fixing is illegal *per se* – the Court there held that price fixing is conclusively presumed to be unreasonable and, as Justice Douglas said 13 years later in the *Socony-Vacuum Oil* case, where a practice is conclusively presumed unreasonable under the rule of reason, it is considered illegal *per se*.[61]

The basic difference between *per se* cases and rule of reason cases is this: In an ordinary rule of reason case, the plaintiff must prove both that an agreement exists, and that the purpose or effect of the agreement is to restrain competition unreasonably. In a *per se* case, however, the plaintiff need only prove the agreement; there is a conclusive presumption that the agreement has an unreasonable purpose or effect on competition.

In a rule of reason case, proof of the purpose or effect of the agreement on competition can be difficult and time consuming. The court will consider the facts peculiar to the business involved; its condition before and after the restraint was imposed; the market shares of the parties involved, and the shares controlled by other firms in the business; the reason the restraint was imposed and its intended effect; the duration of the restraint; and whether there are alternatives that could accomplish similar results with fewer anti-competitive effects.[62] Indeed, the cases require the trier of fact to review and balance the anti-competitive effects of the restraint against any pro-competitive effects accruing from the restraint.[63] As noted, however, the Supreme Court has repeatedly held that, in assessing the reasonableness of a restraint, a court cannot consider beneficial effects other than those to the competitive market. Thus, in the *Professional Engineers* case,[64] the defendant trade association attempted to justify an ethical prohibition against competitive bidding for engineering services on the ground that such bidding would lead to unsafe construction design. The

---

60   *United States v Trenton Potteries Co.* 273 US 392 (1927).
61   *United States v Socony-Vacuum Oil Co.* 310 US 150, at 221 to 223 (1940).
62   *Chicago Board of Trade v United States* 246 US 231 (1918); *United States v Columbia Steel Co.* 334 US 495 (1948); *United States v Addyston Pipe & Steel Co.* 85 F. 271 (6th Cir. 1898) (Taft, J.), aff'd as modified, 175 US 211 (1899).
63   *Continental T.V., Inc. v GTE Sylvania Inc.* 433 US 36 (1977).
64   *National Society of Professional Engineers v United States* 435 US 679 (1978).

Court held that this purported justification could not be considered by the finder of fact as a reason to allow the restraint. Similarly, in the *Fashion Originators* case,[65] the charge was that certain dress companies had agreed not to deal with companies which were guilty of design piracy. Although the Court conceded that pirating designs of dresses could well constitute a state law tort, it held that this would provide no defence to a boycott charge, since horizontal group boycotts are illegal *per se*. And in the *Klor's* case,[66] in which a retail seller of radios complained of a boycott by department stores and manufacturers, the Court's holding that such a boycott was *per se* illegal allowed the plaintiff to forgo proving injury to the public, as would have been required in a rule of reason case.

There are advantages and disadvantages in trying cases under the rule of reason and under the *per se* rule. A *per se* rule has two basic advantages. First, these rules are easy for businessmen to comprehend and to follow. For example, businessmen in the United States are aware that agreements with their competitors fixing prices are always illegal, and they must conduct their businesses accordingly. Second, *per se* rules are easy to apply in litigation, and thus detailed industry analyses are not ordinarily required. Rule of reason cases do not have these advantages. Rule of reason trials are often protracted, and businessmen find it difficult in conducting their businesses to distinguish between the legal and the illegal. Nevertheless, the rule of reason, unlike the *per se* rule, has the important advantage of flexibility. Some agreements, such as mergers, will benefit competition in some cases and harm competition in others. A *per se* rule that draws a clear line irrespective of the actual effect on competition would obviously be inappropriate in such cases.

Since the consequences of holding that a practice is illegal *per se* are so drastic – the practice is forbidden no matter what the circumstances or justifications may be – the Supreme Court has recently been conservative in extending *per se* prohibitions. The Court has held that a practice should be declared illegal *per se* only where it has a pernicious effect on competition and lacks any significant redeeming virtue.[67] Normally, the courts will rule that a practice is illegal *per se* only where they have had sufficient experience with it to draw the necessary conclusive presumption. In some circumstances, however, the anti-competitive effect of the practice will be so obvious that no extensive experience will be required.

Although the Supreme Court has recognised rules of *per se* illegality, it has not yet expressly recognised any rule of *per se* legality. A number of commentators, however, have suggested that certain agreements should be regarded as legal *per se*, and the Supreme Court may well adopt that view in future cases.[68]

Certain practices which the Supreme Court has declared to be illegal *per se*

---

65   *Fashion Originators Guild v FTC* 312 US 457 (1941).
66   *Klor's, Inc. v Broadway-Hale Stores, Inc.* 359 US 207 (1959).
67   For example *Broadcast Music, Inc. v Columbia Broadcasting System* 441 US 1 (1979).
68   See for example Posner, *The Next Step in the Antitrust Treatment of Restricted Distribution: Per Se Legality* 48 U. Chi. L. Rev. 6 (1981).

will now be detailed. The practice that is perhaps most clearly illegal *per se* is horizontal minimum-price fixing. It was first conclusively presumed to be unreasonable in the *Trenton Potteries* case and was described as illegal *per se* in *Socony-Vacuum*. It is important to recognise that, Justice Douglas explained in the *Socony* case, price fixing includes more than explicit agreements as to specific prices. It includes any agreement or understanding among competitors which affects the price. Thus, the traditional language with which the Antitrust Division charges a price fixing violation is to allege that the effect of the agreement involved was to 'fix, maintain or stabilize' prices. Perhaps the best example of price fixing without the parties' fixing a specific price is found in the *Socony-Vacuum* case itself. There, the agreement among the competing oil companies was not that the price of oil would be fixed, but rather that 'distress' oil would be purchased by the group in order to keep it from coming on the market and driving the price down.

The Supreme Court has recently had two opportunities to discuss the scope of the prohibition against 'price fixing'. In *Broadcast Music, Inc. v Columbia Broadcasting System*[69] CBS, the television network, attacked BMI and ASCAP, the two principal music performance licensors, as price fixing organisations. Both ASCAP and BMI obtained the right to license performing rights of copyrighted musical works from copyright holders. Both organisations offered blanket licences, which allow the licensee the right to use any of the works within the licensor's portfolio, and per use licences, which provide for specific performances of specific works. CBS charged that, because the exigencies of the television business made it difficult if not impossible to know when a particular piece of music would be performed, and therefore when a licence would be required, a blanket licence was a practical necessity. Yet the blanket licence required CBS to buy the right to use thousands of works that neither it nor any of the people preparing programmes for it would ever conceivably choose to perform. CBS contended that BMI and ASCAP were therefore fixing prices by offering only a blanket licence or a single-use licence since the latter was impractical and the former was a method of containing or stabilising prices. The Court of Appeals ruled in CBS's favour on the ground that it was not impractical for ASCAP and BMI to offer less than a blanket licence and therefore they were indeed fixing prices. The Supreme Court refused to accept this characterisation of the practice. Rather than find the practice to be price fixing and therefore illegal *per se*, the Court chose to tailor the concept of price fixing narrowly. It said that price fixing was illegal *per se* because the Court had determined after much experience with it that there was no redeeming value in it. On the other hand, the Court had not had great experience with licensing systems such as the one used by ASCAP and BMI; therefore, it remanded the case to the lower Court for a determination of the legality of these practices under the rule of reason.[70]

---

69   441 US 1 (1979).

70   The lower Court subsequently ruled that, tested under the rule of reason, the licensing practices of ASCAP and BMI were reasonable and therefore legal. 620 F.2d 930 (2nd Cir. 1980); cert. denied 101 S. Ct 1491 (1981).

The other recent case of interest in the definition of price fixing is the *Catalano* case.[71] There the plaintiffs alleged that there was a conspiracy to change the terms on which beer was sold to wholesalers, eliminating preferential credit terms. The defendants contended that this was not price fixing, because the most that was alleged by the plaintiffs was that a portion of the price was fixed. They contended that since there was active competition on the base price, it was immaterial that a specific element, such as the credit terms upon which the sale was made, was the subject of an agreement among competitors. Although this defence prevailed in the Court of Appeals, the Supreme Court summarily reversed, holding that fixing one term of sale could constitute a price fixing violation. Because the practice of fixing prices is illegal *per se*, no actual market impact need be shown.[72] Indeed, for example, an agreement between two petrol station owners to increase prices is illegal even though there may be hundreds of other stations in the city and the two conspirators therefore could never, in fact, succeed in raising the price.[73]

Certain other practices that have been found to be illegal *per se* will be identified briefly. Horizontal maximum price fixing has recently been reaffirmed to be illegal *per se*.[74] Vertical price fixing, whether of maximum or minimum prices, has been held to be illegal *per se*.[75] It should be noted that vertical price fixing is the only vertical restraint that is at present illegal *per se*. All other vertical restraints are now subject to the rule of reason. Finally, horizontal group boycotts[76] and division of territories[77] have been held to be illegal *per se*.

There will be no attempt here to define all of the cases in which the rule of reason has been applied. Indeed, the rule of reason applies to all cases that are not subject to the *per se* rules. Two points should be noted. First, it is clear that the Supreme Court can reverse itself, and change an earlier labelling of a practice as illegal *per se*. In 1967 the Court held in the *Schwinn* case[78] that vertical agreements between a manufacturer and its wholesalers and retailers granting exclusive territories and applying customer restrictions were illegal *per se*. There followed a flood of scholarly criticism, and in 1977 the Supreme Court reversed itself in the *Sylvania* case,[79] holding that vertical territorial restrictions are subject to the rule of reason. Thus it allowed Sylvania to defend its practice of granting exclusive territories to various dealers on the ground that otherwise the Sylvania brand, which accounted for a very small percentage of the market

71   *Catalano, Inc. v Target Sales, Inc.* 446 US 643 (1980).
72   See for example *Klor's Inc. v Broadway-Hale Stores, Inc.* 359 US 207 (1959).
73   *United States v Socony-Vacuum Oil Co.* 310 US 150, 224 n.59 (1940).
74   *Arizona v Maricopa County Medical Soc'y* 50 USLW 4689 (1982). See also *Kiefer-Stewart Co. v Joseph E. Seagram & Sons* 340 US 211 (1951).
75   *Dr Miles Medical Co. v John D. Park & Sons Co.* 220 US 373 (1911); *Albrecht v Herald Co* 390 US 145 (1968); *California Retail Liquor Dealers Ass'n v Midcal Aluminium, Inc.* 445 US 97 (1979).
76   *Klor's Inc. v Broadway-Hale Stores, Inc.* 359 US 207 (1959); *Fashion Originators Guild v FTC* 312 US 457 (1941).
77   *United States v Topco Associates* 405 US 596 (1972).
78   *United States v Arnold, Schwinn & Co.* 388 US 365 (1967).
79   *Continental T.V., Inc. v GTE Sylvania Inc.* 433 US 36 (1977).

for televisions, would not be promoted by any dealer. The loss of intraband competition between various Sylvania dealers by the application of exclusive territories was more than compensated by increased interbrand competition.

The second point is that practical problems may result from the amorphous nature of the rule of reason. It is difficult to criticise any rule that is called the 'rule of reason', but as noted above, the rule has been subjected to substantial criticism by those who prefer certainty and clear lines to flexibility.

An interesting case illustrating how the rule of reason is applied is *Berkey Photo Inc. v Eastman Kodak Co.*,[80] a 1979 decision by the Court of Appeals for the Second Circuit. The principal issue in the case was whether Kodak was guilty of monopolising in violation of section 2 of the Sherman Act. The court reversed a jury verdict finding that Kodak had violated section 2, but it upheld the jury verdict finding certain other conduct by Kodak to be unreasonable under section 1.

The section 1 charge related to the joint development by Kodak of new flash systems for cameras with General Electric (GE) (the 'flipflash') and Sylvania (the 'magicube'). The plaintiff in the case, Berkey Photo (a competing camera manufacturer), claimed that the joint development agreements were unreasonable because they prohibited GE and Sylvania from disclosing their flash inventions to other camera manufacturers until after Kodak had introduced cameras into the market utilising the inventions.

In the context of the monopolisation charge, the Court of Appeals had ruled that a unilateral refusal to 'predisclose' its innovations was lawful – despite Kodak's complete market dominance – because requiring predisclosure would eliminate Kodak's incentive to innovate. However, when the context was joint development, the legal analysis was necessarily different.[81] This was 'an agreement among a few firms to restrict to themselves the rewards of innovation'.[82] In light of Kodak's monopoly power, the agreement had a very substantial adverse effect on competition in the camera market, and the agreement's secrecy provisions were not 'reasonably necessary'[83] for the achievement of Kodak's legitimate business objectives in the light of the existing available alternatives. Accordingly, the court ruled that the jury's finding of unreasonableness was not improper.

Anti-Trust Damages in Private Treble Damage Actions

The law is unequivocal with respect to the plaintiff's right to treble damage recovery where an anti-trust violation has injured his business or property. Section 4 of the Clayton Act provides that

---

80   603 F.2d 263 (2nd Cir. 1979); cert. denied 444 US 1093 (1980).
81   *Idem* at 301.
82   *Idem*.
83   *Idem* at 303.

[a]ny person who shall be injured in his business or property by reason of anything forbidden in the antitrust laws may sue therefor and shall recover threefold the damages by him sustained, and the cost of suit, including a reasonable attorney's fee.[84]

The statutory language 'shall' is mandatory, not discretionary. Indeed, as the Supreme Court recently stated '§ 4 contains little in the way of restrictive language'[85] and '[w]e must take the statute as we find it'.[86] In each Congress between 1953 and 1961 bills were introduced which would have put the imposition of treble damages at the discretion of the trial court,[87] as it is in trademark infringement violations,[88] and in patent infringement violations.[89] None of these bills was ever reported out of committee, much less passed by one of the houses of Congress.

Though the language of the provision is clear and sweeping, there have been a number of important issues raised which should be surveyed briefly since private treble damage actions are for most companies the most traumatic anti-trust enforcement mechanism after the criminal anti-trust prosecution.

First, does 'any person' in section 4 mean any person? The answer is yes. In *Reiter v Sonotone Corp.*,[90] the defendants, who sold hearing aids, contended that the plaintiffs in the case – hearing aid consumers – could not sue under section 4 because, as defendants interpreted the statute, it allowed redress only for commercial injuries. The defendants maintained that individual consumers suffered no commercial injury. The Supreme Court unanimously rejected this position. Indeed, every purchaser of goods or services may sue under the anti-trust laws and (with one exception – the United States Government) may recover treble damages. The United States Government is limited to the recovery of single or actual damages.[91] The Supreme Court has held that foreign governments are not so limited, and may recover treble damages as 'any person',[92] and the states of the United States are also included within the term 'any person'.[93]

One of the most important treble damage issues relates to who is liable for any judgment and for what portion of that judgment. At common law, joint

---

84   15 USC § 15. Section 7 of the Sherman Act was the original private treble damage right of action. That private right of action was expanded in Section 4 of the Clayton Act to provide for a private treble damage action for violation of the anti-trust laws as defined therein.

85   *Reiter v Sonotone Corp.* 442 US 330, 338 (1979). See also *Pfizer, Inc. v Government of India* 434 US 308, 312 (1977).

86   442 US at 345.

87   H.R. 4597, 83d Cong., 1st Sess. (1953); H.R. 6875, 84th Cong., 1st Sess. (1955); H.R. 978, 85th Cong., 1st Sess. (1957); H.R. 1184, 86th Cong., 1st Sess. (1959); H.R. 190, 87th Cong., 1st Sess. (1961).

88   15 USC § 1117.

89   35 USC § 284.

90   442 US 330 (1978).

91   15 USC § 15a.

92   *Pfizer, Inc. v Government of India* 434 US 308 (1977). In December 1982, Congress amended Section 4 of the Clayton Act limiting foreign states to single damages in many instances.

93   15 USC § 15c(a); see also *Georgia v Evans* 316 US 159 (1942).

tortfeasors were jointly and severally liable for the entire damage award. While this rule has been modified or eliminated in many states, either by statute or court decision, the rule in anti-trust cases remains. Each defendant is liable for treble the entire damages inflicted by the conspiracy. The Supreme Court refused to adopt any modification of this rule in the recent *Texas Industries* case,[94] and the issue has been hotly debated in Congress for the past year.

Although, as previously stated, section 4 allows suits by 'any person', there are substantial limits on the private treble damage action that have arisen from the courts' attempts to interpret the language 'injured . . . by reason of anything forbidden in the antitrust laws'. One important example is the *Hanover Shoe* case,[95] where the Supreme Court dealt with the question of whether a purchaser of a good whose price had been illegally inflated could still recover three times the overcharge after he had resold the product at a profit. In *Hanover*, the buyer of the shoe machines had used the machines to make shoes. The defendant contended that even though the price of the shoe making machines might have been illegally increased, Hanover had suffered no injury since it has passed along the overcharge when it set the price of its shoes. The Supreme Court rejected the defence and held that Hanover could recover treble the overcharge. The *Hanover Shoe* case has come to stand for the broad proposition that 'pass through' of the overcharge is not a defence even where the plaintiff is a wholesaler who resells the very same product at a profit.

The Supreme Court addressed another important aspect of this question in the *Illinois Brick* case.[96] In *Illinois Brick*, the charge was that there had been a conspiracy to increase the price of brick contracting. The State of Illinois had purchased many buildings which contained brick, but the state had not dealt directly with the defendant brick companies. Rather the state had hired a contractor which had subcontracted the brick work. Even though the contractor had calculated its bid based on the bid it had received from the brick subcontractor, the Supreme Court, applying *Hanover Shoe*, held that Illinois could not recover. Unless there was a pre-existing contract between Illinois and the general contractor whereby the brick subcontracting work had to be included in the overall contract price with a specific mark up (a pre-existing cost plus contract), only the general contractor would be allowed to sue. Just as there was no way of knowing whether Hanover Shoe would have sold its shoes for less, if there had been no illegal overcharge on shoe machines, there was no way of determining whether the general contractor would have bid less for the job had there been no brick conspiracy. If he would have bid the same amount with or without the conspiracy, then he was damaged by the full overcharge. The Supreme Court refused to allow such speculation. Thus, under *Hanover Shoe*, a direct purchaser can sue for treble damages even though his actual out of pocket loss may be passed on to his customers; and, under *Illinois Brick*, the

---

94 *Texas Industries, Inc. v Radcliff Materials, Inc.* 451 US 630 (1981).
95 *Hanover Shoe, Inc. v United Shoe Mach. Corp.* 392 US 481 (1968).
96 *Illinois Brick Co. v Illinois* 431 US 720 (1977).

customers – indirect purchasers – cannot sue. This result was roundly criticised and bills were immediately introduced in Congress to overrule *Illinois Brick* and allow those ultimate purchasers of the product who bore the brunt of the illegal overcharge to recover even though they were not direct purchasers from the conspirators.[97] While there was initial enthusiasm for this approach, it was never passed by Congress and its prospects at present seem dim.

Although *Hanover Shoe* and *Illinois Brick* merely allocated the anti-trust recovery among various possible claimants, two doctrines have had a marked limiting effect on the scope of treble damage recoveries. Section 4 of the Clayton Act requires the plaintiff to prove that it was injured by reason of something forbidden by the anti-trust laws. 'Anti-trust injury' is, therefore, a prerequisite for recovery. In *Brunswick Corp. v Pueblo Bowl-O-Mat*,[98] the Supreme Court was confronted with a case in which the plaintiff, a bowling alley operator, sought treble damages from Brunswick, the industry's giant, when Brunswick acquired a near-bankrupt competitor of the plaintiff. The plaintiff claimed that Brunswick's acquisition of the competitor violated section 7 of the Clayton Act and that with Brunswick's help, its competitor had successfully taken business away, thereby depriving the plaintiff of profits it would have made had the competitor disappeared or remained weak. The Court held that regardless of the legality of the acquisition under the anti-trust laws, the plaintiff's lost profits did not constitute 'anti-trust injury', because they were not the result of something forbidden by the anti-trust laws. In other words, the plaintiff's lost profits were attributable to an increase, not a decrease, in competition and were thus not attributable to something the anti-trust laws were designed to prevent.

A companion doctrine which limits the number of potential anti-trust plaintiffs is the standing to sue doctrine. A significant anti-trust conspiracy may have ripple effects throughout a section of the economy. For example, a conspiracy to drive a competitor out of business, if successful, injures not only the competitor but also those companies which sold supplies to the competitor, those which sold supplies to the suppliers and so on. Standing requirements have been imposed by lower courts as a means of limiting the availability of anti-trust recovery to those most directly injured by an anti-trust violation. Thus, the courts have used catchwords like 'impact,' 'remoteness,' and 'target area' to help them analyse individual cases. Over the years a fairly large split has arisen between the various lower federal courts. Some lower courts require the plaintiff to have felt a 'direct' impact from the alleged violation; those courts have been relatively liberal about granting standing. Other courts state that the plaintiff must have been within the 'target area' of the alleged violation or that he cannot have been too 'remote' from the violation; those courts have been relatively conservative in allowing standing to sue. For those who read the *European Competition Law Review*, this split is illustrated by cases discussed in past issues relating to the standing of employees who are sacked for refusing to participate in an anti-trust

---

97   S. 1874, 95th Cong., 1st Sess. (1977); H.R. 8359, 95th Cong., 1st Sess. (1977).
98   420 US 477 (1977).

violation.[99] Since the employee in such cases was injured by the act of the alleged conspirator (his employer) he has incurred 'direct injury', but he was not the 'target' of the conspiracy — the target was the purchaser of the product. At present two courts of appeals have reached opposite conclusions on this question, and it may be resolved by the Supreme Court.[100]

The Supreme Court recently addressed the standing issue for the first time in *Blue Shield of Virgina v McCready*.[101] There the plaintiff was a health insurance subscriber who had been denied reimbursement for a visit to a psychologist under a rule of her insurer's which provided compensation only for visits to psychiatrists — who compete with psychologists in providing psychotherapy services. The plaintiff alleged that the rule was the result of an anticompetitive conspiracy between the insurer and the psychiatrists. Despite the defendant's argument that the plaintiff was not within the target area of the conspiracy (which was, if it existed, aimed at psychologists), the Supreme Court found that she had standing to sue.

In so ruling the Court dealt with many of the arguments which had been used in the past to justify strict standing requirements. Because her psychologist had already been paid, the Court noted, he had not been injured and so could not sue. Thus there was no reason to fear duplicative recovery. Nor was her injury too 'remote', since denying her reimbursement was the very means used by the conspirators to achieve their illegal ends. Finally, because the subscriber bore the increase in costs caused by the illegal conspiracy her injury 'flowed from that which made the defendants' acts illegal' and thus was anti-trust injury within the meaning of the *Brunswick* case. Whether *McCready* will be broadly construed to expand the scope for potential plaintiffs will be a question closely watched by all anti-trust lawyers and all potential anti-trust defendants.

---

99   See [1982] ECLR 166 and 244.
100   Compare *Ostrofe v H.S. Crocker Co., Inc.* 1982-1 Trade Cas. ¶ 64,643 (9th Cir. 1982); cert. pending No. 82-174 (filed 2 August 1982) with *Bichan v Chemetron Corp.* 1982-2 Trade Cas. ¶ 64,807 (7th Cir. 1982).
101   50 USLW 4723 (21 June 1982).